SLOW TRAVEL

North York Moors & Yorkshire Wolds

Including York & the Coast

Local, characterful guides to Britain's special places

Mike Bagshaw

EDITION

Bradt Guides L
The Globe Pequot P

Third edition published January 2023
First published March 2014
Bradt Guides Ltd
31a High Street, Chesham, Buckinghamshire, HP5 1BW, England
www.bradtguides.com
Print edition published in the USA by The Globe Pequot Press Inc,
PO Box 480, Guilford, Connecticut 06437-0480

Text copyright © 2023 Bradt Guides
Maps copyright © 2023 Bradt Guides Ltd; includes map data © OpenStreetMap contributors
Photographs copyright © 2023 Individual photographers (see below)
Project Manager: Emma Gibbs
Cover research: Pepi Bluck, Perfect Picture

ISBN: 9781804690093

British Library Cataloguing in Publication Data
A catalogue record for this book is available from the British Library

Photographs © individual photographers credited beside images & also those picture
libraries credited as follows: Alamy.com (A); Shutterstock.com (S); Superstock.com (SS)

Front cover View towards Roseberry Topping (Jez Campbell/A)
Back cover York Minster seen from the city walls (Mike Towers/S)
Title page Whitby (allouphoto/S)

Maps David McCutcheon FBCart.S
Typeset by Ian Spick, Bradt Guides
Production managed by Zenith Media; printed in the UK
Digital conversion by www.dataworks.co.in

AUTHOR

Mike Bagshaw is a Lancastrian by birth and a zoologist by training. After four years as a student in Sheffield he qualified as a biology teacher and taught full-time for the rest of his career, all bar two years of it in Yorkshire. Most of this was in an outdoor education centre near Whitby, introducing children and adults to the delights of watersports, mountaineering, forest education and how to understand and appreciate the natural world.

Now officially retired, he still travels the wild places of the world as a naturalist and explorer, often in a canoe or kayak, and writes about his experiences for outdoor magazines. He contributes monthly nature columns to local newspapers and volunteers for local nature conservation organisations.

CONTRIBUTING AUTHOR

Caroline Mills, co-author of the York chapter, is a freelance writer of travel guides including the Bradt guide *Slow Travel The Cotswolds* and two Bradt *Camping Road Trips* guides, and contributes to various national magazines on travel, food and gardens. Though not officially of Yorkshire stock, she has many family connections with the county she classes as her second 'home'. Caroline writes, 'It has been great to return "home" for this guide. When you live in an area, it's easy to take your surroundings for granted and stop exploring. Returning to Yorkshire, I've visited with a fresh pair of eyes and have been able to talk with residents about places they didn't know were on their doorstep.'

ACKNOWLEDGEMENTS

A big thank you goes to all the people that have helped me with this book. All those Yorkshire contributors who shared a little of their lives and passions and allowed me to quote them, Caroline Mills for her help with the original York chapter, and my wife Lois for her forceful encouragement and indexing skills. Also, of course, everyone in the Bradt team: Anna Moores, Jennifer Wildman, Claire Strange, Sue Cooper, James Lowen, David McCutcheon, Ian Spick, Kate Howard and, especially, Emma Gibbs for her professionalism and patience.

DEDICATION

To the memory of my very dear friend
Angela Miller - a true Yorkshire lass.

Mike Bagshaw

AUTHOR'S STORY

On the face of it, a Lancastrian 'townie' writing about rural Yorkshire is an unusual phenomenon, but the truth is that I have spent more of my life in this adopted county than in the one of my birth.

My first experience of Yorkshire, a seaside holiday to Whitby in the late 1960s, was a shocking one; for a ten-year-old boy used to the Gulf Stream waters of Wales, swimming in the North Sea came as a very rude awakening.

Fast forward three or four years and I am back over the border again, this time on the other side of the county in Dentdale, where we teenagers enjoyed many residential stays in the school's country cottage. With hindsight, those first exposures to real country life – windswept hills, clean rivers and undisturbed wildlife – were life-changing experiences, for which I am eternally grateful.

Following that initial love affair with the Yorkshire Dales, I have revisited every Easter since, accompanied by a handful of like-minded school friends, and during that time we reckon to have visited just about every hilltop and decent pub in the area. That, coupled with my 35 years living and working in the North York Moors, led me to believe that I knew pretty much all there was to know about North Yorkshire. How wrong I was.

The very welcome opportunity to write this guide has allowed me to see familiar places in a new light, and discover corners that for years I had unwittingly missed. It also gave me the incentive to go and do some of those things that I'd always promised myself, like kayaking under the bird cliffs at Flamborough or walking a long-distance trail like the Yorkshire Wolds Way. Best of all, it's rekindled my desire to go out exploring again, and see what else I might have missed in this wonderfully varied county.

CONTENTS

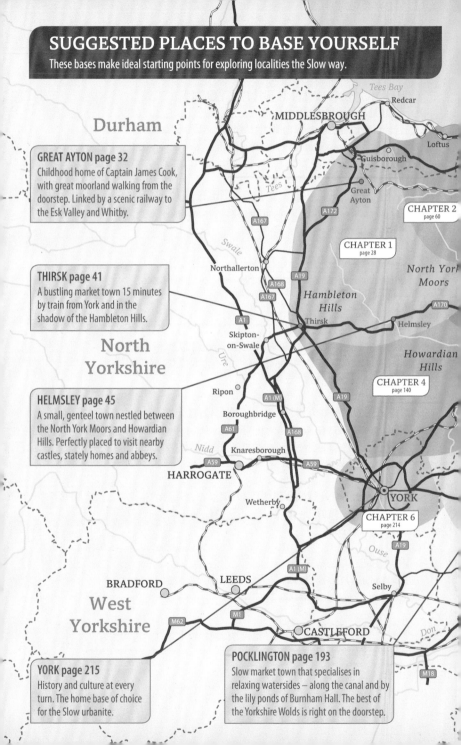

SUGGESTED PLACES TO BASE YOURSELF

These bases make ideal starting points for exploring localities the Slow way.

Durham

GREAT AYTON page 32
Childhood home of Captain James Cook, with great moorland walking from the doorstep. Linked by a scenic railway to the Esk Valley and Whitby.

THIRSK page 41
A bustling market town 15 minutes by train from York and in the shadow of the Hambleton Hills.

North Yorkshire

HELMSLEY page 45
A small, genteel town nestled between the North York Moors and Howardian Hills. Perfectly placed to visit nearby castles, stately homes and abbeys.

YORK page 215
History and culture at every turn. The home base of choice for the Slow urbanite.

POCKLINGTON page 193
Slow market town that specialises in relaxing watersides – along the canal and by the lily ponds of Burnham Hall. The best of the Yorkshire Wolds is right on the doorstep.

West Yorkshire

CHAPTER 1
page 28

CHAPTER 2
page 60

CHAPTER 4
page 140

CHAPTER 6
page 214

North York Moors

Hambleton Hills

Howardian Hills

Tees Bay

Redcar

Loftus

MIDDLESBROUGH

Guisborough

Great Ayton

Northallerton

Thirsk

Helmsley

Skipton-on-Swale

Ripon

Boroughbridge

Knaresborough

HARROGATE

Wetherby

YORK

Selby

BRADFORD

LEEDS

CASTLEFORD

Tees

Swale

Ure

Nidd

Ouse

Don

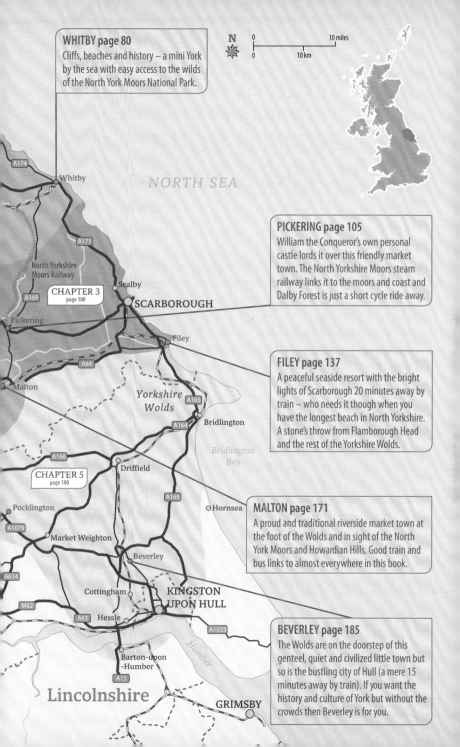

WHITBY page 80

Cliffs, beaches and history – a mini York by the sea with easy access to the wilds of the North York Moors National Park.

N

| 0 | | 10 miles |
| 0 | 10 km | |

NORTH SEA

A174

Whitby

A171

North Yorkshire Moors Railway

A169

CHAPTER 3 page 100

Scalby

Pickering

SCARBOROUGH

PICKERING page 105

William the Conqueror's own personal castle lords it over this friendly market town. The North Yorkshire Moors steam railway links it to the moors and coast and Dalby Forest is just a short cycle ride away.

A64

Filey

Malton

Yorkshire Wolds

A165

A164

Bridlington

FILEY page 137

A peaceful seaside resort with the bright lights of Scarborough 20 minutes away by train – who needs it though when you have the longest beach in North Yorkshire. A stone's throw from Flamborough Head and the rest of the Yorkshire Wolds.

A166

Bridlington Bay

CHAPTER 5 page 180

Driffield

Pocklington

A165

A1079

Hornsea

Market Weighton

MALTON page 171

A proud and traditional riverside market town at the foot of the Wolds and in sight of the North York Moors and Howardian Hills. Good train and bus links to almost everywhere in this book.

Beverley

A614

Cottingham

KINGSTON UPON HULL

M62

A63

Hessle

A1033

Barton-upon-Humber

Humber

BEVERLEY page 185

The Wolds are on the doorstep of this genteel, quiet and civilized little town but so is the bustling city of Hull (a mere 15 minutes away by train). If you want the history and culture of York but without the crowds then Beverley is for you.

A15

Lincolnshire

GRIMSBY

GOING SLOW IN

NORTH YORK MOORS & WOLDS

North Yorkshire is England's largest county, and an astonishingly diverse region. Over 100 miles separate the lofty peaks of the Pennines west from the sea-cliffs and sandy strands of the east, with pastoral limestone dales, rich farmland and rolling heather moors nestled in between. In the first version of this book, which appeared as *Slow North Yorkshire*, I attempted to cover most of the county in one volume. A Slow appraisal of a place shouldn't skim, but needs to look at the detail, so inevitably some very deserving places didn't make it in.

For this new, more focused guide, the western side of the county has been dealt with separately in *Slow Travel Yorkshire Dales*. There is no such place as northeast Yorkshire, but if it did exist it would be the subject of this book, comprising the North York Moors, the Howardian Hills, the Yorkshire Wolds and York itself. I could hardly leave out the county town, especially as it is also one of the most fascinating, historic and 'Slow' cities in the country. In this latest edition, the city of Hull has also managed to make a cameo appearance, having been drawn to my attention as the 2017 UK City of Culture.

My old neighbour Frank, God rest his soul, led an extraordinary life that many of us in this day and age could not imagine, not because of what he did, but for what he didn't do. During all of his 70-odd years, Frank never left Yorkshire, not a single step over the border for one minute. He was born on a farm in Goldsborough, near Whitby, worked there all his life and brought his family up in the

1 The North York Moors National Park above Ravenscar, looking out towards Robin Hood's Bay. 2 York Minster from the city walls. ▶

THE SLOW MINDSET

Hilary Bradt, Founder, Bradt Travel Guides

**We shall not cease from exploration
And the end of all our exploring
Will be to arrive where we started
And know the place for the first time.**

T S Eliot, 'Little Gidding', *Four Quartets*

This series evolved, slowly, from a Bradt editorial meeting when we started to explore ideas for guides to our favourite part of the world – Great Britain. We wanted to get away from the usual 'top sights' formula and encourage our authors to bring out the nuances and local differences that make up a sense of place – such things as food, building styles, nature, geology, or local people and what makes them tick. Our aim was to create a series that celebrates the present, focusing on sustainable tourism, rather than taking a nostalgic wallow in the past.

So without our realising it at the time, we had defined 'Slow Travel', or at least our concept of it. For the beauty of the Slow movement is that there is no fixed definition; we adapt the philosophy to fit our individual needs and aspirations. Thus Carl Honoré, author of *In Praise of Slow*, writes: 'The Slow Movement is a cultural revolution against the notion that faster is always better. It's not about doing everything at a snail's pace, it's about seeking to do everything at the right speed. Savouring the hours and minutes rather than just counting them. Doing everything as well as possible, instead of as fast as possible. It's about quality over quantity in everything from work to food to parenting.' And travel.

So take time to explore. Don't rush it, get to know an area – and the people who live there – and you'll be as delighted as the authors by what you find.

house next door. In his spare time he played football and cricket for the village, and occasionally took exotic holidays – to a caravan on another farm in the Yorkshire Dales. When I asked Frank why he hadn't travelled more, his reply was that he had no need to, that Yorkshire was as good as anywhere else, and gave him all he wanted for a happy and contented life.

Frank and his beloved Goldsborough are not unique, and that's what makes North Yorkshire so special in the Slow stakes. While many places are rediscovering the value of the traditional, real and genuine, and renewing connections with their history and landscape, many corners of rural North Yorkshire never lost them in the first place. This old-fashionedness has attracted some good-natured humour, and not a little malicious ridicule in its time but, as far as I'm concerned (all the more so the older I get), it's an attribute rather than a fault.

So-called progress has brought us cheap, mass-produced goods sold in supermarkets the size of villages and even bigger shopping malls. Thankfully, a backlash is taking place, and rural North Yorkshire is at the forefront of the push to preserve those things that make places different, interesting and… well, real. Folk are fighting hard to keep their village shops open, promote locally produced, high-quality food and drink, and encourage their own artists and artisans. These are the special people – the brewers, potters, shop-keepers, fishermen, farmers, wood-carvers, butchers, bakers and candlestick makers – that have managed to capture a little of the essence of their corner of this singular county, and enable you to feel it, smell it, taste it or even take a little of it away with you.

I hope this book inspires you, not just to read about this corner of North Yorkshire, but to live it – to come and meet these people, spend some Slow time where they live and get to know it as they do.

Climb a few hills, stroll through the woods and meditate in a ruined abbey, eat a pork pie by the river from the village butchers and finish the day in an old stone pub, with a glass of your favourite tipple and a crackling fire to toast your feet on – I can think of worse ways of passing time. Maybe Frank had it right – why go anywhere else?

THE NORTH YORK MOORS NATIONAL PARK

When William Smith produced the first geological map of England, he was particularly fascinated by outcroppings of Jurassic rocks that run in a broad band from the Dorset coast, diagonally up the country to meet the sea again in North Yorkshire. Just before they disappear beneath the cold, grey waves of the North Sea, these rocks bulge up in a range of rolling, flat-topped hills.

The sandstone that capped these uplands produced a thin, acid soil that could only support sparse forest, which Bronze Age people found relatively easy to clear. This natural woodland has never returned, but hundreds of square miles of alien coniferous forest were planted in the 1930s. Although not popular with many naturalists and landscape purists, these woods are now maturing into a certain Scandinavian-style beauty, which I feel adds more to than it detracts from the character of the region. Certainly the Forestry Commission now comes across as a much more enlightened, visitor-friendly and Slow organisation than it has done in the past.

Across the rest of the hill tops, acid-tolerant **heather** has taken over, resulting in the largest uninterrupted expanse of upland heath in England, with an abundance of Bronze Age settlement remains. The North York Moors (as in, moors north of the city of York, not moors in North Yorkshire) were designated as a national park in 1952, primarily to preserve this internationally important habitat. Britain has 70% of the world's heather moorland but, ironically, what many people think of as a truly wild landscape is nothing of the sort. Common heather or ling (*Calluna vulgaris*) only dominates the North York Moors because we let it. Without human management, by controlled burning or mowing, and sheep grazing, these upland heaths would soon revert to their natural vegetation of broad-leaved woodland – and an increasing number of people believe we should allow it to do just that.

An awful lot of landowners' time, effort and money goes into keeping these vast acres covered in heather, not for us to ooh and aah over their colour in August, or for long, uninterrupted views on our walks, but to encourage the populations of one species of wild bird – the red grouse. Grouse are very specific in their habitat requirements, needing young heather shoots to eat and old heather bushes to nest in, and so a moorland gamekeeper's job is to maintain a mosaic of different-aged patches of heather on the land.

What's good for grouse is, fortunately, also attractive to lots of other unique wildlife, and this area is a real stronghold for adders, lizards, curlews, golden plover, short-eared owls and, my favourite of all, a dashing little falcon called the merlin. Another bird of prey, the hen harrier, should also make an appearance on this list, but has been illegally persecuted to extinction in Yorkshire by unscrupulous grouse moor managers – a perennial problem for the National Park Authority and police.

The **National Park Authority** has a delicate balancing act to perform, working with farmers and the big grouse-shooting estates that actually own and maintain most of the moors, and trying to ensure that they do it legally and in an environmentally positive fashion, while opening up these glorious acres for visitors to enjoy.

On the whole, despite political pressures and chronic underfunding, it does a magnificent job, especially in educating visitors about what you can see and do here, and giving practical help to get you out experiencing it. It produces downloadable leaflets detailing a variety of **cycle** routes around the park, and similar help for **horseriding**, with links on its website to cycling organisations, riding centres and the British Horse Society.

If **walking** is your thing, then you will be very well looked after; the park provides free, downloadable leaflets on walking, details of 15 routes accessible to wheelchair users and invaluable information regarding access to wild country. The right of access to open land, which became law in 2005, has been a welcome arrival for those of us that enjoy exploring our country's uplands; for lovers of the North York Moors it has been a revelation. This right means that you can walk just about wherever you wish, across swathes of spectacular moorland, once jealously guarded by the shooting estates and out of bounds to the public. The national park gives detailed advice for responsible use of this privilege, online and at moorland access points marked on OS maps.

For more **information** about what the North York Moors National Park has to offer to Slow visitors, log on to its website (⊘ northyorkmoors. org.uk) or get hold of a copy of its annual guide/newspaper, *Out and About in the North York Moors*.

WILDLIFE OF THE MOORS & WOLDS

The landscapes of northeast Yorkshire are surprisingly varied. Within the geographical boundaries of this guide's six chapters are heather moorlands, mature broad-leaved woodlands, coniferous forests, chalk grasslands, upland rivers, lowland flood meadows, estuaries, intertidal rocky shores and towering sea cliffs. The happy consequence of all this variation is a diversity of flora and fauna that few regions can match – no 'A-list' celebrity nature reserves (Bempton excepted) but enough grassroots wildlife to keep even the most serious naturalists well entertained.

It's one thing knowing that interesting and exciting animals and plants exist in the region but it's another getting to see them: you have to be in the right place at the right time. Below are my recommended places and times to see the best of the region's wildlife.

THE NORTH SEA

As mammal recorder for the Whitby Naturalists Club I receive regular reports of whales and dolphin sightings along the North Yorkshire coast and the tally is very impressive. Harbour porpoises are the most common cetacean sighting, usually close inshore and often visible from land. Since 2018 a pod of bottlenose dolphins has moved into the area and is now often seen from both the shore and boats, especially in summer. The stars of the show though are minke whales which have been seen from clifftops but are much better viewed from a boat as they tend to congregate further offshore. What brings them here are shoals of herring during their spawning season between August and October – this is when the whale watching boats operate from Staithes (*All My Sons* and *Three Sisters*; page 25) Whitby (*Summer Queen* and *Esk Belle lll*; page 82) and Scarborough (*Skylark*; page 134). The successful sighting rate is very high – one boat from Whitby spotted whales on 60 consecutive days in 2015 and on one memorable day logged four different species: minke, humpback, fin and sei. For sheer numbers, 2022 was the best year on record with 83 minke whales seen from the clifftop at Staithes on one day alone.

FLAMBOROUGH HEAD

Flamborough Head (page 208) is an enormous finger of resistant chalk sticking out into the North Sea and the cliffs on its northern side in particular are home to spectacular colonies of seabirds between the months of April and July. Enormous numbers of guillemots and kittiwakes nest on rock ledges here but the two species everyone comes to see are puffins, at their most southerly nesting location on the east coast, and gannets. The gannet colony is on the highest section of cliff near the village of Bempton, where the RSPB has a reserve and visitor centre. The gannetry here is doubly unique – it is the only one in England and the only one in the UK not on an offshore island; consequently, these are the most accessible gannets in the country.

---

1 Wildflowers at Wharram Quarry. **2** Visit Dalby Forest for a chance to see goshawks. **3** A guillemot at RSPB Bempton Cliffs. **4** A common spotted orchid. **5** Otters can be found at Pickering Beck. ▶

RICHARD WATSON/A

ERNI/S

GIEDRIUS/S

ANDREW FLETCHER/S

KARL WELLER/S

RAVENSCAR

Grey seals are one of the UK's signature animals with 95% of the European population living around our shores. The species was afforded protection in 1970 and numbers nationally have been on the rise since, with big colonies like those in Northumberland and north Norfolk reaching capacity in recent years and overflow colonies being founded. Ravenscar (page 127) is one of these and is now home to 300 to 400 grey seals all year round, with even more during the breeding season months of October to January.

There are three ways to get to see Ravenscar seals: on foot along the flat shoreline from Stoupe Beck Beach (four-miles return – be very careful with tides); on foot from Ravenscar village along the clifftop (one-mile return but on a very steep footpath); or by boat from Whitby (⌀ whitbycoastalcruises.com). Whichever way you go, don't get too close, leave your dog at home and listen to the advice of the Yorkshire Seal Group volunteers if they are there.

DALBY FOREST

To the west of Scarborough, the connected woodlands of Dalby, Wykeham, Langdale and Broxa (let's call it Greater Dalby Forest) constitute a huge area of mainly coniferous woodland under the stewardship of the Forestry Commission. Much of the underlying rock is Jurassic limestone and consequently the flora is quite rich, especially on the forest-track verges which are thankfully mown sympathetically. Orchids are particularly well represented, with common spotted, northern marsh, bee and fly all thriving here. Dalby Forest (page 120) is however best known for its birdlife , particularly birds of prey. There is a healthy population of goshawks and also breeding honey buzzards and hobbies. The best place to view them from is the Raptor Viewpoint in Wykeham Forest, especially in early spring when courtship displays are in full swing. Midsummer is the time for two other birds of note: nightjars, which sing at dusk in clear-felled areas, and turtle doves likewise at dawn – the tiny hamlet in Harwood Dale where the former Mill Inn stood (YO13 0LA) is a hotspot for the latter.

SCALING DAM

This small reservoir (page 66) owned by Northumbrian Water sits alongside the busy A171 Guisborough–Whitby road but is backed by the heather moorland of Roxby High Moor. It is a popular watersports and angling venue but the western end has been designated as a nature reserve with a hide overlooking it from next to the boat park. Birdwatching is good here all year round. In summer, breeding birds include marsh harrier, little ringed plover, cuckoo, hundreds of greylag geese and recently the odd pair of barnacle geese. Ospreys are seen regularly on passage in spring and autumn and there are hopes that they will one day stay and nest. Winter sees good numbers of visiting wildfowl, particularly whooper swans, goldeneye ducks, white-fronted geese and nationally important numbers of lapwings. Raptors are often seen over the moors behind the dam and Beacon Hill is a favourite migration stop-off for dotterels during May.

LEVISHAM ESTATE

In the main, National Park Authorities don't actually own any land, which makes the Levisham Estate (page 115) unusual. The purchase of this ex-grouse shooting estate was completed by the North York Moors National Park in 1985 and it has managed it ever since, not as a profit-making business but for its biodiversity, archaeological and leisure-amenity value. There are fewer grouse here than more intensively managed moorlands elsewhere but more of everything else. As part of its Higher Level Countryside Stewardship Scheme, the park is reversing the damage done by past drainage schemes and reforesting the bracken-covered slopes while still maintaining heather on the tops. This is done mainly by mowing rather than the damaging practice of burning, and some patches of heather are allowed to develop to maturity – an excellent habitat for nesting merlins (and hen harriers if they return). Other birds doing well on the moor are ring ouzel, snipe, lapwing, curlew and golden plover.

Overgrazing is a major problem in many areas of the National Park but on the Levisham Estate some areas have been allowed to develop into low scrubland and these have good populations of stonechat, whinchat and yellowhammer. Patches of ancient woodland in the valleys have all three species of UK woodpecker, plus redstart and tree pipits. Otters hunt along Pickering Beck and it's hoped that a nearby population of water voles will find their way back here as well. Floral specialities here are the most southerly dwarf cornels in the UK, at the Hole of Horcum, and un'improved' wet meadows with green-winged orchids, meadow saxifrage, common meadow rue (not common at all!) and blunt-flowered rush. If you are coming by car or bus the best access point to the estate is the car park at The Hole of Horcum (page 118) on the A169. Alternatively, catch a North Yorkshire Moors Railway train and get off at either Newtondale Halt or Levisham Station.

WHARRAM QUARRY

Disused chalk and limestone quarries often support a wonderful array of wildflowers. The Yorkshire Wolds is dotted with scores of old chalk quarries and this one is probably the best of them for wildlife, which is why the Yorkshire Wildlife Trust decided to look after it. There are carpets of beautiful blooms to see from May to August but the best time to visit is June or July as this is when the orchids (common spotted, pyramidal and bee) are in flower. Other rarities include clustered bellflower, red hemp nettle and parasitic thistle broomrape. This floral wealth is bound to attract pollinating insects galore, with butterflies the most obvious: marbled white, common blue, small heath, meadow brown and dingy skipper all breed here in good numbers. Entry is free and access is half a mile from Wharram le Street (page 201) on the Birdsall road, but no dogs are allowed.

WHELDRAKE INGS

In its final 12 miles before it empties into the Ouse estuary, the Derwent is a wild and untamed river. Wintertime sees it escape the bounds of its banks entirely and inundate large areas of floodplain that make up the Lower Derwent Valley National Nature Reserve. The most accessible part of the NNR is known as Wheldrake Ings and is run by the Yorkshire Wildlife Trust. A combination of seasonal flooding and traditional farming encourages a rich and very rare meadow flora that attracts large populations of birds – breeding waders like black-tailed godwits, water rails and spotted crakes in summer and thousands of ducks, geese and swans in winter. Otters and water voles live here all year round. Wedged as it is between the River Derwent and the Pocklington Canal (page 195), the reserve can be accessed from the minor road between Wheldrake and Thorganby but is also visible from the canal towpath. Car parking is available at Bank Island (Natural England) and the end of Ings Lane (YWT). Free entry, no dogs.

SAVOURING THE TASTES OF NORTH YORKSHIRE

Beyond Yorkshire pudding and Wensleydale cheese, England's largest county has never been particularly famous for its food but, in gastronomic matters, as in so many other areas, North Yorkshire surprises with its unexpected mix of rustic no-nonsense and sophistication. What is certain is that there are some truly talented artisans making the most of locally produced, high-quality ingredients.

Yorkshire can't compete in the climate stakes with the West Country and it doesn't have the fertile soils of the Fens, but what it has in spades is variety. Each area covered in this book has a distinct terrain which often determines food production. The heather-covered hills of the North York Moors produce some of the finest honey in the country. Sometimes for sale at the point of production (see Westerdale Heather Honey, page 64), honey is usually on sale at farmers' markets and village shops. Milk from the local dale farm herds goes to produce cheeses, such as those from the Botton Creamery (page 67) and ice cream to die for made by Beacon Farm (page 80) and Ryeburn of Helmsley (page 49).

The big coastal fishing fleets might be a thing of the past, but top quality seafood is still landed all along the Yorkshire coast. In Staithes, catch your own lobster on a Real Staithes trip before cooking and eating your haul in the fisherman's hut (page 97), or perhaps head down the road to Whitby for some traditional Fortunes oak-smoked kippers (page 87). Sea fish are expected, but maybe not local rainbow trout; limestone spring-water near Pickering allows these fish to be cultured at Willowdene Farm (page 108), where an unexpected crop of watercress is also harvested.

Well-drained, limey soils, like those in the Howardian Hills and Wolds, favour fruit production. Apples from the orchards at Ampleforth (page 152) and Suffield (page 134) produce fine juices and ciders, grapes from Ryedale Vineyards (page 190) go to make award-winning wines, and the sloe crop from local hedgerows is made into all sorts of delights by the clever folk at Sloemotion (page 142). Meanwhile, York has a history of importing cocoa beans from the tropics and converting them into fine chocolate. The glory days of Rowntree's, Terry's and Fry's may be in the past, but small-scale, traditional chocolate-making is still happening at the York Cocoa House (page 223).

SQUIDBEAK

 squidbeak.co.uk

Wouldn't it be great if there was a website run by truly independent food enthusiasts who keep abreast of what's happening gastronomically in Yorkshire, and keep us informed. There is?... Hurrah, there is!

Squidbeak is run by Jill Turton and Mandy Wragg, two professional restaurant critics who both live in Yorkshire and share a love of unpretentious, high-quality food. The quirky name came from a sarcastic graffitied recipe in a posh restaurant – 'Squidbeak of a bum-arse on a bed of bum gravy'. Yes, top-end, trendy places to eat are reviewed here but Jill and Mandy also have practical 'Best For' sections with themes like 'walkers', 'gardens' and 'dog-friendly'.

And the beer? North Yorkshire has a really impressive array of breweries and some of the best feature in this book. The Great Yorkshire Brewery in Cropton (page 111) is a large and well-established business that exports so much beer to the Far East that it has a Chinese website; Wold Top Brewery is much smaller, but its beers win awards every year (Benchmark Session IPA – World Beer Awards 2021, Best UK IPA). The Goodmanham Arms (page 192) does brewing as it always used to be done – in the back of the pub, to be drunk by its own customers and those in a few neighbouring pubs.

FARMERS' MARKETS

Apart from farm gate stalls and honesty box eggs and jam by the roadside, farmers' markets are probably the best source of genuinely local, Slow produce. Most of those listed here operate one day a month unless otherwise stated.

Driffield Showground; 1st Sat

Guisborough Westgate; 2nd Sat

Helmsley Marketplace; 3rd Fri

Hovingham The Green; 1st Sat (except Jan)

Humber Bridge Country Park; 1st Sun

Malton Marketplace; 2nd Sat (Mar–Dec). Malton also hosts a cattle market on the last Saturday of the month and an annual week-long food festival (page 176).

Pickering Market Pl; 1st Thu

Stokesley Town Sq; 1st Sat

Thirsk Market Pl; 2nd Mon
Whitby Marketplace; every Thu (Mar–Sep)
Wykeham Downe Arms; every Fri
York St Sampson's Sq; 1st Fri

HOW THIS BOOK IS ARRANGED

MAPS

The map at the front of this book shows the area of land that falls within each chapter. The chapters themselves begin with a more detailed map bearing numbered points that correspond to numbered headings in the text. The ♀ symbol on these maps indicates that there is a walk in that area, and featured walks are also given simple sketch maps.

By far the most complete and useful maps for walking, cycling, horseriding and general sightseeing are the OS 1:25,000 Explorer series. Those covering the region described in this book are as follows:

OL26 North York Moors – Western area
OL27 North York Moors – Eastern area
290 York
294 Market Weighton & Yorkshire Wolds Central
300 Howardian Hills & Malton
301 Scarborough, Bridlington & Flamborough Head

These maps are referenced in the text, preceded by a ✻ symbol.

CAFÉ, PUB & RESTAURANT LISTINGS

Each place heading comes with recommended places to eat, drink and, in some instances, shop. I have chosen standout, high-quality venues, outlets with a 'slow' ethos, my own personal favourites and, when the stars align correctly, some gems that are all three. A village pub or café will sometimes get a mention because there is nowhere else available whereas York, for example, has literally hundreds of great places that I wish I had the space to include.

With Covid and seasonal energy bill pressures, opening hours for many establishments seem to have become very fluid. Consequently I have decided not to give too much detailed information in the listings and recommend that you check by phone or website before visiting. If

no mention is made about special opening times you can reasonably assume that it's open every day and all year round.

ACCOMMODATION

Accommodation has been recommended on the basis of location and because it embraces a Slow approach either in its 'green' ethos or its overall feel.

Hotels and B&Bs are indicated by the symbol 🛏 after town and village headings, self-catering options by 🏠, and campsites by ▲, with a cross-reference to their contact details under *Accommodation*, page 247. For full listings, go to ⌖ bradtguides.com/nymsleeps.

CAR-FREE TRAVEL

TRAINS

York is the hub of the rail network hereabouts. From York Station, you can travel north on the East Coast Main Line for **Thirsk** (*Chapter 1*) or east on the Trans-Pennine Express to **Malton** (*Chapters 4 and 5*) and **Scarborough** (*Chapter 3*). From Scarborough the Yorkshire Coast Line, visits **Filey** (*Chapter 3*) then skirts the **Wolds** (*Chapter 5*), with stations at Hunmanby, Bempton, Bridlington, Driffield and **Beverley**. A circular route can be completed back to York via Hull and Selby.

The only other 'Network' rail line in the region is the wonderful **Esk Valley Line** which runs between Middlesbrough and Whitby, calling at Great Ayton (*Chapter 1*) and of the many places featured in *Chapter 2*. Not counting the miniature North Bay Railway in Scarborough, only one private train line operates in the region and that is the **North Yorkshire Moors Railway** (page 72), a steam railway running from Pickering to Grosmont. On its 18-mile route it calls at Levisham and Goathland and at peak times it continues along the last six miles of the Esk Valley line to Whitby.

BUSES & COACHES

A cheaper (but slower) way of **getting here** is by the excellent Yorkshire Coastliner bus. This service runs every day from Leeds to York (every

---

◀ **1** The farmers' market in Thirsk. **2** Opportunities for horseriding are covered in individual chapters. **3** Bike trail at Roseberry Topping. **4** Derek Fox is a traditional butchers in Malton.

15 minutes) and then on to Malton (every 30 minutes). Here the service splits, with buses travelling to Scarborough (every hour), Whitby via Pickering and Goathland (three times a day) and Filey and Bridlington (three times a day).

Once you have got here, **getting around** by bus is not quite so simple. As is the way with bus services, the smaller and more isolated the place the poorer the service, especially in the less mainstream tourist venues. Buses around the quieter corners of the Howardian Hills and Wolds are particularly sparse.

Below is a list of bus-hub towns, the relevant bus numbers and the villages with no rail access. Check before you use them because some are very infrequent, summer and/or weekends only.

Beverley X46, X47 The Hull–York bus that calls in on Market Weighton and Pocklington.
Great Ayton 18, 28A and 81 to Stokesley, then 80 and 89 for Great Broughton, Carlton, Faceby, Swainby and Osmotherley.
Malton Castleline to Castle Howard via Welburn and Bulmer; 190 for Wharram le Street and Weaverthorpe.
Scarborough X93 for Burniston, Cloughton, Robin Hood's Bay and Whitby; 128 and X28 to Helmsley via Pickering, Sinnington and Kirbymoorside; 10 for Cayton.
Thirsk 59 serves Kilburn and Coxwold.
Whitby X93 for Ugthorpe and Scaling Dam; X4 for Sandsend, Lythe, East Barnby, Runswick Bay and Staithes; X40, 840 for Goathland.

Tour buses

Open-top buses operate in three of the region's towns. York has two companies running tours, Scarborough likewise and Whitby has just the one.

PARK-&-RIDE

Parking can be a headache, especially in popular destinations at busy times. At the time of writing there are three towns featured in the book with successful park-and-ride schemes: York has five options dotted around its ring road (⊘ york.gov.uk) and Scarborough two (⊘ northyorks.gov.uk/scarboroughparkandride). After years of desperate need, Whitby has also finally got one but it struggles to cope at peak times; on very busy days it's still better to leave your car at a village on either the Esk Valley or North Yorkshire Moors rail lines and catch a train into town.

BOAT TRIPS

The harbour towns of the North Yorkshire coast have no ferries to take you from A to B but lots of opportunities exist for trips out and back in the summer months (weather permitting). Scarborough and Whitby offer the most options. All of Scarborough's vessels operate out of the harbour. Numerous boats advertise angling trips, usually with a sandwich board on the harbourside; just turn up and take your pick of the most reputable-looking one. Three enterprises offer pleasure cruises: **Queensferry Coastal Cruises**, **Scarborough Pleasure Steamers** and the *Hispaniola* (a mock sailing ship).

Details of the 19 sea-angling charter boats that operate from Whitby harbour can be found on ↩ whitbyseaanglers.com or through Whitby Tourist Office. As for cruises here, **Whitby Coastal Cruises** has three boats of various sizes (and exposures to the elements!) running trips up the coast, out to sea for whale-watching and up the river when the tide is in. The *Bark Endeavour* is a scale replica of Captain Cook's famous sailing ship that also does short sea trips.

The two small harbours of Staithes, in the north of the region, and Flamborough, in the south, also have charter boats – *All My Sons* **and** *Three Sisters* in Staithes and **North Landing Boat Tours** at Flamborough.

It is also possible to get afloat on inland waterways, of course. River Ouse cruises are available in York (page 236) or you could indulge in a gentle chug on the Pocklington canal (page 195).

CYCLING

The cycling scene in Yorkshire has seen hard times in recent years. The annual 'Tour de Yorkshire', which inspired so much grassroots participation in the sport, has not taken place since 2019 and plans to restart it in 2023 collapsed. At the time of writing, a similar event under a different name was being planned for the summer of 2024 so watch this space or check ↩ cyclingweekly.com.

There are still far more leisure cyclists around the county than in pre-'Grand Départ' times so its legacy is still being felt. Most bike-hire venues and cycle shops have remained open, many taking advantage of the huge upsurge in electric bike riding. Also, other providers like B&Bs, cafes and pubs have not forgotten to be bike-friendly so the future looks bright for cycling in Yorkshire.

FEEDBACK REQUEST

At Bradt Guides we're aware that guidebooks start to go out of date on the day they're published – and that you, our readers, are out there in the field doing research of your own. You'll find out before us when a fine new family-run hotel opens or a favourite restaurant changes hands and goes downhill. So why not tell us about your experiences? Contact us on ☏ 01753 893444 or ✉ info@bradtguides.com. We will forward emails to the author who may post updates on the Bradt website at ♦ bradtguides.com/updates. Alternatively, you can add a review of the book to Amazon, or share your adventures with us on social:
☐ BradtGuides ☐ BradtGuides ☐ BradtGuides

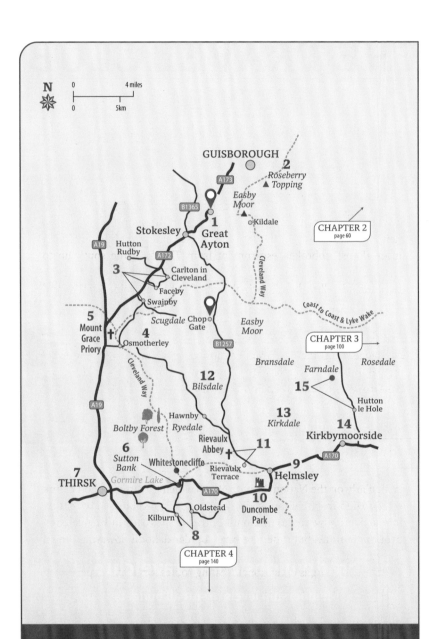

N

0 ____ 4 miles

0 ____ 5km

GUISBOROUGH

2

Roseberry ▲ *Topping*

A173

Easby Moor

▲ Kildale

CHAPTER 2
page 60

B1365

1

Stokesley **Great Ayton**

A19

Hutton Rudby

A172

Carlton in Cleveland

3

Faceby

Swainby

Scugdale Chop Gate

Cleveland Way

Coast to Coast & Lyke Wake

Easby Moor

5 Mount Grace Priory ✝

Osmotherley

4

B1257

CHAPTER 3
page 100

Bransdale

Rosedale

Farndale

15

Hutton le Hole

A19

Cleveland Way

12 *Bilsdale*

13 *Kirkdale*

14 Kirkbymoorside

Hawnby

Ryedale

Boltby Forest

Rievaulx Abbey ✝ **11**

6 *Sutton Bank*

Whitestonecliffe

Rievaulx Terrace

9 A170 Helmsley

7 THIRSK

Gormire Lake

A170

10 Duncombe Park

Kilburn Oldstead

8

CHAPTER 4
page 140

THE CLEVELAND & HAMBLETON HILLS

28

1
THE CLEVELAND & HAMBLETON HILLS

Travelling up or down the Vale of York you are likely to be moving at speed, whether in a car on the A19 or on a train on the East Coast main line. Either way, to the east you will see a range of hills stretching in an almost unbroken escarpment from Thirsk in the south up to Teesside in the north. Occasional crags stand proud from the slopes, tree-muffled valleys bend teasingly out of sight, and ruined castles and priories poke their heads into view. You may be sorely tempted to break your speedy journey, turn off the fast route and go-slow in the hills for a while. Succumb to temptation, because this is low-gear territory par excellence, from the limestone country of Kirkbymoorside, **Helmsley** and **Hambleton** to the brooding sandstone giants overlooking **Osmotherley**, **Great Ayton** and **Guisborough**.

SELF-POWERED TRAVEL
CYCLING
If you are OK with testing hills then **road biking** here is good, particularly on the National Route No 65 which traverses a good chunk of the region from Hutton Rudby in the north to Kilburn in the south, on two alternative routes. A circuit of the minor roads in Farndale is a favourite of mine, but avoid the very popular daffodil flowering time if you want quiet, safe roads.

Off-road biking is exceptional. Testing routes for fit and experienced riders are easy to find; just spread out a copy of the 1:25,000 OS Explorer map OL26 and link together bridleways and green lanes across the moor tops. Some particularly good, but deserted, routes head out of the heads of Farndale and Bransdale. For flatter and easier riding, **Farndale's** high-level disused ironstone railway is a fabulous five miles from Blakey Ridge that can be extended to a ten-mile horseshoe using the Westside

Road green lane. A steep descent will bring you to the pub at Church Houses, a mile from the start point but unfortunately over 1,000ft lower. Another flattish high-level route is the Cleveland Way north of **Sutton Bank**. The first half a mile is footpath so you need to detour to Dialstone Farm or walk the bike, but from Whitestone Cliff there are three loops of four, six and eight miles, easy enough for families, that return along the tarmac Hambleton Road. This last route takes you close to the best forest track riding in the region, in **Boltby Forest**.

 ## CYCLE SHOPS & BIKE HIRE
Bike hire
Sutton Bank Bikes National Park Centre, Sutton Bank ✐ 01845 597759 ⟁ suttonbankbikes.co.uk ⊙ Thu–Mon.
Yorkshire Bike Hire Black Horse Ln, Swainby ✐ 01642 688549 ⟁ yorkshirebikehire.co.uk ⊙ Fri–Tue.

Cycle shops
There are useful bike shops for parts and repairs at:

Bike Scene Park Ln, Guisborough ✐ 01287 610735 ⟁ bikescene.co.uk ⊙ Mon, Tue & Thu–Sat.
NRG Cycles 30 High St, Great Ayton ✐ 01642 723527 ⟁ nrgcycles.co.uk
Westbrook Cycles Stokesley Industrial Estate ✐ 01642 710232 ⟁ westbrookcycles.co.uk ⊙ Mon–Sat.

HORSERIDING
You will find lots of scope to ride here, with or without your own horse, on hundreds of miles of bridleway, green lane and permitted forest track. If you bring your own horse, places offering horse accommodation can be found on the national park's website at ⟁ northyorkmoors.org.uk/visiting/enjoy-outdoors/horse-riding.

 ## RIDING CENTRES
The following riding centres provide trekking or hacking:

Bilsdale Riding Centre Hawnby ✐ 01439 798225 ⟁ bilsdaleridingcentre.co.uk
Boltby Pony Trekking and Trail Riding Centre Boltby ✐ 01845 537392 ⟁ boltbytrekking.co.uk

i TOURIST INFORMATION

Great Ayton Discovery Centre, High St ✆ 01642 723268
Helmsley Castlegate ✆ 01439 770173
Sutton Bank National Park Visitor Centre ✆ 01845 597426
Thirsk Market Pl ✆ 01845 522755

WALKING

The one official National Trail in the region is the **Cleveland Way** (110 miles) with one end (whether it's the start or the finish is your choice) at Helmsley. It follows the whole length of the Hambleton and Cleveland hills before heading to the coast near Skinningrove. Much of the cream of the walking in the area is along this route, taking in as it does the high edges with magnificent views; two of the best areas to head for are Sutton Bank (extremely easy, level strolling along the top from the visitor centre) and in either direction from the B1257 north of Chop Gate (circular walks work particularly well here, joining Chop Gate with the Cleveland Way). Other less official but still very popular long-distance routes are the **Tabular Hills Way** (48 miles), heading east from Helmsley to join the two loose ends of the Cleveland Way together; the **Lyke Wake Walk** (40 miles), a very old traditional route from Osmotherley to Robin Hood's Bay; and the **Hambleton Hillside Mosaic Walk** (36 miles), a circular trail from Sutton Bank.

Shorter sections of all these trails make good day or half-day walks, the perennial problem being transport, as they are not circular routes. Some sections that can use public transport one way are **Kildale to Great Ayton via Captain Cook's Monument** (a pleasant, mainly woodland walk of three miles using the Esk Valley Railway as a shuttle); **Carlton to Swainby via Carlton Bank** (an airy five-mile moorland traverse with extensive views of the Vale of Mowbray; bus 89 gets you back); and **Sutton Bank to Rievaulx or Helmsley** (five or seven miles, along the lovely valleys of Nettle Dale and Ryedale – best done this way as it is downhill; use bus M4 for the return leg). In **Farndale** and **Rosedale** some of the best walking takes in the valleys themselves and the high moors just above, though the route-finding through fields can be very intricate. Once you're up on the Moors, however, it's a different world; visibility is unimpeded by walls and trees and you can wander where you wish, all being open access land.

THE CLEVELAND HILLS

The gradually rising land of the North York Moors has its precipitous swansong in its northwestern corner; a final celebration of altitude in a series of buttresses, overlooking the Cleveland plain. Clustered around the ankles of these hills are a string of old villages, the largest being **Great Ayton** and **Osmotherley**.

1 GREAT AYTON

Soon after your arrival in Great Ayton you may begin to suspect the existence of a famous old boy, one James Cook, whose former presence is writ large, though he only spent nine years of his youth living here. Born in 1728 in Marton (now a suburb of Middlesbrough), James Cook was one of the great explorers, and his sea voyages charted much of New Zealand and Australia. The Cooks moved to Great Ayton when he was a child, and his father worked nearby at Aireyholme Farm on the slopes of Roseberry Topping where the family lived; the Cooks also had a cottage in the village, dismantled stone by stone in 1933 and re-erected in Melbourne, Australia. The **Captain Cook Schoolroom Museum** (✆ 01642 724296 🖰 captaincookschoolroommuseum.co.uk ⊙ Apr–Oct; free entry) is in the very school the young James attended for four years, and has displays about his life and the village's past.

The main street running parallel with the river is overlooked by a Quaker school, founded in 1841, but sadly closed in 1997. The railway line here doubles as the boundary of the national park, with Great Ayton outside and this spectacular branch of the Cleveland Hills most definitely in. Two summits stand out: Easby Moor with its tall memorial pillar, and the unmistakable outline of **Roseberry Topping**.

¶ FOOD & DRINK

For **shopping**, head three miles south to the market town of Stokesley which has two excellent pubs and a Friday market, or four miles north to the much bigger town of Guisborough. This former capital of Cleveland also has a market (Thursday and Saturday).

Cookfellas Winebar and Eatery Westgate, Guisborough ✆ 01287 658700 🖰 cookfellas. co.uk ⊙ Tue–Sat. A modern European-style restaurant in an old pub building. The best place to eat in town and very popular - booking essential.

A walk to the Captain Cook Memorial

❄ OS Explorer map OL26; start: Great Ayton Station, 📍 NZ574108; 4½ miles; moderate.

Captain Cook's Memorial stands proud a short walk southeast of Great Ayton. Thank goodness common sense prevailed in 1827 when sites for a memorial to Captain Cook were discussed, and Roseberry Topping was rejected in favour of Easby Moor. This flat-topped hill is enhanced by the 51ft tower whereas the Topping needs no help in catching the eye. Ringed with old sandstone quarries, capped with heather and a healthy population of red grouse, this is good walking country, though rarely quiet, as the Cleveland Way crosses the top. My preference is to link it with Roseberry Topping to create a five-mile walk from Great Ayton to Kildale, returning by train.

The walk starts at Great Ayton Station, heads east on a minor road then north after 300yds on a green lane towards Aireyholme Farm. A choice of paths and bridleways bypass the farm and head to the summit of Roseberry Topping. The return trip follows the Cleveland Way south to Captain Cook's Monument, followed by another choice of paths through Mill Bank Wood to finish at Kildale.

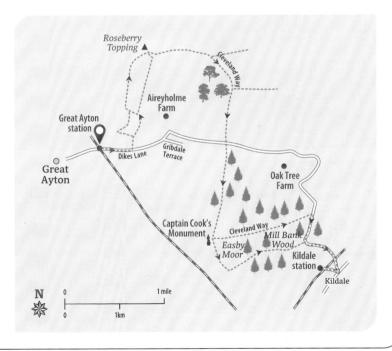

Joplins Restaurant High St ✆ 01642 722773 ⌕ joplinsrestaurant.co.uk ⊙ Wed–Sat.
Local seafood cooked brilliantly: not cheap but definitely worth it.

Pomegranate Persian Tea Room Park Sq ✆ 01642 958764 ⬛ ⊙ Wed–Mon. A
speciality tea room, yes, but one that also serves delicious Middle-Eastern food.

Spread Eagle High St, Stokesley ✆ 01642 710278 ⬛. A small and unspoiled market town
pub with good-value, home-cooked food and a range of real ales including guests from micro-
breweries. The beer garden backs on to the River Leven and has duck-feeding potential.

Suggits Café and Shop High St, Great Ayton ✆ 01642 722522 ⬛ Suggits Ices. An ice-
cream shop since the 1920s, old-fashioned sweet shop and very popular cyclists' café – very
much a local institution. Waterfall Park opposite is a pleasant place to sit and enjoy your
ice cream.

The White Swan West End, Stokesley ✆ 01642 714985 ⌕ whiteswanstokesley.co.uk. A
typical 18th-century, one-room pub with an interesting J-shaped bar. The pub doesn't do
food but the beer is excellent, whether it's from the Captain Cook micro-brewery on the
premises or a local guest ale. Brewery tours by arrangement.

2 ROSEBERRY TOPPING

Some high mountains disguise their altitude with a humble show of
rounded slopes and flat, grassy tops. Roseberry Topping is the opposite,
a hill with delusions of grandeur, sometimes
even referred to as the Matterhorn of   *"A history of reverence*
Yorkshire. Such is its prominence, with an   *is hinted at in the name,*
abrupt conical shape and rocky summit, that   *which probably derives*
it is possibly the most recognised, best-loved   *from Odin's Berg."*
and most often climbed peak in Yorkshire,
probably deserving the title of 'Little Mountain' despite not even managing
the altitude title for the Cleveland Hills, as nearby Round Hill on Urra
Moor is over 300ft higher.

A history of reverence is hinted at in the name, which probably derives
from Odin's Berg, the Vikings associating it with their chief god, but later
generations treated it with far less respect. One local historian commented
that Roseberry Topping is an industrial summary of the North York
Moors… almost everything that has been taken from the ground in
Cleveland has been pillaged from its slopes – jet, coal, alum, sandstone,
fossils, ironstone and basalt. This last surprising mineral product was
quarried up until the 1980s from the Whinstone Ridge, a ruler-straight

◀ **1** Osmotherley. **2** Roseberry Topping. **3** Mount Grace Priory.

igneous intrusion crossing the Moors and breaking the surface here, and also at Egton Bridge, Goathland Moor and Sneaton Forest.

Despite its human ravages, Roseberry Topping provides a fine venue for a walk, inviting from every angle, especially the Cleveland Way extension from the east, and with a panoramic view from the top, hard to beat anywhere else in the country. The most direct route of ascent is from the hamlet of Newton under Roseberry, just north of Great Ayton.

3 CARLTON IN CLEVELAND, FACEBY & SWAINBY

⋏ Lordstones Country Park Carlton Bank (page 247)

Both Carlton and Swainby, and the smaller **Faceby** in between, are close enough to the A19 to cater mainly for the commuters of Teesside, but each has attractions for visitors. All three have a pub, **Carlton's** being the pick of the bunch, and old churches with unusual dedications: St Botolph's in Carlton is the most northerly in the country to be named after this Lincolnshire monk, while Faceby's **St Mary Magdalen's Church** has a fine collection of 'Mouseman' carvings (page 44). Carlton has an outdoor activity centre if you fancy exerting yourself.

Swainby is one of those settlements that moved sites after the ravages of the Black Death. All that is left of the old village of Whorlton are ruins of the 11th-century castle, and nearby, probably even older, church of the Holy Cross. Modern Swainby is an attractive collection of stone buildings lining the banks of Scugdale Beck.

Two roads lead uphill out of the moors end of Swainby, one the scenic back lane to Osmotherley, and the other, the winding, dead-end road up Scugdale. Being a no-through valley, this is a haven of peace and quiet, the only visitors being walkers, and climbers coming to play on its crags.

¶ FOOD & DRINK

The Blackwell Ox Carlton in Cleveland ✆ 01642 712287 🖰 blackwellox.co.uk. A typical village local pub with luxury log cabin accommodation behind the building. The extensive menu is predominantly Thai, and a range of cask ales is always available.

Lordstones Café/Restaurant Lordstones, Carlton Bank TS9 7JH ✆ 01642 778482 🖰 lordstones.com. This iconic venue at the top of Carlton Bank is a café during the day, but becomes 'The Beltie' restaurant on Thursday–Saturday evenings. Local estate Belted Galloway beef goes into the signature steak and burger dishes, hence the name. Quality local meats are also available in the adjacent shop and there are a variety of grades of camping and glamping available if you want to stay the night.

Rusty Bike Café Black Horse Lane, Swainby 🖉 07734 979029
🛈 therustybikenorthyorkshire ⊙ Fri–Tue. Warm (log-burning stove) and welcoming café between the A19 and the village proper (not near the Black Horse pub!). Run by cyclists for cyclists but everyone else passing seems to pop in.

4 OSMOTHERLEY

The most satisfying mode of arrival into this village is on foot from the south along the Cleveland Way. This route treats you to tempting glimpses, from high up on Black Hambleton Hill, of the village tucked into a fold of the valley-bottom fields, and descends through the verdant woods of Oak Dale.

Even using wheeled transport, it is possible to visit Osmotherley avoiding the nearby A19 dual carriageway, by approaching via the spectacular moor road over from Bilsdale, or the minor back road from Swainby. This latter route could well have been the one followed by the Queen of Northumbria and her dead child (see below). According to legend, she buried Oswy at the church in Tivotdale, and joined him soon afterwards when she died herself, of grief and guilt. Tivotdale's name changed to commemorate Oswy-by-his-mother-lay – a rather far-fetched, but poignant story.

However you arrive, you will find yourself at the village green, decorated by an ornately carved market cross and stone barter table, where goods were exchanged. The table is more famous now for one of Osmotherley's many religious connections, as it was used as a preaching pulpit by John Wesley in 1745. He obviously made an impression, as one of the oldest Methodist chapels in the world is hidden away down a cobbled alley across the road.

A DEATH FORETOLD

Many local stories have Roseberry Topping as a backdrop but probably the oldest is the tragic tale of the death of Prince Oswy. It had been prophesied that King Osmund's beloved only son would drown before his second year was out.

In a desperate attempt to thwart the prediction the King sent his infant son, with his mother, as far from water as he could find in his Kingdom of Northumbria – the summit of Roseberry Topping. On Oswy's second birthday, the queen dozed in the sun on the hillside and the boy wandered off. Her frantic search for him on waking ended with the tragic discovery of his body, lying face down in a shallow pool of spring water. Roseberry Well, now merely a marshy patch of ground, is marked on the OS map.

🍴 FOOD & DRINK

Golden Lion West End ✆ 01609 883526 🖥 goldenlionosmotherley.co.uk. A dark-stone inn overlooking the village green and the most popular of the village's three pubs. Inside, wood is the theme in the bar, and the beer is sourced from Timothy Taylor and other Yorkshire breweries. The menu is refreshingly simple, with an excellent range of gluten-free meals, and the wine list is extensive. B&B available.

Osmotherley Tea & Coffee Shop West End ✆ 01609 883419 ☺ Fri–Mon. A very welcoming little cafe next door to the Golden Lion. Sandwiches and cakes popular. Dogs welcome.

5 MOUNT GRACE PRIORY

Two miles north of Osmotherley, DL6 3JG ✆ 01609 883494 ☺ Apr–Oct daily; Nov–Mar variable; English Heritage

Of the bewildering array of orders of monks and nuns to have lived in Yorkshire, the Carthusians, the last to arrive from the Continent, are perhaps the least known. There have only ever been ten Carthusian priories, or Charterhouses, in England and Mount Grace is the best preserved of them all. Its position displays the usual monastic good taste for beautiful locations, tucked as it is beneath the steep wooded slope of Swinestye Hill. What struck me was how different Mount Grace was to more traditional sites like Fountains and Rievaulx; not one, big, dominating abbey church here, but smaller, homely buildings. This reflects the Carthusian philosophy of solitary hermitage, with each monk or nun living silently in their own cell, meeting only for chapel services and one long, communal walk, the only time they could speak – I bet that was a noisy affair.

Mount Grace Priory is owned by the National Trust but, oddly, administered by English Heritage. Areas of interest include a reconstructed cell, an exhibition upstairs in the attached manor house, a shop and activities for children. The gardens are full of wildlife, notably a family of famous stoats that have featured in various BBC wildlife documentaries. Beware, dogs are not allowed on the grounds.

THE HAMBLETON HILLS

When the heathery tops of the Cleveland Hills give way to grass, you will know that you have arrived in the limestone country of Hambleton. The most public face of these hills is its steep, scarp slope, often referred to as **Whitestonecliffe**, which stretches ten miles south from Thimbleby, and looks out west over **Sutton-under-Whitestonecliffe**, to **Thirsk** town and the rest of the Vale of York. At its more hidden, southern end, it tumbles down to **Kilburn**, to then merge imperceptibly with the Howardian Hills.

6 SUTTON BANK

The village of Sutton-under-Whitestonecliffe has two claims to fame, the longest place name in England, and the cliff itself that provides the label. The busy road that passes through Sutton is one of the main routes into the North York Moors, but as the many warning signs insist, it is not recommended for lorries or towed caravans. Sutton Bank, the hair-pin section up Whitestonecliffe, is blocked by stranded vehicles with monotonous regularity. At the top of Sutton Bank you will find the **national park visitor centre** of the same name ($\mathscr{O}$ 01845 597426 $\mathring{\partial}$ northyorkmoors.org.uk), with a shop, exhibition centre and tea rooms inside. A very entertaining half-hour can be spent with a cup of tea or coffee, gazing out of the window at one of the busiest bird feeding stations that I've ever seen (keep an eye out for the locally very rare turtle doves that occasionally turn up).

From the centre, six waymarked **walking trails** can lead you between two and nine miles astray, the best to my mind being a five-mile circuit taking in Gormire Lake; or just for a blast of air and the sublime views, head across the A170 on the dead-level, dead-easy stretch of the Cleveland Way, which heads along the top of the great cliff that is Sutton Bank for a very easy mile or so towards the **White Horse of Kilburn**. On your walk, don't just gaze down to the lake, woods and Vale of York, but glance upwards every now and again, and you may be treated to the sight of a glider drifting silently overhead. If it seems like an idyllically peaceful way to travel, and you fancy having a go – the good news is that you can! The **Yorkshire Gliding Club's** base is hidden away in the trees less than a mile from Sutton Bank, and it offers trial lessons where, under the expert guidance of an instructor, you can actually fly the glider with no previous experience. My wife bought me one for my birthday and it was the most exciting hour's experience I've had for a long time, especially the take-off.

A map detailing six circular bike routes from the centre, between 11 and 23 miles, is also available.

RICHARD BOWDEN/S

STEVE ALLEN/S

ELECTRIC EGG/S

WORLD OF JAMES HERRIOT/WORLDOFJAMESHERRIOT.COM

VETERINARY
SURGEONS'
PREMISES
EASE LEAVE
CLEAR

Gormire Lake

Beneath the Hambleton Hills scarp and one of the few natural lakes in North Yorkshire, this is also one of its most beautiful. With the pale cliff above and surrounding lush forest reflected in its crystal-clear limestone spring waters, the name hardly seems deserving, as it literally means 'filthy swamp'. Gormire is not only a haunting and evocative place, it's a prized haven for wildlife. The rich limestone woodland surrounding it is managed by the Woodland Trust, mainly for its flora, and the lake itself supports important numbers of winter waterfowl, like goosanders, tufted duck, pochard and kingfishers. The whole area is designated as a Site of Special Scientific Interest (SSSI).

Probably because lakes are such a rarity in this part of the world, many legends have grown up around Gormire Lake, some involving it being bottomless, or telling of it swallowing witches or geese and spitting them out in wells miles away (Gormire has no in- or out-flow river). The most common theme though, a white mare leaping off the cliff and into the water, complete with doomed rider, possibly derives from White Mare Crag, the alternative name for Whitestonecliffe. This refers to the shape of a horse that used to be visible in the rock face, not the White Horse at nearby Kilburn.

¶¶ FOOD & DRINK

The Hare Scawton ⌀ 01845 597769 ⌂ thehare-inn.com ◷ evenings only Thu–Sat. An inn reputedly once used as a brewhouse by the monks of Rievaulx Abbey in the 13th century, and now a Michelin recognised restaurant. B&B available.

Yorkshire Gliding Club Low Town Bank Rd, Sutton Bank ⌀ 01845 597237 ⌂ ygc.co.uk ◷ Tue–Sun. The clubhouse has a café and bar open to the public and selling great-value drinks, snacks and light lunches – an ideal vantage point to watch the gliders come and go. Gliding courses and lessons are available.

7 THIRSK

🏠 **Merry Hall** Boltby (page 247)

This small town has ticked along, minding its own business, for over a thousand years. Nothing momentous has ever happened here, no battles or royal visits to the castle (because there's no castle), just a

◀ **1** Gormire Lake, seen from Sutton Bank. **2** The White Horse of Kilburn. **3** James Herriot's Skeldale surgery is now a museum. **4** A carving from the Mouseman of Kilburn.

lower-league manor house and an old, but fairly average, church. For me, it is a celebration of ordinary Yorkshire life through the centuries, centred on trade in its busy market square and surrounding shops and inns. **Market days** are still the high points of the week (Mondays and Saturdays), with the cattle market moved to a purpose-built venue on the trading estate (Thursday) and a farmers' market there on the first Saturday of each month.

How apt then, that the town should earn some outside fame from the venue of a favourite local pastime, its racecourse, and the reminiscences of an ordinary working man, who just happened to write about his experiences particularly well.

"For me, it is a celebration of ordinary Yorkshire life through the centuries, centred on trade in its busy market square."

Alf Wight was the local vet in the 1940s, but the world knows him better under his pen name of James Herriot. His entertaining stories appeared in print in his vet series of books of the 1970s, but it was when they were televised as *All Creatures Great and Small* that a legend was born, and Thirsk became Herriot country.

His original surgery, in Kirkgate, the real-life Skeldale House, has been restored to its 1940s state and opened to the public as the **World of James Herriot** (⌀ 01845 524234 ⌀ worldofjamesherriot.org).

Another museum faces this one in Kirkgate. **Thirsk Museum** (⌀ 01845 527707 ⌀ thirskmuseum.org) celebrates life in the town from Saxon times to the present day, and famous pre-Herriot old boys, like Thomas Lord (of Lord's cricket ground) whose house this was.

¶¶ FOOD & DRINK

Cafés

Bliss Millgate ⌀ 01845 868163 ⌀ blisscafethirsk.co.uk. Informal and friendly with dogs made very welcome. Vegan options.

The Pantry Millgate ⌀ 01845 522423 ⌀ thepantrythirsk.co.uk ☉ Mon–Sat. Very friendly and good value. The homemade cakes go down particularly well.

Teatime Cafe Market Pl ⌀ 01845 523869 ⌀ teatimeyorkshire.co.uk ☉ Mon–Sat. Formerly called Arabica, this is a small, modern café with a good range of coffees and very attentive staff. Dog friendly.

Yorks of Thirsk Market Pl ⌀ 01845 526776 ▪️. A traditional café serving quality Taylors teas and coffees, and substantial snacks – not cheap but very good.

Pubs

As you would expect of an active market town, Thirsk's eight pubs rub shoulders with each other around the marketplace and Kirkgate. Unfortunately, in this case, competition hasn't pushed up standards so only one makes it into my listings:

Little 3 (Old 3 Tuns) Finkle St ✆ 01845 523782 ⏁ littlethree.co.uk. A quirky mixture of traditional (oak beams, great real ale and dogs in the bar) and hip (live music scene).

Travelling out of town you will find the following:

Carpenters Arms Felixkirk YO7 2DP ✆ 01845 537369 ⏁ thecarpentersarmsfelixkirk.com. Don't come here if you want a traditional village pub but do if you want to be very well fed because the emphasis is on high-quality food. There is also accommodation available, in luxurious garden rooms behind the building.
King's Arms Sandhutton YO7 7RW ✆ 01845 587887 ⏁ thekingsarmssandhutton.co.uk. Still very much a locals' pub, the King's Arms also serves excellent meals using seasonal local produce. Gluten- and dairy-free requirements are well catered for, and a wide range of vegetarian and vegan options are offered. Local micro-brewery beers are always on tap and accommodation is available.

Pick-your-own

Spilman Farming Church Farm, Sessay YO7 3NB ✆ 07754 857284 ⏁ spilmans.co.uk. Soft fruits for sale in June and July; including strawberries, raspberries, gooseberries, redcurrants and blackcurrants – all grown on the farm. Lots of pumpkins in Oct. There's also an on-site café.

ART

Rural Arts Westgate ✆ 01845 526536 ⏁ ruralarts.org ⏲ Tue–Sat. The old town courthouse is abuzz six days a week with all things art and crafty. There's a shop, gallery and performance space where events and regular workshops take place. Very child-friendly.
Zillah Bell Gallery Kirkgate ✆ 01845 522479 ⏁ zillahbellgallery.co.uk ⏲ Mon–Sat A nationally renowned gallery housing the largest collection of work, outside of his studio, by Norman Ackroyd CBE RA. Regularly changing exhibitions usually feature other Yorkshire artists.

8 KILBURN & OLDSTEAD

The unofficial emblem of the Hambleton Hills, logo of a local brewery and name of numerous local pubs, is carved into the side of Roulston

Hill above the village of Kilburn, and consequently bears the name the **White Horse of Kilburn**. Impressively large and visible for many miles (from York Minster tower for instance) it was created in 1857 by a local schoolmaster with the aid of his pupils.

The village itself has something of a Cotswoldy charm, with a beck gurgling down the side of the main street (in a deep unfenced trench – so beware), but is very small, and would be relatively unknown except for a famous former resident, Robert 'Mouseman' Thompson, woodcarver. **The Mouseman Visitor Centre** (✆ 01347 869102 ⌂ robertthompsons.co.uk) has outgrown his old workshop and is now in the old blacksmith's buildings over the road.

The Hambleton escarpment takes a sharp turn to the east above Kilburn, and at this corner an ancient drover's road descends to the valley, where **Oldstead** village nestles. The name Scotch Corner commemorates the

THE MOUSEMAN OF KILBURN

There's no doubt that Robert Thompson was an extremely talented woodcarver, whose skills alone may well have earned his fortune, but from the moment he came up with the inspired idea of carving a mouse on to every item he produced, his international fame was well and truely assured.

He was born in 1876 and, as a young man, took over his father's joinery business in Kilburn. His early work was mouse-less but his reputation grew, and Thompson carvings began to appear in many local churches and Ampleforth Abbey. The idea for the emblem apparently came when his carving companion, while working on a church screen, commented that their jobs left them as 'poor as church mice'. Robert had a light-bulb moment and carved his first mouse there and then.

By the time of his death in 1955 'Mousey' Thompson's work was to be found all over the country, including York Minster and Westminster Abbey. Such is his fame that a letter sent from Australia with just a picture of a mouse and the word 'woodcarver' on the envelope, was delivered safely to his workshop. The Mouseman Visitor Centre is still an operating workshop employing 30 craftsmen, but also a shop and café. Some of the furniture isn't cheap, but they produce smaller items such as napkin rings that make excellent souvenirs.

Robert's other legacy has been an upsurge of interest in quality, hand-carved furniture in the area. Ten workshops are included in the Thirsk Furniture Trail (⌂ thirskfurnituretrail. co.uk), each of which has its own motif carved on to every item, of course. You will have fun finding the hidden unicorn, fox, wren or beaver, but I suspect none will ever have the impact of that original humble church mouse.

nationality of many of the drovers and, in times gone by, an old farm-cum-pub sat here. Now the only building to be seen is a chapel – an amazing place created single-handedly and almost from scratch in 1957, by the sculptor John Bunting whose artwork adorns the walls and grounds. Its story is told brilliantly by his daughter Madeline, in her book *The Plot*.

¶¶ FOOD & DRINK

Black Swan Oldstead YO61 4BL ✆ 01347 868387 ⌂ blackswanoldstead.co.uk ☺ Very limited hours, so check in advance. It's well worth the mile stroll, or cycle, over from Kilburn to this 400-year-old gem. A Michelin star tells you all you need to know about the food, and the beer is good too. Low beams, roaring fires and wooden floors make this a comfortable space and, in 2017, the Black Swan became the first ever UK establishment to be named 'world's best restaurant' in the Tripadvisor Travellers' Choice awards.

Forresters Arms Kilburn ✆ 01904 947570 ⌂ forresterskilburn.co.uk. The food can't quite compete with the Black Swan's on quality, but then it is half the price. The beer, however, is in a different league with three cask Yorkshire ales usually on offer. En-suite rooms available.

THE WESTERN DALES

Three valleys bite into the southern slopes of the Cleveland Hills and channel their rivers and becks to the Vale of Pickering. The upper reaches of Farndale, Bransdale, Bilsdale and Ryedale are rural in the extreme, with some of the most inaccessible acres in the whole of the national park. Where these hills meet the Vale's rich farmland is where you'll find most of the villages, as well as the area's two small towns, **Helmsley** and **Kirkbymoorside**.

9 HELMSLEY

🏠 **Helmsley Garden Cottage & Railway Carriage** Helmsley (page 247)

Helmsley possibly attracts more visitors in relation to its size than anywhere else in the North York Moors. It has achieved this pulling-power without resorting to anything 'fast' or tacky, having unconsciously carved itself a niche as an upmarket resort and, perhaps incongruously, a destination for touring motorbike clubs, who almost fill the market-square car park some weekends. Families will not find a huge amount here to entertain young and active children, but it has a wealth of historic buildings, serene walled gardens, aristocratic connections and quality, speciality shops.

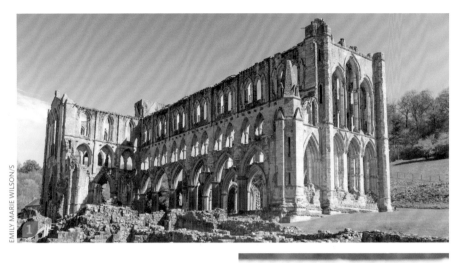

When Helmsley is at its busiest the crowds spoil the experience for me, so I try to visit on off-peak days. My favourite is on Friday when the street market is held, and the town is bustling and vibrant without being heaving. This is a very small town so almost all the interest is around the market square or, in the case of the outrageously ornate **Feversham monument**, smack bang in the middle of it. Here is where all four of Helmsley's old coaching inns are, along with most of its ten cafés and two exceptional **food shops**: Hunters and Perns (run by the Star at Harome).

Behind the library you will find yourself in Castlegate; carry on around the castle walls to the **tourist office**, which doubles as the entrance to **Helmsley Castle**. Signs here will direct you to **Helmsley Walled Garden**, once part of the **Duncombe Park Estate**, supplying the big house with a large variety of seasonal fruit and vegetables, and now hiding away behind the castle.

Two more venues away from the centre are worth seeking out; one for daytime entertainment and the other evenings. **Helmsley Arts Centre** ($\mathcal{O}$ helmsleyarts.co.uk) lies a short walk up an alley off Bridge Street. This old Quaker meeting house is the town's very active theatre, putting on a wide variety of plays, films, concerts and readings. The volunteers that run it are never less than really welcoming and the place always seems full. Slightly further afield is a welcome rarity for outdoor swimmers. The River Rye is not quite big enough for wild swimming but **Helmsley open-air swimming pool** ($\mathcal{O}$ 01439 326008 $\mathcal{O}$ helmsleyopenairpool. org), in Baxton Road, opens afternoons and early evenings, late June to early September.

Helmsley Castle
$\mathcal{O}$ 01439 771580; English Heritage

This jagged ruin may not have the spectacular position of Scarborough or the royal connections of Pickering, but it does merit a brief peep, if only to brave the bridges spanning an incredibly deep inner moat. The castle was founded by a character with one of my all-time favourite names from English history – Walter the Woodpecker, or Walter l'Espec as he was known to his Norman compatriots. He was succeeded by Robert de Roos who was responsible for most of the fortifications,

◀ **1** Rievaulx Abbey. **2** Helmsley town centre. **3** A Steller's sea eagle at the National Centre for Birds of Prey. **4** Helmsley Walled Garden with views towards the castle.

and later the Manners family built the Elizabethan mansion which is still partly intact. English Heritage now maintains it and has provided complete wheelchair access at ground level with some good hands-on exhibitions in the mansion range.

Helmsley Walled Garden

⌀ 01439 772314 ⌀ helmsleywalledgarden.org.uk ⊘ 10.00–16.00 Wed–Sat

My first visit to this place was during a 'Green Day', a festival of sorts to celebrate all things environmental and earthy (which are no longer run). The place was cluttered with information desks about recycling and nature reserves, stalls selling local honey, cheese and pickles and everywhere the sounds of folk music, sizzling sausages and happy people. It was great, but it was busy, busy, busy.

The second time I went was an altogether different experience, and what walled gardens are all about. I sat on a bench in a quiet, sunny corner – it's easy to find solitude in a five-acre space. The only sounds were the buzzing of the bees on the nearby roses and a wren trilling within the wall ivy. In the baking heat I could actually smell the apples on the branch hanging over my head just before I dozed off. To think this lovely garden nearly disappeared, but for the efforts of a determined group of locals led by a lady called Alison Ticehurst, who in 1994 started the long job of restoring the orchards, vine house and orchid house. The gardens are now back in full production, continuing Alison's vision of horticulture as therapy for local people in need. Almost everything grown in the gardens is available for you to buy.

Its demise up until recent years is a sad and poignant story. From its construction in 1758 until 1914 it supported 19 full-time gardeners and supplied produce to Duncombe Park House. At the start of World War I, the earl and all the gardeners went to serve their country – the earl was killed and few gardeners returned. This peaceful place is a fitting memorial to their sacrifice.

ⵙ FOOD & DRINK

Bantam Bridge St *⌀ 01439 770479 ⌀ bantamrestaurant.co.uk ⊘ Wed–Sun.* Opened in 2021, Bantam made it into the Michelin Guide within a year. Unusual, but very good, Mediterranean-style cuisine.

Beadlam Grange Farm Shop and Tearoom Pockley YO62 7TD *⌀ 01439 770303 ⌀ beadlamgrange.co.uk.* A resident butcher serves locally produced beef, lamb, pork, poultry and game, with fruit and veg and Yorkshire cheeses on the deli counter. The café is in the upstairs granary.

Feathers Hotel Market Pl ✆ 01439 770275 ⏾ feathershotelhelmsley.co.uk. Although Helmsley has more select hotels, this is by far the most welcoming and comfortable as a pub. The public bar, called Pickwick's, always serves Black Sheep and Tetley's with two guest beers, usually local brews.

Helmsley Brewery Tap Bridge St ✆ 01439 771014 ⏾ helmsleybrewingco.co.uk/brew-tap. Quite simply the best beer in town, draught and bottles. Brewery tours available.

Mannion & Co Castlegate ✆ 01439 770044 ⏾ mannionandco.co.uk ⏰ Thu–Mon. Another outlet from the Mannions of York bistro/deli/kitchen stable (page 222), though not open evenings. Specialises in high-quality, continental-style brunches, lunches and sandwiches.

Ryeburn of Helmsley Church Farm, Cleveland Way ✆ 01439 770331 ⏾ ryeburn.com ⏰ Tue–Sun. Delicious homemade ice cream in a bewildering range of flavours... oh, and posh Belgian chocolate, too.

Vinehouse Café Helmsley Walled Garden ✆ 01439 771427 ⏾ vinehousecafehelmsley. co.uk ⏰ Tue–Sun. Within the walled garden, the newly restored Victorian vinery houses an atmospheric café beneath the climbing vegetation. Most of the produce is organic, home produced, vegetarian or fair trade. Dog friendly.

🛍 SHOPPING

The Stickman Cleveland Way ✆ 01439 771450 ⏾ thestickman.co.uk ⏰ Thu & Fri. Keith Pickering is a walking-stick maker operating from a workshop just outside the Walled Gardens. He has impressive credentials: he made the Archbishop of Canterbury's crook.

10 DUNCOMBE PARK

YO62 5EB ✆ 01439 770213 ⏾ duncombepark.com ⏰ parkland year-round, gardens open mid-Apr–Aug 10.30–17.00 Sun–Fri. The house is not open to the public.

Lord and Lady Feversham probably wouldn't thank me for saying this, but Duncombe Park is, in essence, a second division Castle Howard. I don't mean that as an insult, because I actually prefer the Duncombe experience, but just as a measure of scale. They are both massive, opulent, privately owned and run 18th-century houses with surrounding parklands to match, but the Feversham estate is slightly lower key, the house and gardens smaller and, in terms of visitors, much quieter.

The origins of the house are unusual in that it was built from scratch by a commoner. Sir Charles Duncombe was a London goldsmith who made his fortune with more than a whiff of suspicion of insider dealing. He bought the whole Helmsley estate from the Villiers family after the death of the infamous Charles, Duke of Buckingham. Helmsley Castle he declared 'un-liveable' and built The Great House on a green-field site further up the hill, finishing it in 1713, three years after Castle Howard. Since then the two major events in the life of the house were a catastrophic fire in 1879 and a 60-year spell on let as a girls' boarding school. This chapter ended in 1986 when the Feversham family decided to return the house to its former glory and open it to the public.

The parklands cover nearly 3,000 acres, a large chunk of which is a National Nature Reserve, primarily to protect some of the oldest and biggest hardwood trees in the country, and the rare invertebrates and birds that depend on them. Two waymarked walks will take you through the best of the wild areas; the **Country Walk** and **River Walk** are both about three miles long but can be easily combined to create a five-miler for those who fancy a decent stride out. The hub of the garden landscape design is a half-mile-long terrace adorned at each end by two classical 'temples' – strikingly similar in conception to Rievaulx Terrace, three miles up the valley above Rievaulx Abbey.

Like Castle Howard, many outdoor special events are held here throughout the year, but mainly in the summer. You may want to time your visit to coincide with point-to-point racing, or a brass band concert, or a steam fair… or avoid them altogether for a quiet day away from the crowds.

The entrance to the Duncombe estate is also the entrance to the **National Centre for Birds of Prey** (✆ 0844 2422035 ⊘ ncbp.co.uk ⊙ mid-Feb–Oct 10.00–17.30 daily). If you have a couple of hours to spare I would really recommend paying a little extra to visit this place, but make sure you time it to catch one of the flying displays (three a day). If you are lucky you might get to see the centre's speciality bird, the huge Steller's sea eagle, in action. Those that fancy being even more hands-on can sign up for a Hawk Hike, an hour's walk around the estate where you get to fly a trained Harris hawk from your fist. The **Owl House Café** is the only place for a brew and a snack on the estate.

11 RIEVAULX ABBEY & RIEVAULX TERRACE

Rievaulx Abbey Rievaulx ✆ 01439 798228 ⊘ mid-Feb–Oct daily; Nov–mid-Feb 10.00–16.00 Wed–Sun; English Heritage **Rievaulx Terrace and Temples** Rievaulx ✆ 01439 798340 ⊙ Apr–Sep; National Trust

With a name like that, there has to be a French influence. It was 12th-century Cistercian monks who brought themselves, and the name, over from the Continent to settle in this breathtakingly beautiful bend of the valley of the River Rye and found **Rievaulx Abbey**. They were granted vast areas of land by the then Lord of Helmsley, Walter l'Espec, and quickly became very rich and powerful landowners. The monastery's influence peaked in the early 1400s when the community numbered more than 200, and then went into steady decline, with the Black Death hitting particularly hard. By the time Henry VIII spoilt the party completely, numbers were down to 23. Even though the abbey was significantly dismantled during the Reformation, it remains a stunning building – 'the most beautiful monastic site in Europe', according to the landscape painter, Turner. English Heritage also obviously rates it highly as it scores £1 more than Helmsley Castle on its strange sliding scale of entrance fees.

"They are a rich riot of spring and summer colour: cowslips, yellow rattle and early purple orchids in May."

Traffic can be unpleasant on the narrow lanes around Rievaulx but the M4 Moorsbus does call here on Sundays in summer, from Helmsley or Sutton Bank. By far the nicest way to get here, though, is to walk or bike the three miles from either Helmsley, Scawton or Old Byland.

Arguably the best views of the abbey are from a landscaped grassy walkway on the hillside above, called **Rievaulx Terrace**, although no access exists from one to the other, except via the road. Ownership here is a confusing issue; both the abbey and the terraces were the possession of Duncombe Park Estate, but they sold the former to English Heritage and the latter to the National Trust, along with the two **Neoclassical temples** that grace either end of the walk: a rotunda called the Tuscan Temple and a lavish banqueting hall called the Ionic Temple and resplendent with painted ceiling and wood carving. The Trust keep the main part of the terraces mown as per its original design, but manage the verges as flower meadows. They are a rich riot of spring and summer colour: cowslips, yellow rattle and early purple orchids in May and spotted orchids, betony and cranesbills later in the year. The obvious similarity to the terrace at Duncombe Park is not coincidental; it was once all part of the Duncombe estate and was laid out in 1758 by Thomas Duncombe III, the grandson of the creator of the Duncombe Park version.

12 BILSDALE

🏠 **Laskill Country House** near Hawnby (page 247)

Too few motorists bother to stop and explore here, which is a shame, because walking on both sides of the valley, and neighbouring upper Ryedale, is as good as anywhere else in the moors. In particular you might revel in exploring the remains of **jet mines** here. In my ignorance I always assumed that the jet industry was confined to the coast around Whitby, so was staggered at the number of jet mine spoil heaps I found lining the side of Tripsdale (♥ NZ5897).

Hawnby is the largest village hereabouts, with a very pleasant pub, a bridge, which replaced one lost in the flash floods of 2003, and a horse trekking centre. Woodland walking just to the north of the village, along the banks of the infant River Rye, is tremendous.

🍴 FOOD & DRINK

Hawnby Stores and Tea Room Hawnby YO62 5QR ☎ 01439 798223. This is one of those cornucopia places: a general store with lots of local information and a café that does particularly good cream teas and breakfasts.

The Owl at Hawnby Hawnby YO62 5QS ☎ 01904 208000 ☝ theowlhawnby.co.uk. A light and airy bar, usually serving three Yorkshire ales, which can also be enjoyed in the beautiful beer garden, weather permitting. The menu features local game, often cooked in a Continental style. Children and dogs welcome. Very comfortable B&B available.

13 KIRKDALE

In its infancy, Hodge Beck flows through the very isolated fields of Bransdale, which in its lower reaches does something very unusual for a valley – it changes its name, twice. It becomes Sleightholmedale for a while, but lower down still, between Kirkbymoorside and Helmsley, it takes on its most widely-known label of Kirkdale, and is visited most for its minster and a cave.

St Gregory's Minster is a tiny church with no village to accompany it, but the fact that it qualifies as a minster, and has a valley named after it, hints at its historical importance. Its south wall carries its most remarkable feature, a **Saxon sundial**, carved into a single block of sandstone 7ft in diameter, and set above an outside doorway. It is the most complete one of its kind in the world and its creator also left us a very informative inscription detailing his name (Hawarth), the owner of the church (Orm) and the priest (Brand).

A walk around Bilsdale Head

❄ OS Explorer map OL26; start: Chop Gate ♀ NZ559998; 6 miles; moderate .

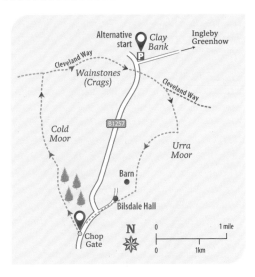

The best of Bilsdale Head can be taken in during a six-mile circular walk, including Urra Moor, the Wainstones climbing crag and Cold Moor. Being circular, this walk could be started anywhere and done in either direction. I have described it clockwise starting at the hamlet of Chop Gate, although Clay Bank car park (♀ NZ573035, near where the B1257 crosses the Cleveland Way) is a good alternative starting point.

Head north on the bridleway by the Methodist Chapel, to the top of Cold Moor then along the ridge to where it ends with panoramic views over Teesside. From here follow the Cleveland Way eastwards, down and up a couple of big dips, to the top of the steep slope above Clay Bank. Here a bridleway branches off from the Cleveland Way and follows an ancient earthwork as it contours around Urra Moor. Take this route for 1½ miles until it meets another bridleway which plunges down the hill to your starting point. The highest point on this route, the top of Chop Gate pass, is quite a geographical landmark, as it marks the watershed between two major river systems; to the north all waters flow into the River Tees, while southwards it's a much longer journey to the Humber estuary.

The views throughout this breezy moorland route are glorious and constantly changing, although its finest section is undoubtedly along the Cleveland Way.

Fascinating and charming as it is, don't restrict your Kirkdale visit just to the church; a mere 200yds from St Gregory's you will find a small hole, partway up a quarry wall. This is the entrance to **Kirkdale Cave**, which, although the longest cave in the North York Moors, is far more famous for what was found in it. In 1821 when quarry workers

JET-SETTERS, WHITBY-STYLE

A chat-up line that I would love to try out is 'Did you know that your dangly, black earrings were once part of a log, floating down a river 180 million years ago?' I'm not sure how successful that would be though.

Jet is fossil wood, but from one particular species of tree only, the *Araucaria* or monkey-puzzle tree. This very particular specification makes it beautifully carveable and polishable but also rare – the only place in Britain where it can be found is under the North York Moors.

A common misconception is that the Victorians invented jet jewellery in Whitby. They were certainly the first to mechanise the process, and Queen Victorian's morbid obsession with all things black popularised it, but jet artefacts have been found in Bronze Age tombs and at almost all Roman excavations. As for its presence at the coast, these are merely the most visible exposures of the seams; more than half the jet that ended up in the Whitby workshops was dug from beneath the western moors. Wherever river valleys had cut down far enough through the rock strata to expose the jet series, miners would tunnel 'drifts' into the hillsides, leaving a telltale line of spoil heaps today, in Bilsdale, Scugdale, Farndale and along the Cleveland escarpment. A happy geological accident resulted in a thin band of hard limestone being laid down just above the jet, and this Top Jet Dogger made a very convenient strong mine roof, allowing the drifts to penetrate deep underground. Working so far underground by candlelight, miners could not distinguish the black jet from dark-grey shale, so the whole lot was wheeled out in a barrow and sorted in the daylight.

Jet is still collected from the coastal cliffs to supply the small-scale workshops in Whitby, mainly by professional fossil hunters like Mike Marshall (page 94) and storm-bound fishermen, but on nowhere near the scale of the Victorian boom-time, when 1,500 jet workers were employed in the town. Over in the Cleveland Hills, the only evidence of this industry are lines of collapsed tunnels on the valley sides and pub names like the Jet Miners Arms in Great Broughton.

If you do find any black pebbles on the beach or hillside that you suspect may be jet, here's the test; scratch it on to a piece of pale sandstone and examine the colour of the mark. If it's black, bad luck, you have a piece of coal; if it's chocolate brown you have maybe struck it rich!

exposed the entrance, they found it full of the bones of prehistoric, and largely extinct, mammals from around 70,000 years ago. It turns out that this cave was a hyena lair, and the bones were the remains of their many meals, including hippo, lion, elephant and rhino – Yorkshire was obviously a warmer place back then. The cave is not officially open to the public, and a deep exploration is not recommended, but a short scramble up, to crouch in the entrance and peer into the blackness, is an atmospheric experience. Kirkdale valley upstream from the cave and minster makes an excellent walking objective. You can follow **Hodge Beck**, one of those disappearing and reappearing limestone watercourses, and enjoy rich woodland, full of flowers in springtime. A maze of paths on both sides of the beck gives you a range of options for return loops.

14 KIRKBYMOORSIDE

'Kirby', as it is known to local folk, is a small but busy market town, leaning on the southern slopes of the North York Moors – hence the name. It has many similarities to Helmsley seven miles down the road; it is roughly the same size, with a castle, a market square surrounded by old coaching inns, and a nearby stately home and estate. Are the two places friendly, co-operative neighbours then? Not a bit of it. A traditional rivalry exists between the towns that poor old Kirby always seems to lose out on. The castle is a feeble bit of wall built into a younger building, and the pubs, although busy, aren't quite as genteel as those of the 'posh' place. Even the National Park Authority seems to have been deliberately insulting; their headquarters are in Helmsley, whereas the park boundary takes a deliberate detour to completely exclude Kirby. None of this bad press is warranted of course because this is an agreeable little town, especially around the marketplace, and a start point for some pleasant walks in the hills behind – and a particular favourite bike ride of mine.

"A traditional rivalry exists between the towns that poor old Kirby always seems to lose out on."

Take either of the tiny but cycleable routes of Park Lane or Swineherd Lane from Kirby, and you will find yourself joining Back of Parks Road to Gillamoor (rehydrate in the Royal Oak), thence to Fadmoor and back to Kirby by a choice of minor roads (five or six miles in total).

¶¶ FOOD & DRINK

Cafés & farm shops

Newfields Organics The Green, Fadmoor YO62 7HD ℰ 01751 431558 ℰ newfieldsorganics.com. A wide variety of organically grown vegetables for sale direct from the farm.

Summit Bakery & Wholefoods Market Pl, Kirkbymoorside ℰ 01751 430033. Formerly a bookshop, now an organic bakery and a very pleasant café.

Pubs

The four pubs on Market Place have had mixed fortunes in the last few years but they are all open and selling good beer as I write. Even so, you may feel that it's worth a journey of a couple of miles up the road to Gillamoor for real quality.

The Royal Oak Gillamoor ✆ 01751 431414 ⊙ theroyaloakgillamoor.co.uk. A solid 17th-century stone inn on the village green noted for its food, wines and Black Sheep beer. En-suite rooms available.

15 HUTTON LE HOLE & FARNDALE VALLEY

Hutton or 'Hightown' presumably refers to this village's elevated attitude in relation to nearby Kirkbymoorside and 'le Hole' the pretty hollow it sits in. This is one of the national park's honeypot villages, with many visitors drawn here by the excellent Ryedale Folk Museum, but more than a few just to enjoy strolling around the village green, or calling in the pub or café for refreshment. The delightful river that tumbles over the limestone ledges of Ravenswick is the Dove, fresh from its journey further upstream through Farndale.

As quiet as anywhere in the Moors for 11 months of the year, **Farndale Valley** bursts at the seams with visitors in late March and early April. The reason for this popularity is the best display of **wild daffodils**, or lenten lilies, in the country. Most of the valley has been designated a National Nature Reserve to protect the millions of blooms; strangely no-one really knows how they got here and why there are so many of them, although one theory has the monks of Rievaulx introducing them from France. To cope with the 40,000 admirers that arrive during the four-week flowering season, paths have had to be paved, a shuttle-bus service from Hutton le Hole put on and the seasonal Daffy Café opened.

"Most of the valley has been designated a National Nature Reserve to protect the millions of blooms."

The official **Daffodil Walk** runs from Low Mill to Church Houses but it can be extremely crowded; for almost as many daffs all to yourself, follow either of the public footpaths alongside the River Dove upstream from Lowna Bridge on the Hutton to Gillamoor road.

◄ **1** A six-mile walk around Bilsdale Head takes in Wainstones climbing crag. **2** St Gregory's Minster, Kirkdale. **3** Ryedale Folk Museum.

Ryedale Folk Museum

Keld Lane, Hutton le Hole YO62 6UA ✆ 01751 417367 ryedalefolkmuseum.co.uk
mid-Mar–mid-Nov Sat–Thu.

The small and unassuming frontage to this museum, on the village main street, gives no clue to the delights hidden behind. Over 20 buildings, strung-out down a long, thin, three-acre site, house recreations of Ryedale country life through the centuries, all the way back to a thatched Iron Age roundhouse. Many of them are genuine historic buildings moved from their original sites, and rebuilt stone by stone, to house the artefacts of many rural craftsmen and craftswomen, like blacksmiths, wheelwrights, coopers, saddlers and dairymaids. Trails and activities are provided for children, and many hands-on events are put on throughout the year, usually with an old-fashioned theme; the ancient boardgame of Merrills, for instance, once had its world championships held here. Recent attractions have included a cottage cooking weekend, harvest festival, dry-stone walling taster, bee-keeping workshop and maypole dancing. The Ryedale Folk weekend is a regular feature in May.

FOOD & DRINK

The Barn Tearoom Keld Lane ✆ 01751 417311 thebarnguesthouse.com. All three cafés in the village are good but I think this one is the best; the fried breakfast is particularly tasty. A discount is offered if you show your Ryedale Folk Museum ticket. Also does B&B.

The Crown Keld Lane ✆ 01751 417343 crownhuttonlehole.com. Busy and welcoming village pub serving Black Sheep beer and wholesome traditional food. Rooms available but no breakfast.

Feversham Arms Inn Church Houses, Farndale East YO62 7LF ✆ 01751 433206 fevershamarmsinn.co.uk. An archetypal country pub, with stone flag floors and horse-brasses, serving simple but wholesome pub food and Yorkshire cask beer. Hugely popular at daffodil time. Good value, and offers self-catering accommodation.

The award-winning Slow Travel series from Bradt Guides

**Over 20 regional guides across Britain.
See the full list at bradtguides.com/slowtravel.**

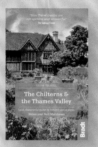

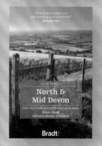

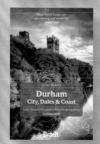

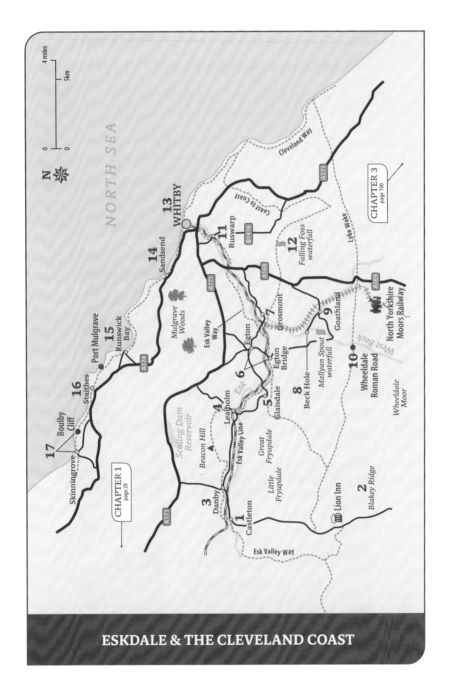

ESKDALE & THE CLEVELAND COAST

2
ESKDALE & THE CLEVELAND COAST

Eskdale, the 'valley of the winding river', is at the heart of the North York Moors, and the River Esk is the life-blood of the dale. It is only 25 miles long but it punches way above its weight; it has more charm, variety and points of interest than many rivers twice its size. Until recently the Esk was the only salmon river in Yorkshire, and is the only site in eastern seaboard England with a population of freshwater pearl mussels.

What I love most about the modern River Esk are its moments of wild inaccessibility. Long stretches where it wanders away from civilisation, often plunging into narrow ravines and crag-shadowed gorges where no tarmac road dare follow, and the only way to explore it is by foot or by canoe.

Eskdale ends at the point where the river enters the sea, the entrance to **Whitby** harbour, with this last leg of its journey in a surprising direction. Because of a geographical quirk, this stretch of the Yorkshire seaboard faces due north, so consequently, the coastline to the left, towards Teesside and Scotland, runs away westwards – and what a coastline it is.

The first two miles of it is beach, until the sand ends at a village called simply **Sandsend** – the first of a string of small, former fishing communities, tucked into what little shelter they can find behind rocky headlands, known locally as 'nesses' or 'nabs'. Resembling a giant crocodile's snout, Sandsend Ness is the first of these, and the start of the dark, Jurassic, shale cliffs rising progressively higher the further west you go. **Runswick Bay** is the next haven, hiding behind the heights of High Lingrow, followed by the derelict iron-mining harbour of **Port Mulgrave**. Further west still, at **Staithes** a beck has cut a way through the cliffs to form a spectacular, natural walled harbour. Beyond looms the huge bulk of **Boulby Cliff**, the highest point on the east coast of England, and reputedly the burial place of famed Saxon warrior Beowulf.

SELF-POWERED TRAVEL

CYCLING

If you can cope with occasional very steep hills, **cycling country lanes** in and around Eskdale is great, especially up the quieter side dales. A circuit of Little and Great Fryupdales is my particular favourite, mainly because the slopes are fairly forgiving, but also as the pass between the two dales navigates the delightfully named Fairy Cross Plain where bikes can be hired. The national park website (northyorkmoors.org. uk) has two downloadable routes – Esk Valley East and Esk Valley West – both about 20 miles long and with some serious hills in places.

The picture for the coastal strip is less attractive as few alternatives to the horribly busy A174 exist, except the lane over the top of Boulby Cliff, linking Cowbar and Skinningrove.

Off-road biking is sparse down in the valley bottoms, and tends to be muddy for most of the year anyway, but bridleways and former miners' tracks abound on the moor tops. Danby Beacon and Glaisdale Rigg are two good areas with less challenging routes and are ideal for families.

 BIKE HIRE & SHOPS

AL Suspension Station Works, Lealholm ✆ 07376 251169 ⊘ alsuspensionltd.co.uk. Bike service and repair; MTB suspension specialist.

Yorkshire Cycle Hub Fryupdale ✆ 01287 669098 ⊘ yorkshirecyclehub.co.uk. A major hub for all things cycling, both road and off-road. There's a shop, repair service, bike hire, regular social rides, a café and comfortable bunkhouse accommodation.

HORSERIDING

Hundreds of acres of moorland, and mile upon mile of bridleway, bode well for potential horseriders, though opportunities for hiring are limited.

 RIDING CENTRES

Borrowby Equestrian Centre Borrowby TS13 5EH ✆ 07545 259590 ⊘ borrowbyequestriancentre.co.uk. The only trekking stable in the region. Rides of half an hour or longer for any ability over four years of age. Children's riding parties can be arranged.

WALKING

Walkers are very well served here. For long-distance yompers, the Coast to Coast Walk and the Cleveland Way both skirt the edge of the area,

> ***i* TOURIST INFORMATION**
>
> **Danby Lodge National Park Centre** Danby ✆ 01439 772737
> **Whitby Tourist Office** Langbourne Rd ✆ 01723 383636

but the **Esk Valley Walk** lies wholly within it. Starting at the Lion Inn on Blakey Ridge above Castleton (the highest pub in the North York Moors) and marked by leaping salmon signs, it follows the complete length of the river from its source to the sea at Whitby. The number of shorter walks, to suit all levels of fitness and enthusiasm, is almost endless. You could for example try a short section of the **Coast to Coast Walk**, like Glaisdale to Grosmont, or vice versa, and take the train back to your start point. As ever, for **information**, the national park website or visitor centre at Danby are the places to pick up details of waymarked walks or walking guidebooks.

One gem of a walk worth a special mention is the **Rail Trail** from Grosmont to Goathland; rich wildlife, safe river access for children to go paddling, and the route is wheelchair accessible along most of its three-mile length.

ESKDALE

The River Esk flows from west to east, starting at the head of the dale, which the Vikings, not known for their imagination or sense of irony, named Westerdale, and ending gradually by mixing itself with the sea for its last two miles between **Ruswarp** and **Whitby**. In between nestle a string of thoroughly Yorkshire villages; solid but unassuming, chiselled from dark sandstone and growing up the dale-side at each important crossing point. They include rural idylls like **Lealholm** and **Egton Bridge**, the ancient fortified settlements of **Castleton** and **Danby**, and two survivors of a brutal industrial past, **Grosmont** and **Glaisdale**.

The mother river is fed by a series of tributary becks along its length, each with its own mini-dale. The largest of these, the Murk Esk, actually qualifies for 'river' status itself, albeit briefly at only 2½ miles long, and navigates even wilder country than the Esk. This is especially so in its upper reaches, through the moorlands and forests near the village of **Goathland**.

1 CASTLETON

Don't come here expecting turreted ruins: the building that gave this place its name is long gone, with the mound site now occupied by a private manor house. The village is mainly just a service centre for the upper dale, with two pubs, two shops and a petrol station. Visitors don't tend to stop here as Castleton can't really compete in the tourism stakes with neighbouring Danby, which ironically does have a castle.

Most of Castleton village isn't actually in Eskdale bottom, but strung out along a road escaping up the valley side towards Blakey Ridge, arguably the most dramatic moor-top crossing, and a fantastic bus journey to or from Hutton le Hole.

¶¶ FOOD & DRINK

Deli 23 High St ✎ 01287 669000 ⬧ deli23.co.uk. A great little shop selling a wide range of foods from small-scale, local, rural producers. Even the take-away coffee is roasted in Malton and Stokesley.

The Eskdale Station Rd ✎ 01287 660333 ⬧ theeskdale.co.uk. Both pubs in Castleton are good but this has the edge, with an idyllic river- and rail-side position just out of the village. Real ales from Yorkshire breweries and the excellent restaurant food merits its inclusion in the Michelin Guide. B&B available.

Westerdale Heather Honey The Bungalow, Westerdale YO21 2DE ✎ 01287 660208. Locally produced heather honey sold from the door.

2 BLAKEY RIDGE

A lonely moorland road from Castleton to Hutton le Hole heads along the exhilarating Blakey Ridge, which wonderfully encapsulates the wildness of the North York Moors. At the top stand a scattered collection of standing stones, guiding travellers across the moor at the head of three valleys – Westerdale, Danbydale and Rosedale. The tallest stone, named Young Ralph Cross, is the symbol of the national park and, along with two others, is said to commemorate the survival of three medieval travellers, lost in a deadly fog – Ralph the guide, and Fat Betty and Margery, two nuns from Rosedale.

Not far from the crosses is **Loose Howe**, a Bronze Age burial mound where a 3,000-year-old body was found, prepared for his voyage into the afterlife, armed, clothed and interred in a dug-out boat. In sight of Loose Howe, and surrounded by even older Neolithic burial mounds, the **Lion Inn** makes a most unexpected sight in an astonishingly inhospitable position and 1,325ft above sea level; like the similarly remote Tan Hill Inn in the Dales it was built to serve miners – those working in coal and iron in this case.

¶ FOOD & DRINK

Lion Inn Blakey Ridge YO62 7LQ ☎ 01751 417320 🖑 lionblakey.co.uk. A 16th-century inn in a superb, isolated moor-top location. The building, though very large, has low ceilings and open fires which give it a homely feel. Beer is from Theakstons and other guest breweries, and the wholesome meals are very popular. B&B available.

3 DANBY

Five miles from its source, the River Esk is straddled by a pair of conjoined twin villages, joined at a venerable bridge. Both communities sit comfortably in the valley bottom, with old pubs at their centre, the Duke of Wellington on the north bank in Danby, and over the water, the Fox and Hounds in Ainthorpe. The river here is still very young and narrow, and a good running leap could clear it in places, but it carries enough water to power Danby Watermill, whose wheel still turns the internal machinery, but sadly not within public view.

A long history of settlement is evident in the vicinity, with a wealth of Bronze Age earthworks and field systems on adjacent hills (Danby Rigg in particular), a Norman castle, and a medieval packhorse bridge. Despite all this, however, Danby's most influential building today, the Moors Centre, is predominantly Georgian. **Danby Castle** overlooks the village from nearly a mile away, and has its own access road crossing the river via a structure even older than that in the village. Duck Bridge, built in the 1300s as Castle Bridge, was renamed much later after a local stonemason who renovated it.

The minor road beyond Danby Castle leads into the wonderfully named **Little Fryupdale**, which itself is linked to **Great Fryupdale**. Both valleys, named in honour of the Viking goddess Freya, not a plate of bacon and eggs, offer great potential for foot and pedal exploration. Road cycling is quiet and gentle, a superb off-road route follows the Cut Road around the dale heads, and walking is excellent, especially on the central hill of Heads, which separates the two Fryupdales. It boasts a heathery cap and stunningly beautiful forest in Crag Wood at its northern end. Facing Danby Crag on Heads, across Eskdale, is the prominent **Beacon Hill**, complete with modern commemorative beacon, accessible by tarmac road to the summit. This road continues over to **Scaling Dam reservoir** (page 16), the largest lake in the Moors, and a good birdwatching venue – breeding greylag geese and little ringed plovers are specialities, with ospreys as regular passage migrants.

Danby Lodge National Park Centre

Lodge Lane, YO21 2NB ℘ 01439 772737 ⊙ Jan–mid-Feb Sat & Sun; mid-Feb–Dec daily

This building originated as the palatial shooting lodge for the Dawnay Estate and is now the flagship visitor centre for the North York Moors National Park. You could easily spend a whole day here, especially in fine weather, as there is just as much to do outside as in. Within the grounds, short, wheelchair-accessible walks follow the riverside and delve into Crow Wood, an orienteering course and climbing frame can entertain energetic children, the artistic will enjoy the sculpture trail and there are acres of lawn space for sitting and picnicking. For those happy to wander further afield, five waymarked walks start at the lodge. Recently revamped, the building contains an indoor climbing wall, a gallery with changing exhibitions of arts and crafts inspired by the local landscape, a shop and a tea room.

Danby Castle

Danby YO21 2NP ℘ 01287 669219 ◈ danbycastle.com

In a long and eventful life since it was built in the 12th century, this petite castle has passed through the hand of many aristocratic owners; Catherine Parr, who married into the Neville family, lived here as a young woman long before her recruitment as Henry VIII's sixth wife. As part of the Danby section of the Dawnay Estate, like the Moors Centre, it is owned by Viscount Downe. After many years of part-ruin, attached to a hillside farm, Danby Castle's latest chapter involves a neat juxtaposition of ancient and modern. Every October the Danby Court Leet, one of the few still in existence, meets in the jury room of the castle, as it has for centuries, to administer the affairs of the local common lands. The same room doubles as a wedding chapel operated by Esk Valley Weddings, a family enterprise comprising Carolyn and Phillip who live in the farmhouse (the southeast tower).

The castle is not officially open to the public, but you can nose around the outside of the ruins, and if you give them a ring they will be happy to let you in.

¶¶ FOOD & DRINK

Camphill Village Trust Botton Farm YO21 2NJ ✆ 01287 660871 ⬧ cvt.org.uk. Camphill community shop and café has home-produced Botton bread, cakes, milk, yoghurt and cheese. Botton Creamery cheeses have a fine reputation all over the county.

Danby Bakery Briar Hill, Danby ✆ 01287 669126 **f**. Speciality breads, cakes and confectionery to take-away or eat in the café.

Duke of Wellington Danby ✆ 01287 660351 ⬧ dukeofwellingtondanby.co.uk. A large, rambling but homely village pub on the central crossroads. Cask beer is Whitby Saltwick Nab, Daleside and a guest; evening meals are very good and, although lunches aren't served, the landlord is happy for food from the bakery next door to be eaten inside.

Fox and Hounds Brook Lane, Ainthorpe YO21 2LD ✆ 01287 660218
⬧ foxandhoundsainthorpe.com. A big 16th-century coaching inn with quoits pitch nearby (page 76). Cask Yorkshire beers and basic pub grub.

4 LEALHOLM

Back in the 1990s I was always baffled as to why Lealholm was not more popular as a place to visit. Granted, the riverbank and quoits pitch would be dotted with picnickers on a sunny weekend, but nothing like the hordes that would descend on Goathland or Grosmont rain or shine. Back then, there was only enough custom to support the pub and one tea shop at the Shepherd's Hall. Now

> *"Three places supply those wanting to indulge in a cup of tea and a scone, and the pub is busier than ever."*

numbers must have perked up, or people are drinking more, because three places supply those wanting to indulge in a cup of tea and a scone, and the pub is busier than ever.

I guess the reason for the influx is that more people are using the Esk Valley line and hopping off at the station here, the growing reputation of the revitalised Board Inn, or the fact that word has got out about the excellent walking and cycling routes from the village.

Two circular jaunts from Lealholm I would recommend are a low-level route and another longer one, partly on the moors above the valley. The beauty of them is that, following bridleways and minor roads, they can be done on foot, bike or horseback. The shorter of the two starts along the track just below the car park, and following the river eastwards (downstream). At Underpark Farm, the route heads under the railway and uphill to Rake Lane. The farmyard can be a bit 'clarty' – the Yorkshire dialect's understated way of saying that you may find yourself up to the knees in a mixture of mud and cow muck. A left turn at the quiet dead-ended Rake Lane takes you back to Lealholm via Lealholmside. The longer high-level route climbs up Danby Beacon and back via moorland track and Oakley Walls Road.

¶¶ FOOD & DRINK

Board Inn Village Green ☏ 01947 897279 ⊗ theboardinn-lealholm.godaddysites. com. An 18th-century alehouse in a glorious riverside position, with a quoits pitch out front. Lunchtime bar meals Tue–Sat, pizza night Fri, burger night Sat and Sunday lunch. B&B available.

Shepherds Hall Tea Rooms Main St ☏ 01947 897011 ⊗ shepherdshalltearooms.co.uk ⊙ Thu–Mon. Reopened after a period of closure, with a craft and local produce gallery attached. Beware steep steps to get in.

🛒 SHOPPING

Lealholm Village Shop Main St ☏ 01947 897310. A veritable cornucopia with tiny tea room attached.

Poets Cottage Shrub Nursery Main St ☏ 01947 897424 ⊗ poetscottage.co.uk. A serene hideaway just behind the village store, named after the 19th-century Irish-born poet, John Castillo, who lived here.

5 GLAISDALE

A more rural picture would be difficult to imagine, but the Glaisdale of 150 years ago was an altogether different scene: the river polluted, the air full of black industrial smoke, the clank and rattle of heavy machinery and rail carriages, and its erstwhile pub full of ironstone miners and foundry workers. Glaisdale's industrial revolution was short-lived and the scars have healed, but sharp-eyed industrial archaeologists will still have plenty to find.

The history of this long, straggling village goes way back beyond the Victorian iron boom as the graceful 17th-century packhorse bridge over the river testifies. It was constructed on the instruction of one Thomas Ferris, originally a poor farmer's son, who fell in love with the Squire of Glaisdale's daughter, but was refused her hand in marriage unless he

1 The River Esk at Lealholm. **2** Beggar's Bridge at Glaisdale. **3** The famous Egton Gooseberry Show. **4** Grosmont is at the junction of two railway lines. **5** Young Ralph Cross – the emblem of the North York Moors National Park. ▶

SS

SMILER99/S

EGTON BRIDGE OLD GOOSEBERRY SOCIETY

ATGIMAGES/S

DEJAVUDESIGNS/S

went away and made his fortune. When he succeeded in the task he returned, married his love and built 'Beggar's Bridge' to commemorate his wading of the swollen river to see her during their courtship, and to ensure that later needy suitors kept their feet dry.

At the point where Beggar's Bridge reaches gracefully over the river, a small railway viaduct does the same, though not quite so delicately. Glaisdale Beck joins the Esk through one of its arches, having just flowed down through West Arncliffe Wood. Strangely, this beck has been nowhere near Glaisdale village, which actually resides in Eskdale; the valley of Glaisdale, where the beck originates, is a rarely visited corner nearby. Its one minor road loops up one side of the dale, and back down the other, providing an excellent, gentle, family cycling circuit.

Every August, Glaisdale is host to an extraordinary event which I have attended on more than one occasion and would wholeheartedly recommend. It takes place in the Robinson Institute building which temporarily becomes the Esk Valley Theatre for 3½ weeks, during which time a professional theatre company puts on a play (Mon–Sat, including matinees). The standard of production is always high and 2022 even saw a world premiere of *All Lies* by Alan Ayckbourn.

🍴 FOOD & DRINK

R H Ford & Son Butchers High St ✆ 01947 897235. Beef and lamb from its own farm; other local farms supply pork for bacon, shop-made sausages and shop-salted hams. The black pudding is legendary and, of the numerous kinds of pie available, Monty Don once declared the pork pie to be the best he had ever tasted. All in all, a pretty good butchers.

6 EGTON & EGTON BRIDGE

🏠 **The Witching Post Inn, Egton** (page 71)

The trees that gave 'oak town' its name are gone, but one survivor from the village's past is alive and well. **Egton Show**, on the last Wednesday in August, is the largest of its kind in the North York Moors, and is such an event in the country calendar that for many people it is the one and only time they visit during the year. Others may call in for a drink at either of the village pubs while passing through, but not much else will hold your attention.

A mile down the road, the ancient river crossing at **Egton Bridge** attracts far more visitors. It has double the number of pubs of its hilltop neighbour, one on either side of the river, with a delightful stepping-

GROWING GIANT GOOSEBERRIES

A world record was broken in Egton Bridge in 2009. It wasn't one that made the national news, but among the soft-fruit growing fraternity, the biggest gooseberry ever seen was a major event.

The Egton Bridge Old Gooseberry Society (🖥 egtongooseberryshow.org.uk) has been holding an annual show on the first Tuesday in August for over 200 years, making it the oldest in the country. Come along in the afternoon for public viewing of the 600 or so entries and prizes for the winners. You will learn about reds, whites, yellows and greens and the relative merits of the Lord Derby, Lord Kitchener and Montrose varieties but you're not likely to see the like of Bryan Nellist's monster 35-dram (two-and-a-bit ounces) Woodpecker in the foreseeable future.

stone and island-hopping potter between them. A steady stream of admirers always seem to find their way to Egton Bridge, some just happy to gaze at the magnificent 18th-century redwood trees by the river, or to saunter along its banks. Downstream, a flat and just-about wheelchair accessible track leads to Grosmont, while the other direction takes you into the spectacular Arncliffe Gorge and a glorious woodland trail to Glaisdale along the Cleveland Way. Other visitors are Roman Catholic pilgrims visiting **St Hedda's Church**, one that seemed to miss the Reformation and is large enough to be dubbed the Cathedral of the Moors. Despite these attractions, the only time it really gets crowded here is at Gooseberry Show time.

¶¶ FOOD & DRINK

It's very rarely that I feel I can recommend every pub/hotel in a place for food, drink and accommodation but these four deserve it:

Horseshoe Hotel Egton Bridge 𝒷 01947 895245 🖥 thehorseshoehotel.co.uk. Serene rural location by the river. On warm days most folk prefer the large beer garden but the snug bar with fishing memorabilia is the place on wet days or winter evenings. Six comfortable, en-suite, dog-friendly rooms available.

Postgate Inn Egton Bridge 𝒷 01947 895241 🖥 postgateinn.com. Small and cosy pub by the railway station that doubled as the 'Black Dog' in *Heartbeat* but in real life is named after a local Catholic martyr. B&B available.

The Witching Post Inn Main St, Egton 𝒷 01947 895537 🖥 thewitchingpostinn.co.uk. If ever a bloke was born to be a cheery, banterful pub landlord it's Pete. He is the driving force behind this great place but the rest of the staff are also incredibly welcoming and professional. Food is very good value, beers are Theakstons plus a guest, and dogs aren't just welcomed, they are encouraged.

Wheatsheaf Inn Main St, Egton ✆ 01947 895271 🖉 wheatsheafegton.com ⊙ Tue–Sun. A comfortable village pub with a traditional bar and highly regarded restaurant. Best on a winter's evening with a roaring fire in the bar corner range. B&B plus dog-friendly self-catering.

7 GROSMONT

In the past two centuries life has almost gone full circle for Grosmont, from rural backwater to industrial centre and back again. Almost but not quite because, although the ironstone mines and blast furnaces are gone, the railways (two of them) still remain.

The smoke-stained buildings of Grosmont sit at the confluence of two river valleys, the Esk and then the Murk Esk, and are consequently the junction of the two railway lines in those dales. The Esk Valley line is three stations away from Whitby here, and is joined by the **North Yorkshire Moors Railway**, now a very popular private steam and diesel line crossing the moors from Pickering. Up until recently this was the terminus for steam services, but old locomotives puffing their way through Sleights and Ruswarp to Whitby are now regularly seen in summer.

"In the past two centuries life has almost gone full circle for Grosmont, from rural backwater to industrial centre and back again."

Such was the impact of the railway when it arrived in Grosmont that its common name changed to 'Tunnel', after the line's short underground journey. It was during the digging of the first small tunnel for a horse-drawn tramway that ironstone was first discovered, and this route has since become a footpath to the **railway engine sheds**. Another footpath, over the top of the tunnels, then follows the rest of the track bed of the old line, planned and built by George Stephenson, the 'railway king'. The Rail Trail crosses the Murk Esk four times on its three-mile journey to Goathland via Beck Hole.

Grosmont Engine Sheds

The public face of the North Yorkshire Moors Railway is the station and level crossing in the village main street, but if you want to see what makes this organisation really tick, stroll over the footbridge across the river and through the Stephenson's Tunnel footpath. This takes you to the

Grosmont Engine Sheds where the locomotive restoration, maintenance and servicing takes place, and where hard-core enthusiastic volunteers work; there's probably enough oil under their collective fingernails to keep a small car on the road. A public viewing platform lets you watch the work going on and the shed shop sells enthusiasts bric-a-brac.

¶ FOOD & DRINK

Old School Coffee Shop 'Up the path to the church' ✆ 01947 895758 ⬧ grosmontcoffeeshop.co.uk ⊙ Fri–Tue. 'Old school' not as in old fashioned but in the old primary school building by the church. Proper coffee, lunches and light bites, plus a flask-filling service for walkers on the Rail Trail. Dogs welcome.

ARTS & CRAFTS

The Geall Gallery Front St ✆ 01947 895007 ⬧ chrisgeall.com ⊙ Tue–Sat. A showcase gallery for talented local landscape artist Chris Geall and others.

8 BECK HOLE

Almost every approach to this tiny hamlet involves a precipitous hill, to where its dozen or so houses nestle at the bottom of a natural excavation – no surprises where the name came from. Becks Hole (plural) would be more accurate, as this is the point where Eller Beck, still visibly and audibly excited after its recent fall over Thomason Foss, joins West Beck to create the River Murk Esk. As at Grosmont, ironstone was worked here, and many old buildings served the miners and furnace workers, some as alehouses.

Only one pub remains, but the **Birch Hall Inn** is the heart and soul of the village; that and the quoits pitch, scene of many sepia-coloured triumphs decorating the walls of the pub. Of all my visits over the years, the most memorable have been on wet winter nights, with a fire blazing in the big bar, a wet dog steaming in front of it and just a handful of locals to share the craic. For me, the Birch Hall is as near perfection as a pub can get, and my favourite anywhere in the country.

On a quiet day, the best sort here, you can hear steam engines pass without stopping on the 'new' line higher up the hill but Beck Hole's station is a 'ghost' on the 1836 route, at the foot of the feature which caused its closure. The incline up to Goathland was way too steep for horses or locomotives to pull carriages up, so ropes and cables did the job, first using an ingenious water-filled counterweight tank coming down, then a big, fixed engine at the top. Rope and cable failure caused mayhem on more than one occasion so, after a crash causing two deaths and 13 injuries, in 1864 the line was re-routed to bypass the incline.

Scope for walking around Beck Hole is extensive, especially half-day rambles that use part of the old railway track at some stage. For a glorious two-mile woodland and heather circuit, go west to circumnavigate Randy Mere Reservoir (♀ NZ812018). Steam enthusiasts will enjoy following the railway to Darnholm and the incline back (another two miles) or of course the full three-mile **Rail Trail** from Goathland to Grosmont is a classic, following the original route the railway took (including up an inclined plane for its final section into Goathland), and you can travel back on the train.

¶¶ FOOD & DRINK

Birch Hall Inn Beck Hole YO22 5LE ♪ 01947 896245 ☐ ☐ Sun, Mon & Wed–Fri. This little alehouse is a genuine national treasure, made up of two tiny bar rooms, served by hatches, and a sweet shop sandwiched in between – virtually unchanged for 70 years. Three beers are usually available, Black Sheep, the house brew 'Beckwatter' from the North Yorkshire Brewing Co and a guest, and food is simple but wholesome; Botham's roll butties and Radford's pies.

9 GOATHLAND

I was always a little surprised at the popularity of Goathland even before *Heartbeat* hit our TV screens, as I don't think it has anywhere near the charm and neatness of Lealholm or the character of Grosmont. Now though, its visitor-pulling power is in a different league since it became Aidensfield, and its railway station starred as 'Hogsmeade' in the first *Harry Potter* film. I prefer to pass through and visit some of the glorious countryside nearby, like **Wheeldale** or the gorges of Eller Beck, towards Beck Hole, and West Beck nearer at hand.

A signpost opposite the church (♀ NZ827007) indicates the direct route down to the surprisingly verdant netherworld of **West Beck**, with a waterside footpath that takes you past the silky tresses of **Mallyan Spout waterfall**, or under it if you're feeling bold or hot, or both. If you are up for a challenge, then the mile of public footpath upstream from here is for you, as it follows a deep, narrow and boulder-strewn ravine up to New Wath Bridge on the Egton road. This can be a serious scramble, especially when wet or icy, and West Beck floods the path after heavy rain. Come here on a warm summer afternoon though, and it shows its other face; wood warblers singing in the tops of the oaks, dippers zipping up the rapids and dragonflies snatching a meal from the clouds of gnats that dance over the chattering waters – a glorious place.

¶¶ FOOD & DRINK

The Homestead Kitchen Opposite the church ⏿ 01947 896191
⏿ thehomesteadgoathland.com ⏰ noon–14.00 & 18.30–20.30 Wed–Sat, noon–15.00 Sun. Two ex-Star Inn chefs (page 158), both named Peter, teamed up at the Homestead and within three months of opening made the Michelin Guide. They make a point of sourcing food and drink locally and seasonally where possible but don't scrimp on the quality.

10 WHEELDALE ROMAN ROAD & WHEELDALE MOOR

South of Goathland, a vast tract of land rises as whale-backed hills, pimple-topped with Bronze Age burial mounds and smothered in what is part of England's largest continuous area of **heather moorland**. Two Howes Rigg, Simon Howe and **Wheeldale Moor** are all Access Areas where you can in general walk where you please: for lovers of peace and tranquillity in the natural world it is a slice of heaven. I have spent many a day up here, striding through the heather or squelching across bogs, with the spicy scent of sweet gale in the air and the bubbling of curlews in my ears, and often not seen another human all day.

"I have spent many a day up here, striding through the heather or squelching across bogs, with the spicy scent of sweet gale in the air."

Hot summer days are best for wildlife, with the air alive with bees and dragonflies, green tiger beetles scurrying across the sandy soil and an excellent chance of seeing lizards or adders. In August add the bonus of the spectacular flowering of the heather; trillions of tiny blooms combining to form a purple blanket across the hill. Take care from the 12th of the month onwards though, as areas of moor may be closed for shooting.

Wheeldale Moor has a half-mile stretch of the best preserved and excavated **Roman road** in the country. The easiest access is at the Stape Road end where an interpretive board describes the local legend of Wade the giant and his labour of love. Wade lived in Mulgrave Castle near the coast at Sandsend but his wife Bel lived in Pickering Castle. To make visiting easier they decided to build a road linking the two,

QUOITS

Nothing better reflects the dogged insularity of the Yorkshireman than the game of quoits. It is played virtually nowhere else in the world other than this corner of northeast England, and Eskdale is its heartland.

Norse in origin, as are most things hereabouts, the game involves tossing a metal ring from one end of a pitch to the other, aiming to 'hoopla' a metal pin (a two-point 'ringer'); touch it for one point or at least thunk into the surrounding square of clay nearer than your opponent's quoit.

The tiny hamlet of Beck Hole has had more than its fair share of 'world' champions in its time, so I asked Mike Mendelsohn, a multiple winner of that prestigious title, what made a great quoits player.

'A good strong arm's important. That ring weighs five pound, which is a fair weight to be slinging. You don't want to be straining to reach the pin. It's best to have a bit of distance to spare, which is why me father had us throwing full sized quoits as bairns to build us up. What else do you need? A good eye, a nasty streak and a willingness to go down the pub regularly and practice!'

Almost all the region's quoits pitches are in front of a village pub, and many a visitor has been seen puzzling over the wooden covers and peeping at the mysterious clay beneath. Turn up on a Saturday and all will be revealed; and what better way to spend a summer evening than discussing the day's walk and sipping a beer to the clink of metal on metal, as local rivalries

but with only one rock-breaking hammer between them, they had to throw it across the Moors to each other. The road is still known locally as Wade's Causeway, but the less romantic reality is that it linked the Roman garrison town of Malton to a chain of coastal signal stations.

11 RUSWARP

Twice a day the River Esk does something odd: prompted by the rising tide it flows backwards away from the sea and a mile inland to the village of Ruswarp (pronounced Ruzzup). Its short journey winding under two big viaducts over the estuarine floodplain is a joy, and one that you can follow on foot, by train or, best of all, by boat. Some of the boat trips will venture up the river at high tide and there are possibilities for paddling or rowing your own boat. You're at the richest section of the whole river for wildlife and on the right day it can be a memorable experience: very rare saltmarsh plants like wild celery and hemlock water dropwort grow on the banks alongside vitamin C-rich scurvy grass, which sailors took as a preventative supplement on voyages. The water teems with are settled in an inter-village fixture. You never know, you may even be asked to join in. One of my proudest moments was making up the numbers in a Goldsborough team at home to Fryupdale. I was accosted by my neighbour Alwyn, as I sauntered over to the Fox and Hounds for a swift half one evening. 'Do you fancy a game, Mike?' he asked. I laughed and muttered something about leaving it to the experts and having a pint waiting. 'No,' he said, 'I'm serious. Will Lewis is on a coastguard shout and we're down a man.'

So, the upshot was that I was given a quick resumé of the rules, watched what the others were doing and attempted to copy them. My practise throws were a bit wayward, a couple of under-thrown bouncing bombs and an over-corrected heave that cleared the clay and rebounded into the fence behind. By the time the opposition had arrived and the match got under way I had sort of found my distance and, while I never mastered the finer points of throwing 'Frenchman' or laying a 'gater', I didn't let the team down; 'steady away' was the verdict in the bar afterwards. If memory serves me rightly, we came out 21–19 winners.

To find the local quoits venues and match days, go to ⊘ tradgames.org.uk or to have a go yourself visit one of the many village shows in summer, as they often have a come-and-try-it quoits stall. You never know – you might be a natural and take it up permanently.

tiny opossum shrimps, attracting fish, which in turn bring herons, cormorants, dabchicks and kingfishers. When the sea-trout and salmon are running, seals follow them up the river and otters are here, although dawn and dusk are the only times you are likely to see them, such is their shyness.

Up until the 15th century the Esk was tidal all the way to Sleights along what is still known as The Carrs, meaning flooded woodland, but for 600 years a watermill weir has stopped the tide at Ruswarp. You can get welcome respite from the crowds of Whitby here while still finding things to occupy you: a circuit of the miniature steam railway, feeding the ducks on the mill pond or just watching the river go by from the Bridge Inn beer garden or Riverside café. Sadly, no footpath follows the river for its next languid mile upstream, but half-hourly buses or, better still, the train four or five times a day can take you to **Sleights** where a bridleway picks up the Esk Valley Walk route. The River Esk trickles when it's low or roars at high levels, over another weir at Sleights with a fish ladder at the side. In flood conditions the salmon don't bother

MARK BULMER/S

MIKE KIPLING PHOTOGRAPHY/A

MATT TURNER/S

RADOMIR REZNY/S

with their staircase but jump straight up the main wave, and this is the best place on the whole river to watch them do it. The nearby pub, not surprisingly, is called the Salmon Leap.

Rowing & paddling at Ruswarp

Various options exist for you to get afloat at Ruswarp and explore the river using your own muscle power. **Ruswarp Pleasure Boats** (✆ 01947 601610 ⌂ ruswarppleasureboats.co.uk) hires out rowing boats or sit-on-top kayaks to explore the non-tidal mile of flat river upstream to Sleights.

If you have access to your own canoes or kayaks you can arrange launching with Ruswarp Pleasure Boats and stay on the flat water or descend the friendly weir and run the tidal section of river to the public slipway at Whitby marina, returning by train. Alternatively, launch at Whitby an hour or two before high tide, drift up with the flood, spend a relaxing hour in Ruswarp, before coming back down river with the ebb-tide.

If all that sounds tempting but the lack of a boat is stopping you (as boats from the hire company only go upstream) then the whole trip can be arranged by **East Barnby Outdoor Education Centre** (✆ 01947 893333 ⌂ outdoored.co.uk). You choose the route and do all the paddling but transport, equipment (including possibilities for wheelchair users) and a guide are provided.

¶¶ FOOD & DRINK

The River Gardens Briggswath YO21 1RR ✆ 07785 573625 ⌂ perrysplants.co.uk ◷ Mar–Oct. Plant nursery and riverside café. The crab sandwiches and local Radford's steak pies are particularly noteworthy.

Ruswarp Riverside Café The Carrs, Ruswarp YO21 1RL ✆ 01947 600109 ⌂ chainbridgeriverside.com ◷ Apr–Oct. The name sums it up – lots of duck-feeding potential while you have a brew. Self-catering accommodation available.

12 FALLING FOSS

Just over three miles south of Ruswarp, May Beck's tumble over a 67ft shale cliff creates Falling Foss, the highest waterfall in the North York Moors, and the centrepiece of a secretive wooded valley. It is possible

◀ **1** The river at Ruswarp is rich in wildlife. **2** Falling Foss. **3** Mallyan Spout waterfall, Goathland. **4** Eskdale is the heartland for the game of quoits.

to drive and park close to the falls but I find it much more satisfying to arrive here on foot along the beck, with the noise of the cascade gradually developing from a distant hiss to a spray-filled roar as I approach.

Of the two routes in, the northerly upstream one is probably the more trodden, as the final mile joins up with the Coast to Coast Walk. It can be started from Sleights railway station (♥ NZ868081) and follows a tributary of the River Esk which has a confusing habit of changing its name. It is Iburndale Beck for its first mile, then Little Beck as it passes through the rich rainforest-like woods owned by the Yorkshire Wildlife Trust. Just before you arrive at the falls, look out for The Hermitage, a remarkable hollowed-out boulder shelter, complete with seats.

The southerly downstream approach starts at Sneaton Forest car park (♥ NZ893024) and follows our stream under its third pseudonym, May Beck, on either bank, along a half-mile nature trail to Midge Hall and its tea rooms on the lip of Falling Foss.

Other very popular Forestry Commission trails head in the opposite direction from May Beck car park, visiting more waterfalls as they enter the vast expanse of Sneaton Forest, a great place to see reptiles and amphibians. Adders and lizards are common in heathery clearings and the plethora of round ponds (World War II bomb craters) boil with frogs, toads and newts in springtime.

¶¶ FOOD & DRINK

Beacon Farm Sneaton YO22 5HS ✆ 01947 605212 ◈ beaconfarmicecream.co.uk. A farm that has diversified into Yorkshire dairy ice-cream production with a café attached. Also offers self-catering cottages and a campsite.

Falling Foss Tea Garden Midge Hall, Sneaton Forest YO22 5JD ✆ 07723 47929 ◈ fallingfossteagarden.co.uk ◷ Apr–Oct. The former gamekeeper's cottage of Midge Hall houses an Edwardian tea garden in a most idyllic woodland site. Sympathetically renovated and restored in 2008, to sell drinks and light meals, it also provides pooh-sticks for the nearby bridge and lots of other activities to entertain children.

13 WHITBY

🏠 **La Rosa Hotel** (page 247); 🏰 Whitby Lighthouse (page 247)

'If you want a quiet day in Whitby, try a wet Tuesday in February, with *Love Island* on telly', was Jim the taxi driver's advice, and his reasoning is plain to see. Whitby is an extremely popular destination, bursting at the seams every weekend, and even midweek if the sun appears. The root of the town's pulling power is its possession of a little bit of something for everyone, seeming to combine in a melting pot all the best that Yorkshire has to offer with a dash of Cornish fishing port and more than a drop of Transylvanian blood. The place is dripping in history, it oozes from the pores of every building like a little York-by-the-sea with Tudor halls, Gothic ruins, Saxon churches, smugglers' pubs and fishers' cottages – they all have their stories to tell. And then, cheek by jowl, you will find the other, more modern Whitby of buckets and spades, amusement arcades and fish and chip shops, but even this has a dated and quaintly retro feel to it.

Three figures stand tall in Whitby's past: a woman who famously arrived on a mission, a man who left three times and changed the world, and a character who never even came here, because he didn't really exist. The woman was a Northumbrian princess called **Hild** who came in the year AD656 and founded a Saxon monastery on East Cliff, the first Whitby Abbey. The seafarer who repeatedly left in the 18th century, along with shiploads of crewmates, was **Captain James Cook**. He returned twice, but never made it back from his third voyage, having been clubbed to death on a Hawaiian beach – the sort of thing that always upsets your travel plans. Ironically, the most well-known of the three characters is a fictitious literary creation of the Victorian novelist **Bram Stoker**, the infamous Count Dracula. The horrifically evocative Chapter 7 of Stoker's novel *Dracula*, where the Count, in the form of a black dog, leaps off a ship grounded in the harbour, and bounds through the alleyways of the town, should be read on a bench in the churchyard overlooking the scene, for full effect. Dracula's link with Whitby has inspired one of the town's most lively and entertaining annual events, the Goth Festival, which takes place on the weekend nearest to Halloween each year (so popular that there's now another one every spring).

Whitby owes its existence to the **River Esk** and the fact that it is a natural sheltered anchorage for ships using the North Sea. This is still what it always was, a working harbour, and going to sea in boats will always be at the heart of the town. In the 18th century fleets of sailing ships left these shores, not just explorers in Cook's *Resolution*, *Discovery* and *Endeavour* but whalers of world renown like the captains (father and son) Scoresby. In the early 20th century when herring fishing was at its peak, hundreds of boats packed the harbour and it was said you could walk from one side to the other without getting your feet wet.

THE WHITBY LOBSTER HATCHERY

℘ 07965 642884 ⊘ whitbylobsterhatchery.co.uk

Historic overfishing and government mismanagement of the quota system have all but killed the white-fish industry in Whitby. There are no big offshore boats now and all the small inshore fleet have moved to lobster and crab potting. Inevitably this has put pressure on local stocks of these species and many people are concerned that history is in danger of repeating itself. As a result, a small group of knowledgeable and dedicated folk have created a charity called The Whitby Lobster Hatchery to try and ensure a sustainable future for marine life in the area and the fishermen and women whose livelihoods depend on it.

Based in the old fish market on Pier Road, the hatchery plans to hatch, raise and release 100,000 young lobsters into the wild annually and a visitor centre is currently under construction to give us all the chance to see the scheme in operation (due to open sometime in 2023). 'Conservation, education and research are at the heart of all this,' insists Joe Redfern the project manager. 'We plan to conserve the marine environment, protect the fishing industry and, in doing so, provide something that will benefit the whole town.'

Hundreds of craft still use Whitby Harbour but nowadays many of them are pleasure boats such as yachts, cruisers, scuba-diving inflatables and trip boats. Ironically, some of the most popular trips out of the harbour these days are to take people to see creatures that were once the hunters' quarry – **whales**. In late summer and early autumn good numbers of minke, humpback, and even fin and sei whales, follow shoals of breeding herring down the Yorkshire coast, and boats like the *Summer Queen* (⊘ whitbywhalewatching.net) will take you out to see them. Successful viewing rates are as good as anywhere in the country so consequently these trips are very popular – book early.

The river both unites and divides the town, even more so pre-1767 when no bridge linked the two sides. Separation breeds suspicion and the inhabitants of each bank used to refer to each other as 't'other side o' watter dogs'. Such was the mistrust that when the first bridge was opened, locals celebrated with a pitched battle in the middle. Even today, old-established families say they come from East Whitby or West Whitby, not Whitby. The first bridge lifted to allow boats through but the Victorian replacement that survives today is a swing bridge and is the focal point of the town. Whitby has so much to see that

I would recommend splitting it into two trails to visit on foot, both starting here.

Scarborough Borough Council produces two excellent **town trail** books, one for each side of the river and available from the tourist office. The *West Side Trail* takes in Baxtergate's yards, a lifeboat museum, the whalebone arch (recalling the town's former connection with the whaling industry), Captain Cook's statue and the fish quay but it fails to mention what, to me, should always be a compulsory prime objective, weather and phobias permitting – the end of the **pier**. This is as far out to sea as it is possible to get without a boat and an exhilarating experience in rough weather. **Whitby harbour** faces due north and is one of the few places in the country where watching the sunrise and sunset over the sea is possible on the same day – you are allowed to go for a cup of tea in between. On your way out or back, look out for dinosaur 'fossils' carved into the concrete by local stonemason Darren Yeadon.

The east side is my favourite; more compact and with fewer new intrusions, this is where I can best let my historical imagination run riot. The *East Side Trail* mentions the jet shops, old inns, lifeboat pier, **Captain Cook Memorial Museum** (with displays about his voyages of discovery that started from Whitby), market square (still operational Tuesdays and Saturdays) and 199 steps up to the church and abbey but stops again at the foot of the pier. Carry on though (weather permitting) because the East Pier is a wild and evocative place and sanctuary for large numbers of sheltering purple sandpipers in winter.

Off the trail, and around the corner under the cliffs, a short mile's wander along the wave-cut platform to Saltwick Bay makes a tremendous diversion, with the return to the abbey via the clifftop Cleveland Way. Small boats anchored just offshore here may be carrying sub-aqua divers visiting the wreck of the *Rohilla*, a World War I hospital ship which hit Whitby Rock on a stormy night in 1914 with the loss of 85 lives. One survivor, a nurse, had only ever been on a ship once before – the *Titanic*. I don't suppose she ever went to sea again.

Whitby Abbey
🕿 01947 603568; English Heritage

If ever a place could be described as having a chequered history, then this is it: founded by Saxons, destroyed by Vikings, rebuilt by Normans, dismantled by Tudors and bombarded by Germans.

When Princess Hild was sent from Hartlepool in AD656 she arrived in the tiny fishing hamlet of Streoneshalh (Whitby was a later Danish name) and became first Abbess of the wooden Columban abbey of St Peter. She later became the patron saint of the town and had many wells and a fossil named after her. *Hildocerous bifrons* is an ammonite common in the cliffs below the abbey and commemorates the legend that St Hilda turned snakes infesting the headland into stone and threw them over the cliff. Medieval monks even carved heads on to them and sold them as 'snake-stones'. During her time a dispute between the Roman and Celtic churches over the date of Easter was settled at the Synod of Whitby and we still use their convoluted formula today.

After the Vikings razed the original structure, the Normans rebuilt, in local sandstone, the present Benedictine abbey. At the Dissolution much of the abbey stone was used to build the Manor next door which now houses the Abbey Visitor Centre.

In one last twist of fate, during World War I, a flotilla of German battleships bombarded the east coast of England. Scarborough and Hartlepool were also targeted but the abbey was particularly badly damaged during Whitby's shelling. This won't be the final chapter: when the abbey was built it stood half a mile from the sea but in the intervening 900 years that distance has been reduced to 200yds by the erosional power of the North Sea. In a few more centuries, the stones of the abbey will be on the beach growing seaweed.

St Mary's Church

I have a soft spot for St Mary's, as it was here my daughter was baptised. That said, I can still safely claim, without being accused of bias, that this is one of the most fascinatingly quirky churches in the country.

Being next door to the abbey, you might expect it to be dedicated to St Hilda instead of St Mary. The reason lies in the church's antiquity – it was already here, complete with name, when the Princess came calling. The fact is that the heart of this building is older than its neighbour but has been added to piecemeal ever since. The outside is full of interest – Norman arches aplenty and a strange ship's-deck-style roof – but go inside and you could be in a museum. A rare set of 17th-century box

---

1 Whitby Abbey. **2** Exhibits at Whitby Museum. **3** Pick up locally caught seafood by the harbour. **4** Climb 199 steps for superb views over Whitby. ▶

pews, a three-decker pulpit with ear trumpets for a deaf vicar's wife, a multi-locked treasure chest, and more, all candle-lit and heated from a central pot boiler.

Don't confine yourself to the building but wander around the graveyard surrounding it. Like a mouthful of loose and rotting teeth, this has to be the perfect horror film set. Those gravestones still legible tell of boat sinkings and drownings, master mariners and lifeboat men. One of the eeriest is the Huntrodds memorial, to a husband and wife born on the same day, married on their birthday and dying within hours of each other on… you guessed it, their birthday again.

Whitby Museum

Pannett Park ✂ 01947 602908 ✂ whitbymuseum.org.uk ◴ 10.00–16.30 Tue–Sun

If you enter this building expecting a high-tech, hands-on multi-sensory modern museum, you will be disappointed. The words hotchpotch and higgledy-piggledy could have been invented for Whitby Museum; it is unashamedly old-fashioned, cramped, politically incorrect, poorly set out, and full of glass cases, but that is what sets it apart and gives it its charm. It is not only a museum of things, but a museum piece of museums.

Themes seem infinitely varied: model ships, stuffed birds, local archaeology, fossils, military clothing, and a brilliant weather-forecasting machine based on leeches called a tempest prognosticator – a little bit of everything but not much of anything. Don't get the impression that it's all junk in here though. One of the model ships made from food-ration chicken bones by Napoleonic prisoners of war is reportedly worth £250,000 and the carved jet collection is the best in the world, featuring two wonderful jet chessboards.

What I like best about this place, though, is the chance to explore and discover things for myself. I read elsewhere of a sea kayak in here, the only one of its design in the world, so I searched and eventually found it, on top of a wall cabinet, unlabelled – that's this place to a tee. There's a great little cafe downstairs (◴ 10.00–15.00 Tue–Sat).

🍴 FOOD & DRINK

Cafés & restaurants

Whitby doesn't really do posh restaurants but quality cafés are a different matter. Of the scores of good ones available here are my favourites:

Elizabeth Botham and Sons Skinner St ☏ 01947 602823 ⌂ botham.co.uk. The nicer of its two long-standing tea rooms in Whitby; a family-run craft bakery since 1865.

Humble Pie n' Mash Church St ☏ 01947 606444. All it does is pie, mash and peas, which might seem a very limited menu, but the homemade pie selection is extensive. Vintage theme, great value and you can bring your beer over from the neighbouring pub.

Sherlock's Flowergate ☏ 01947 603399. A snug and cosy coffee shop with a great Dickensian-style atmosphere. More importantly, the food and drink are really good.

The Singing Kettle Angel Yard ☏ 07985 238046 ⌂ singingkettlewhitby.co.uk. A no-nonsense café serving the best full English breakfast in town, in my opinion.

Pubs

Of over 20 pubs in the town centre, many of which with a rich history, these are three crackers:

Black Horse Inn Church St ☏ 01947 602906 ⌂ the-black-horse.com. An unspoiled architectural gem, possibly the oldest pub in town with the original Victorian bar. Traditional in every sense of the word, with up to five cask ales including Whitby Brewery beers, Yorkshire cheese and seafood 'tapas' to eat, and snuff to sniff. Room-only accommodation available.

Duke of York Church St ☏ 01947 600324 ⌂ greatukpubs.co.uk/duke-of-york-whitby. An all-round good pub with fine food and well-kept beer, but its best feature is its location at the bottom of the 199 steps, with panoramic views of the harbour. B&B available.

Station Inn New Quay Rd ☏ 01947 603937 ⌂ stationinnwhitby.co.uk. A popular inn with very welcoming staff and lots going on (live music and a Thursday quiz). No food, but a wide range of real ales and ciders, including the house beer brewed in Whitby. Adult-only accommodation.

Fish & chips

Whitby is renowned for its fish and chips. Some are over-priced and/or overrated, but these two definitely aren't.

Magpie Café Pier Rd ☏ 01947 602058 ⌂ magpiecafe.co.uk. World-famous café serving superlative seafood, especially fish and chips. Be prepared to queue.

Royal Fisheries Baxtergate ☏ 01947 604738 ⌂ royalfisherieswhitby.co.uk. The locals' favourite take-away chippy since 1968 when the Fusco family moved here from Pickering. Known as 'Fuscos' in town.

Speciality foods

Fortune's Smokehouse Henrietta St ☏ 01947 601659 ⌂ fortuneskippers.co.uk. Traditional kipper-smoking shed with shop. Kippers sold in pairs, wrapped in newspaper.

ART & CRAFTS

Wash House Pottery Blackburn Yard ✆ 01947 604995. Customised tiles, planters, house plaques and plates made on site.

Whitby Jet Heritage Centre Church St ✆ 01947 821530 ⌂ whitbyjet.co.uk. An original Victorian jet works (page 54) with working craftspeople.

Whitby Kiln (formerly Doodlepots) Skinner St ✆ 01947 878587 ⌂ whitbykiln.co.uk. Paint your own plain plate/cup/pot/bowl, etc, and then have it fired to pick up later.

THE CLEVELAND COAST: SANDSEND TO SKINNINGROVE

A few years ago from the back of a ferry leaving Newcastle, I saw through binoculars a dark line on the horizon to the southeast. What I was seeing 40 miles away was the great bulge of the northern North York Moors meeting the sea in a line of dark crags. Marauding Vikings approaching from the North Sea over a thousand years ago had the same view, prompting them to name this part of England the Land of Cliffs – Cleveland. This wall of rock stretches seemingly unbroken, from Saltburn southeast to Whitby and beyond. Prehistoric erosion has breached the wall in a handful of places, allowing the coastal communities of **Sandsend**, **Runswick Bay**, **Staithes** and **Skinningrove** to develop. In the past all have relied for their livelihood on the silver harvest of the sea and the mineral wealth from the cliffs themselves, but now to a greater or lesser degree each depends on tourism.

14 SANDSEND

⛺ **Lythe Caravan & Camping** Lythe (page 247)

This village is certainly aptly named: two miles of golden beach stops abruptly at the foot of The Ness and this cluster of sandstone cottages, hotels and shops huddle in what little shelter it provides. A closer look reveals two hamlets here; one for each of the small streams that flow into the sea 200yds apart.

East Row, at the beach end, is older but smaller, and hosts the White Hart pub, two cafés, a restaurant and the main entrance to **Mulgrave Woods**. At the cliff end, most of Sandsend proper hides up the little valley of Sandsend Beck, with a sleepy hobbit village air to it. Even at the height of summer when the beach is crowded, and boy does it get crowded, all stays serene and peaceful up here, with little to disturb the grazing goats.

What the original valley inhabitants were hiding from was the full force of the North Sea. Houses and shops along the seafront are now protected from the worst by a concrete sea wall, but even this doesn't stop the road being shut at least once a year, when waves from a high spring tide and northeasterly gale combined can send spray over the top of three-storey buildings. The final two buildings at this end of the village are the old railway station and the remains of an alum works, now a café and car park. Beyond lies an industrial archaeologist's wonderland, visited by the **Sandsend Trail**.

The Sandsend Trail

Once you have climbed 30 or so steps up from the car park to join the old railway line, and leant on the station platform to catch your breath, you can relax, because you needn't go uphill again during the rest of this walk.

This cindery track bed heads along the cliff edge to what locals call 'The Moon', giving grandstand views of wheeling fulmars and surfers on the famed reef break (known as 'caves' to surfers) below. It weaves its way between vast quarried holes and artificial hills called 'clamps' – remnants of 300 years of the alum industry. Spoil from the works is so disagreeable to plant life that most areas remain completely bare of vegetation, hence the lunar references.

ESPIONAGE, FIRE WATER & URINE – THE ALUM STORY

Back in the 16th century, the only known chemical able to fix dyes in cloth was alum, but the complex process for extracting it from rock was known only to chemists in the Vatican. In the first ever documented case of industrial espionage, Henry VIII managed to steal the formula and the English alum industry began. The shale of the Cleveland coast contains 2% alum and to get it, the rock had to be quarried by pick and shovel, piled up and roasted by fire for months, treated with an alkali and then dissolved in water and dried, to allow the crystals to form.

Here comes the bit of the process everyone always remembers: the cheapest source of alkali was stale urine, and such volumes were needed that every household in Whitby was required by law to put out all their urine for collection. At the height of the industry demand exceeded supply, so barrels of urine were shipped up from London. Rather than send the barrels back empty they were filled with butter for the rich appetites of the folk in the capital. As the barrels were never rinsed, this is said to account for Southerners' taste for yellow salted butter!

The flat trail ends abruptly at a railway tunnel entrance a mile down the line. You can retrace your steps or continue along the Cleveland Way you have been unwittingly following, and brave the big climb over the tunnel. Roof falls and subsidence have made the underground route unsafe but I did get the chance to traverse its three-quarter-mile length once, while searching for a missing person with the auxiliary coastguard. We didn't find anyone, but had a huge scare when torchlight revealed an old wetsuit that some practical joker had stuffed to look like a headless corpse. The air turned blue with relief when we realised our mistake.

ROCK POOLING

No trip to the seaside would be complete without a spot of rock pooling, and it was ever thus. How many of us have vivid childhood memories of mornings splashing in the waves, gritty sandwiches for lunch and then, as the tide recedes, ferreting in warm pools with a net and a bucket?

Without doubt, the prime quarry of most rockpoolers are **crabs**. My old day job used to involve taking school children on to the seashore to introduce them to the intertidal ecosystem, but sooner or later, even with A-level biology groups, proceedings usually degenerated into a 'biggest crab' competition. I have often pondered why we are all fascinated by these creatures, and have come to the conclusion that it is their creepy alienness (walking as they do sideways on eight legs) and the thrill of real danger; even a small crab can give a powerful and painful nip.

You will find four common species of crab without much difficulty, and the **shore** or **green crab** is by far the most abundant. Lift up flat rocks among the seaweed and they will scuttle away, or dangle a piece of meat-baited string into a deep pool and you could tempt them out into the open. These are the characters that are hauled up on crab lines to fill enthusiasts' buckets in Whitby and Scarborough harbours. **Edible** or **brown crabs** can be found lower down the shore, but only small, young specimens. The adults that end up on the fishmonger's slab live in deeper water. Identification is easy – the only crab with a shell the shape of a Cornish pasty and black mittens. **Hermit crabs** are many people's favourite, living as they do in someone else's shell, usually a periwinkle, top-shell or dog whelk. If you want to get a good view of the creature, place its shell upside down underwater and the crab will slide itself almost all the way out when it thinks the coast is clear and turn itself the right way up. You will know if you have found a **velvet swimming crab** or, more to the point, you will know by the excited squeals if someone else has found one. They are beautiful with velvety backs, electric blue claws and bright red eyes but are

Mulgrave Woods

If you can, arrange your visit to Sandsend for a Wednesday, Saturday or Sunday, because these are the days that access is granted to these private woods. This is a big wood and there are still lush, pristine corners, especially since large-scale pheasant rearing was stopped by the estate. It boasts three castles, alum quarries, cement stone mines and a wealth of wildlife – easily a full day's worth of exploration. The woods cloak the two parallel ravines of East Row Beck and Sandsend Beck and the Castle Rigg in between, so a circular walk could take you up one valley and back down the other. Alternatively, a taxi drop-off two miles inland,

without doubt the most aggressive creature on the shore. I have seen one actually jump up off the rocks to attack my approaching hand, and can testify from experience that their pincers are very sharp.

Crabs may be the most extrovert rock pool inhabitants, but they are by no means the only ones. North Sea rocky shores are incredibly rich habitats, so within an hour or two's searching you could easily find an impressive tally of green, brown and red seaweed and over 30 different species, from deep maroon **sea anemones** and small green sea urchins to translucent **prawns** and big knobbly **lumpsucker fish**. Here are some top-tips for the best results:

- Get as far down the shore as you can. A low spring tide is best of all as you can get in among the exposed kelp forest.

- Take a deep white tray to put your finds in for examination.

- A small aquarium net is the only way you will catch fast or slippery prawns and fish.

- Take an identification guide. The Field Studies Council (⊘ field-studies-council.org) producse an excellent waterproof key, and the best field guidebook is *The Seashore*, published by Country Life Books. Online, the Marine Life Information Network (⊘ marlin.ac.uk) is comprehensive.

- The best accessible sites for rock pools along the North Yorkshire coast are between Staithes and Port Mulgrave, Runswick Bay, Robin Hood's Bay, Scarborough North Bay and Filey Brigg.

One last safety note: don't go too close to the cliffs as they are very unstable, take care on wet, slippery rocks and consult tide tables before you stray away from the main beach. Happy searching.

where the East Barnby road crosses the woods, would allow you a linear walk downhill to the sea.

ⅼⅼ FOOD & DRINK

Hart Inn East Row ✆ 01947 893304. An attractive little pub popular with locals and visitors alike. Decent beer and food served by very friendly and helpful staff.

The Lickerish Tooth High St, Lythe ⌂ thelickerishtooth.com ◷ 11.00–15.00 Thu–Sat. This gin distillery sits a mile up the hill from Sandsend. The shop sells four different flavours of gin and it also runs a highly rated 'Gin School' – a half-day workshop on how to make your own gin.

Sandside Café East Row ✆ 01947 893916 ⓕ. Overlooking the beach, this place rightly describes itself as the 'little cafe with the big view'. If it's hot, sit outside with cake – if it's not, sit inside with a jacket potato and a brew.

15 RUNSWICK BAY

⋏ **Folly Hall Farm** Tranmire (page 247)

Runswick Bay possesses two particularly appealing features, a huddle of pantile-roofed cottages that comprises the village, and the beach. The village resembles a miniature Robin Hood's Bay with its maze of alleys and passageways but the beach is much more attractive than that of the larger near neighbour. Ice creams, buckets and spades, multicoloured windbreaks and crowds of bank holiday sunbathers; Runswick Bay beach does all of that, but venture a frisbee-throw away from the car park and slipways and it shows a much wilder side to its nature. Halfway round the sandy bay, and just past the yacht club, low shale cliffs begin and the guttural cackles of nesting fulmars compete with the 'swosh' of the waves. This place is known as **Hob Holes** locally, after the old jet mines at the crag foot. Legend has it that a hobgoblin lived in the darkness with the unexplained ability to cure whooping cough. A chant of 'Hob, Hob, me bairn's got kink cough. Takk it off, takk it off,' was the brief and to-the-point request that was supposed to do the trick.

The Cleveland Way footpath makes its way to the top of the cliff at Hob Holes, so very few people carry on along the shore beyond this point, but the extra effort is well worth it. Just around the corner is the handkerchief-sized beach of Kettleness Sand, a wonderful secluded corner cowering beneath the battleship-grey walls of **Kettleness** itself.

1 Runswick Bay. **2** Sandstone cottages at Sandsend. ▶

Here the only company you can expect are oystercatchers and turnstones ferreting around in the seaweed, and maybe a nosey seal, head bobbing in the water offshore.

Take care where you lie and sunbathe though; too close to the cliff bottom and you are in danger of being landed on by one of the regular small rock falls. Back in the 1990s one family had a very close call when a huge section of cliff buried half of the beach. Fortunately it came down in instalments so they had time to make their escape down to the water's edge. Apparently their tartan rug and Tupperware are still deep under the rocks – an interesting find for the archaeologists of the future!

Cliff falls are maybe not good news for the average visitor to Kettleness Sand, but they certainly are for Mike Marshall, a professional fossil-hunter operating from his shop and gallery at Lythe (℡ 07831 155665 🖥 yorkshirecoastfossils. co.uk). 'I love going down on the seashore searching,' he said. 'You never know what you're going to find. Mostly it's ammonites of course; there are hundreds of different types in the rocks around here and they are my bread-and-butter – what I make my day-to-day living from. They don't take too long to prepare and polish, then I'll sell them to shops in Whitby, or on my website at £10–£30 or so. The really exciting moments are when big, important specimens turn up. I'm still working on an Ichthyosaur (giant fish-like reptile) that I found 15 years ago, which will probably sell for £15,000 when it is finished; that is my pension fund.'

"Half the fun is in the searching and children can be occupied for hours."

While Mike's sale-quality ammonites and belemnites make great souvenirs, hundreds more lie waiting to be found for free among the beach pebbles here. Half the fun is in the searching and children can be occupied for hours; top-tip, take an old dinner knife to split the soft rock and some paper and wax crayons to take rubbings of fossils embedded in big rocks.

On busy days, parking can be a problem at Runswick Bay, so consider parking at East Barnby and walking the four miles to Runswick (all downhill), via Goldsborough Roman signal station and the Cleveland Way clifftop path. You will be rewarded with magnificent views; the half-hourly number X4 bus takes you back up the hill to East Barnby.

FOOD & DRINK

Black Bull Ugthorpe YO21 2BQ ✆ 01947 840286 ⌂ blackbullwhitby.co.uk ◷ Wed–Mon. 'Where do the locals go to eat?' is what I'd ask, and the answer is here. A very friendly, family-run village local with great value food and fine beer. Book early, especially for the Sunday carvery.

Fox and Hounds Goldsborough YO21 3RX ✆ 07870 406926 ⌂ foxandhoundsgoldsborough.co.uk ◷ Wed–Sun. A great little pub in a hamlet off the beaten track. Popular with Cleveland Way walkers. Food noon–16.00 only.

The Royal Hotel Runswick Bay ✆ 01947 840215 ⬛. Decent food and drink and possibly the best view from any pub in Yorkshire.

16 STAITHES

In many ways Staithes could qualify as a miniature Whitby – a tidal river slicing its way to the sea through steep cliffs, multicoloured fishing cobbles bobbing at their moorings behind the harbour's stone piers, and the same mass of orange pantiled houses, jostling shoulders for space between the cliffs and the water. The two-towns-in-one principle is also at work again, this time officially, with Staithes proper only on the south side of the beck. Not only do the houses on the other bank belong to the separate village of **Cowbar**, they aren't even in North Yorkshire. The county boundary runs across the middle of the small footbridge over Staithes Beck, and Cowbar is in Cleveland. Just to confuse the issue further, the **Staithes lifeboat** is housed here on the Cowbar side.

Staithes' most famous son is undoubtedly James Cook who, after a childhood just inland, probably had his first smell of the sea when he worked as a teenage shop assistant in the village. An old harbourside cottage bears a 'Cook Trail plaque' but the shop he worked in was actually washed away, along with 12 other buildings, in the great storm of 1745.

A few yards from Captain Cook's cottage is the labelled entrance into **Dog Loup**; quite probably the narrowest named thoroughfare in the country, and a good start to a wander around the back alleys, squares and streets. On your exploration, look out for the nautical themes in house names, including imaginative ceramic plaques, and the fascinating **Staithes Story Museum** (⌂ staithes-museum.org.uk) on the High Street. Housed in an old Methodist Chapel, this heritage centre has displays covering the history of the village, a couple of craft outlets and a shop. I also recommend crossing the bridge to climb Cowbar

Bank for the best bird's-eye view of Staithes to one side, and the mighty **Boulby Cliff** on the other, returning via the allotments' footpath and stepping stones.

One of the best short walks in the North York Moors heads off in the opposite direction, but the tide needs to be in your favour to complete it safely (follow the ebb tide out). The route couldn't be simpler; negotiate the steps at the far end of the beach, walk along the rocky shore below the cliffs for a mile to **Port Mulgrave** and then return along the Cleveland Way. En route you should see oystercatchers on the mussel beds of Penny Steel and surfers on one of the most testing reef breaks in the country (if there are waves), ironstone and jet mines, and alum quarries. You can also experience the best fossil and rock-pool pickings along the whole coast.

If you would prefer expert local guidance in this very wild environment, it doesn't come any better than from Sean Baxter ($\mathscr{O}$ 01947 840278 $\mathscr{O}$ realstaithes.com), local fisherman, member of the lifeboat crew and passionate champion of the town. 'There are more fish, whales, dolphins and peregrines around here than ever,' Sean explained, 'and I want to show people this rich natural diversity – and tell them about the amazing maritime heritage of my town.' You can accompany him baiting long-lines and emptying lobster pots, ultimately eating your catch as a picnic at Sean's fisherman's hut in Port Mulgrave.

The fastest, most expensive and best cared for boat in Staithes is named *Sheila and Dennis Tongue lll*, after the generous couple whose legacy paid for it. This is the Staithes and Runswick Inshore Lifeboat, to give it its full title, an 'Atlantic 85' class boat which sits on a trailer attached to its amphibious tractor, in a shed in Cowbar. Being the bustling focal point that it is, with crew members often pottering around, the doors are usually open and you are welcome to go in and nose around there and in the RNLI shop, which is just a couple of doors down. One certainly shouldn't wish for a lifeboat call-out, but if the pager call from the coastguard goes out, the launch is exciting to watch. There's no 'maroon' (a loud firework to alert the crew) to hear these days but the sight of grown adults racing down the hill from all sides of the village is a bit of a giveaway. You'll have to be quick to witness the launch as the Staithes crew pride themselves on being out of the harbour within five minutes

◀ Whitby in miniature at Staithes.

of their pagers going off. More predictable is crew training, 18.00 on Mondays in summer, and 10.00 on Sundays in winter.

¶ FOOD & DRINK

Captain Cook Inn Staithes Lane ℘ 01947 840200 ♂ captaincookinn.co.uk. A very uninviting-looking hostelry at the top of the bank by the old railway (formerly Station Inn) but don't be fooled: the 'Cook' is an oasis. The best selection of real ales within a ten-mile radius, and cheap and cheerful bar food. Regularly hosts a wide range of festivals: folk music, jazz, sea shanties and beer, pies and sausages. Accommodation available.

Cod and Lobster High St ℘ 01947 840330 ♂ codandlobster.co.uk. Notable for its position, this must be one of the closest pubs to the sea in the country – storm-damaged on more than one occasion. Nostalgic photos line the walls, and three or four cask ales usually on tap. Food available.

Dotty's Vintage Tearoom High St ℘ 01947 841096 ◼ dotty's tearoom. A justifiably popular gem – chaotic yet elegant decor, outrageously efficient and attentive staff, and really good quality food and drink.

Restaurant No 20 Port Mulgrave ℘ 01947 459647 ♂ restaurantnumber20.com ⊙ dinner Wed–Sat. Jason and Sue, who ran the fantastic Fox and Hounds restaurant in Goldsborough for 12 years, moved here in 2019 and the food and service Michelin-Guide quality.

ARTS & CRAFTS

Staithes Gallery High St ℘ 01947 841840 ♂ staithesgallery.co.uk ⊙ Wed, Thu, Sat & Sun. A fine display of contemporary artists' work inspired by the old masters from the celebrated Staithes Group. Offers residential weekend courses for artists and co-ordinates an excellent weekend art festival every September (♂ staithesfestival.com).

Staithes Arts and Crafts Centre Church St ℘ 01947 841678 ♂ staithesartsandcraftscentre.co.uk. A fine collection of crafty stalls inside the old St Peter's Methodist Chapel, run by some very talented local artists. Wonderful 'in-situ' tree carvings in the back garden.

17 BOULBY CLIFF & SKINNINGROVE

> The king was borne, hoary hero, to Hronesness (Whale Hill).
> And firm on the earth a funeral-pile.
> Beowulf

Viewed from Staithes, the outline of Boulby Cliff is uncannily like the back of a whale, and I would love to share the belief of some that this was the burial place of that great hero of the Viking age. What is for certain is that his body is no longer there now, after 1,000 years of natural and human erosion. Despite all this cliff reduction, Boulby, at 666ft above the sea, is still the highest cliff on the east coast of England, albeit in two steps because of the huge alum quarries. Alum is no longer worked here but **Boulby Potash Mine** is a modern mineral extraction operation close by that breaks records in the opposite direction. It is the deepest mine in Europe, and at its bottom, nearly a vertical mile down, tunnels radiate out five miles in every direction, including out beneath the North Sea – a scary thought. The potash, destined to become agricultural fertiliser, is transported to Teesside factories on the only remaining section of the Whitby to Middlesbrough railway.

"The former mining village of Skinningrove will never be described as pretty but it has bags of character."

The four-mile traverse of Boulby Cliff from Staithes makes a magnificent walk, or cycle, and the steep descent at the far end will bring you to a very singular place. The former mining village of **Skinningrove** will never be described as pretty but it has bags of character, and your arrival takes you past some of the structures it has become famous for – pigeon lofts. Skinningrove is one of the racing-pigeon centres of the North East with scores of sheds lining the hillside.

At the bottom of the hill, the beck won't fail to catch your eye either, being as it is luminous orange, a result of pollution from the ironstone mines further up the valley – rust, in essence. The entrance to the old mine at the top of the village is worth a visit as it has been converted into the excellent **Cleveland Ironstone Mining Museum** (✆ 01287 642877 🖰 landofiron.org.uk). Not far from the museum, a half-hourly bus (X4) can take you back to Staithes if you have walked. Better still, get the bus here and walk back to Staithes as the views are marginally better. Navigation is easy as the whole route follows the Cleveland Way, which is clearly marked on OS Explorer map OL27.

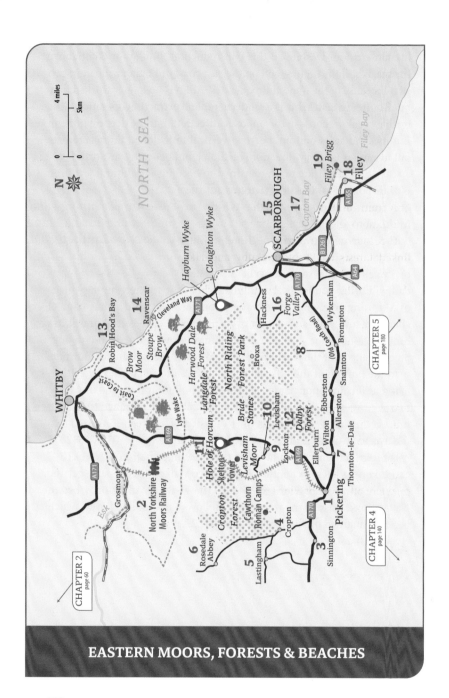

EASTERN MOORS, FORESTS & BEACHES

NORTH SEA

N

0   4 miles
0   5km

WHITBY

CHAPTER 2
page 60

13 Robin Hood's Bay
14 Ravenscar

Brow Moor
Stoupe Brow
Cleveland Way
A171
Hayburn Wyke
Cloughton Wyke

Coast to Coast

Esk

Grosmont

A171

2 North Yorkshire Moors Railway

A169

Lyke Wake

Harwood Dale Forest

Langdale Forest

North Riding Forest Park

Hackness

15 SCARBOROUGH
17

16 Forge Valley
Wykeham

A170

Cayton Bay

B1261

A165

19 Filey Brigg
18 Filey

Filey Bay

A64

Brompton

CHAPTER 5
page 180

Hole of Horcum
11
Skelton Tower
Cropton Forest
Cawthorn Roman Camps
Levisham Moor

Bride Stones

Broxa

8

Dalby Forest

10 Levisham

9 Lockton
A169
12 Ellerburn
Wilton
7 Thornton-le-Dale
Allerston
Snainton
Ebberston

Rosedale Abbey
6

Lastingham
5

Cropton
4

A170
3 Sinnington
1 Pickering

CHAPTER 4
page 140

3
EASTERN MOORS, FORESTS & BEACHES

This southeastern corner of the North York Moors is dominated by forest, not the natural English oak woodland that was originally here, but hundreds of square miles of coniferous plantation. The almost-linked forests of Cropton, Dalby and Harwood Dale constitute the Forestry Commission's North Riding Forest Park, at 500 square miles the second largest in England. It stretches from Rosedale in the west to the North Sea coast in the east, across an area of plateaux and deep valleys that some inspired geographer gave the perfect label of the Tabular Hills. These uplands don't meet the sea gently, but in a line of precipitous cliffs stretching from **Robin Hood's Bay** in the north to Filey in the south. In the few places where these cliffs relent, there is sand, and where there are beaches there are holiday resorts. **Scarborough**, with two sandy bays, is not only the biggest seaside resort on the Yorkshire coast but claims to be the oldest in the world. Next comes little **Cayton Bay**, literally awash with surfers much of the time, and finally, seven miles south of Scarborough, her younger and more modest sister, **Filey**, with the queen of beaches – five miles of glorious Filey sands stretching to the chalk cliffs of **Flamborough Head** and out of North Yorkshire. The only other town in the region is **Pickering**, an old fortified market town sitting just at the point where pancake-flat Ryedale turns hilly: very much a southern gateway to the North York Moors.

SELF-POWERED TRAVEL
CYCLING
I will stick my neck out and suggest that this is possibly the best area in the country for the cyclist, especially **off-road**. It is absolute two-wheel heaven, and **Dalby Forest** is the focus of it all: it is so good that it was selected for staging the World Mountain Bike Championships in 2011.

In the last ten years the Forestry Commission has spent over a million pounds developing biking facilities in the forest culminating in a series of six colour-coded and waymarked trails ranging from the two-mile Ellerburn green trail (easy), a perfect gentle intro for young families, to the black trail (severe), which is a challenge for even expert mountain bikers. The most popular route, and it can get very busy, is the 23-mile red route (difficult), which is possibly the best of its kind in the country. Maps of all the trails are available free in the visitor centre at Low Dalby (page 120).

"I will stick my neck out and suggest that this is possibly the best area in the country for the cyclist, especially off-road."

If you want forest track riding to yourself then just go exploring with the 1:25,000 OS Explorer map OL27. There are literally hundreds of miles of deserted tracks in Cropton, Langdale, Broxa and Harwood Dale forests waiting to be ridden, and the Forestry Commission (bless it) is happy for you to do it as long as you take special care near forestry operations. A rewarding gentle ride, for those allergic to hills, starts at Reasty Hill Top car park near Harwood Dale, and covers a flat four-mile triangular route to Barns Cliff End and back; my children had their first exciting forest bike ride here aged five and seven, and still talk about it. It would be too tame for them now of course, but the route can be extended to Broxa, with the uphill return via the delightful, and delightfully named, Whisper Dales.

Another more testing favourite of mine is a meandering exploration of the northern end of **Cropton Forest**, taking in Needle Point and Killing Nab Scar. You can reach the starting point either by car from the hamlet of Stape, or from Newtondale Halt on the North Yorkshire Moors Railway (bikes can be taken on the train).

Still off-road, but not under trees, there are lots of bridleways and green-lane routes on the moors. The moors are not as extensive here as further north and west, but two are crossed by bridleways that make for good biking territory. Levisham Moor is one and is accessible from Levisham village or the Hole of Horcum on the A169 Pickering to Whitby road. The other is Brow Moor behind Robin Hood's Bay, where you could make a circular route by using part of the **disused railway line** at Stoupe Brow. This line is a fantastic, recognised cycle route in its own right and rideable all the way from Scarborough to Whitby, 20 miles of easy cinder track with great sea views.

Good **road biking** is less easy to find here, but the best of it is a network of quiet minor roads to the west of Scarborough around the village of **Hackness**, which also link up with the tarmac toll road winding its way through Dalby Forest.

Finally, there is a long-distance cycle trail which incorporates lots of what I have already detailed. The **Moor to Sea cycle route** (⌀ moortoseacycle.net) was developed by local bikers for family cycling and provides four days' worth of the best road, forest, lane and rail riding the area has to offer, linking Scarborough, Pickering and Whitby.

⍾ FOOD & DRINK

Bayhire Scarsdale Cres, Scarborough ⌀ 07477 167076 ⌀ bayhire.co.uk. Fully supported hire of mountain and e-bikes for the Cinder Track. Delivery and collection service available.
Bikeabout Filey Hope St, Filey ⌀ 01723 518314 ⌀ bikeaboutfiley.co.uk. Bike hire, accessories and a mobile repair service.
Dalby Bike Barn The Square, Thornton le Dale ⌀ 01751 476633 ⌀ dalbybikebarn.co.uk. Mountain and e-bikes for hire. Also shop, servicing, repairs and guiding.
Dalby Forest Cycle Hub Dalby Forest Courtyard ⌀ 01751 460585 ⌀ dalbyforestcyclehub. co.uk. Shop, repairs, hire and courses; page 121.
Trailways The Old Railway Station, Hawsker ⌀ 01947 820207 ⌀ trailways.info. Bikes, buggies, tandems and trailer bikes for hire. Two hours to multi-day. One-way ride and pick-up by arrangement.

HORSERIDING

The long well-drained tracks here are as good for horses as for bikes, and there are plenty of riding opportunities, whether you have your own beast of burden or need to borrow one. The big forests (Dalby and its neighbours) are wonderful venues for riding, and the Forestry Commission welcomes you with open arms – free entry into Dalby via the toll road for instance. No specific horseriding routes are designated so you are free to use any of the forest roads or bridleways, but colour-coded bike trails are best avoided as they get so busy.

There are trekking/hacking centres at Robin Hood's Bay and Sinnington. If you are bringing your own horse, the North York Moors National Park has a really useful horseriding section on its website (⌀ northyorkmoors.org.uk/visiting/enjoy-outdoors/horse-riding).

RIDING CENTRES

Farsyde Riding Centre Robin Hood's Bay YO22 4UG 📞 01947 880249
🖊 farsydefarmcottages.co.uk. Hacking for experienced riders on moors, fields and forests.
Trekking is also available on the old railway line for beginners.
Friars Hill Riding Stables Sinnington YO62 6SL 📞 01751 432758 🖊 friarshillridingstables.
co.uk. Hacking and trekking for those over the age of eight years (but note: not
absolute beginners).

WALKING

Four **long-distance footpaths** or unofficial 'ways' have a terminus
here. Whether it is the start or the finish is pretty much up to you,
except for the Coast to Coast Walk and Lyke Wake Walk, where the
universally accepted direction to travel is west to east, both finishing at
Robin Hood's Bay. The other two are the much-frequented, horseshoe-
shaped Cleveland Way, which in this area traverses the full length of
the coast between Robin Hood's Bay and Filey, and the lesser-known
48-mile Tabular Hills Walk between Helmsley and Scarborough. This
route is also sometimes referred to as the Cleveland Way Link as it
joins the loose ends of the longer walk to create a circular route of
158 miles.

Shorter day or half-day walks are many and varied, limited only
really by your map-reading skills and sense of adventure, because there
is a huge network of rights of way and a large area of open access land
(page 13). Avoid busy mountain-bike areas, like some of the bridleways
leading into Dalby Forest, and the Moor to Sea cycle route.

Because public transport is so comprehensive here, there are many
opportunities for **point-to-point walks** with a bus or train shuttle. I am
always more comfortable being driven first and walking back as there is
less chance of being marooned and no pressure to make the bus stop or
station on time. If you can wangle it so the engine power does more of
the uphill than your legs, all the better. A good way to do sections of the
Cleveland Way is to use the Scarborough to Whitby bus; Robin Hood's

---

TOURIST INFORMATION

Filey John St 📞 01723 383636
Scarborough Town Hall, St Nicholas St & Stephen Joseph Theatre, Westborough
📞 01723 383636 for both.

Bay to Cloughton perhaps (ten miles), or Cloughton to Scarborough (five miles). The train can do the same job between Scarborough and Filey (seven miles). Away from the coast, a rover ticket on the North Yorkshire Moors Railway allows you to hop off at one station, walk to the next and hop back on – plenty of scope there.

THE SOUTHERN MOORS & FORESTS

Much of this area is virtually uninhabited, wild territory covered by either trees or heather. Around the sole town, **Pickering**, are a clutch of rewarding **villages**: Thornton-le-Dale and the other Old Coach Road settlements on the way to Scarborough, Lockton and Levisham towards Whitby and, up the beautiful valley of Rosedale, Cropton, Sinnington, Lastingham and Rosedale Abbey.

1 PICKERING

🏠 **Cottage Lea's Country Hotel** Middleton (page 248)

Pickering first came to my attention as a case study in a geography lesson at school. It is a textbook example of a ribbon development; a town that grows along an important road instead of spreading sideways. What my geography teacher failed to tell me, though, is that the bits of Pickering away from the busy main road are full of unexpected history and quirky character. By far its biggest visitor attraction is the **North Yorkshire Moors Railway**, of which Pickering is the southern terminus, but the shops and arcades of Market Place and Birdgate come a close second. My favourite part of the town is surprisingly little visited, probably because of the steep walk involved. It is the area where narrow old streets lead up Castle Hill to the town's biggest and oldest building – **Pickering Castle** itself. My recommended route would be up Castle Road, from where it begins near the railway station, and back down Castlegate to take in the Quaker meeting house. It is worth detouring along Hatcase Lane, not just to celebrate such a wacky name, but because it will lead you to the fascinating **church of St Peter and St Paul**. This would be a humdrum building with little interest but for a chance discovery during renovation in 1852. Limewash was removed from an interior wall to reveal 15th-century frescoes underneath, which the architectural historian Nikolaus Pevsner described as 'one of the most complete series of wall paintings in English churches that give one a vivid idea of what ecclesiastical interiors were really like'. The pictures are multicoloured affairs mainly depicting the important saints of the time, St George of pest control fame, St John the Baptist, St Thomas of Canterbury and a particularly tall St Christopher, who was reputed to stand 12 cubits high.

On emerging from the front of the church you will be back into the bustle of Birdgate. If another dose of peace and quiet is required try **Beck Isle Museum** (Bridge St ✆ 01751 473653 ⬧ beckislemuseum.org. uk ☉ Easter–Oct Mon–Sat), at the other end of the marketplace. You don't even need to go in, although it is well worth the small entrance fee, because the beck-side lawn to the front, by the arches of the old bridge, is an ideal place for a tranquil muse or picnic. If you have any interest at all in rural social history, then the 27 rooms of this old agricultural college will keep you well entertained.

Pickering can be a haven of relaxation – it can also be a hive of activity. If you value peace and quiet then don't come here for the Wartime Weekend in October, the Steam Fair weekend in August or whenever the Mountain Bike World Cup is in town. But if you are fine with crowds and noise, then come along and be entertained.

Pickering Castle

Castlegate ✆ 01751 474989; English Heritage

Pickering's royal connections date back to accounts in a late medieval chronicle of a Briton king called Pereduras living here. A very dubious legend connects him and the origin of the town's name, which involves him losing a valuable ring in the river and it turning up later in the belly of a fish served up on the royal table. The fish was a pike; ring in a pike, pike-ring, Pickering – likely? I don't think so, but there is a pike on the town's coat of arms and a beautifully carved one on a wooden panel in the bar of the White Horse Inn. King Pereduras was around far too long ago to have had anything to do with the present castle but it was a royal residence, having been built at William I's instruction for his personal use when hunting in the Forest of Pickering. Possession of the castle has been passed down the royal line ever since, the present owner being the Duke of Lancaster, better known by his Sunday name – King Charles III. English Heritage looks after it for him today.

---

1 Whisper Dales makes wonderful cycling territory. **2** Pickering Castle. **3** St Mary's Church, Lastingham. **4** Thornton-le-Dale. ▶

This is a classic Norman motte-and-bailey castle, with the motte, or mound, crowned by the remains of the keep (the King's Tower). I particularly enjoy the walk on the path around the outside of the walls to detour into the quarries at the back where the limestone for the building was extracted; the North East Yorkshire Geology Trust has placed information boards explaining how these Jurassic rocks were formed under the sea.

¶¶ FOOD & DRINK

With more than ten **cafés**, Pickering is a place where it's easy enough to overdose on tea. My top three are **Elizabeth Botham's** on Park Street (✆ 01751 602823), another gem from the Whitby catering family Botham's of Whitby (page 87); the very popular **Feast** in Market Place (✆ 01751 470121 ⬛ Feast Cafe); and **Cafe Cocoa** on Smiddy Hill (✆ 07908 112087 ⬛), where quiche is a particular speciality and dogs are welcome.

Cedarbarn Farm Shop & Café Thornton Rd, YO18 7JX ✆ 01751 475614
⬧ cedarbarnfarmshop.co.uk. Angus beef and free-range eggs from its own farm plus veg, pies, cheeses and cakes.
The Organic Farm Shop Eastgate Sq ✆ 01751 473444 ⬛ Organic Food and Healthcare. An Aladdin's cave of good things, from home-produced beef to ice cream and groceries.
The Sun Inn 136 Westgate ✆ 01751 473661 ⬧ thesuninn-pickering.co.uk. No accommodation, no food and no pretensions – just great beer in a traditional pub. A winner of CAMRA's local rural pub of the year on more than one occasion. Regular live music, a Thursday quiz and customers are welcome to bring in take-away meals to eat in.
Willowdene Watercress and Trout Farm Westgate Carr Rd, YO18 8LX ✆ 01751 472769. Traditionally grown watercress and spring-water rainbow trout from the door.
Willowgate Bistro Willowgate ✆ 01751 476300 ⬧ willowgatebistro.co.uk ☉ Tue–Sat. For evening eating, this place is hard to beat – not fussy or fancy, just exceptional food and great service. It's very popular so booking is advised.

2 NORTH YORKSHIRE MOORS RAILWAY: PICKERING TO GROSMONT

✆ 01751 472508 ⬧ nymr.co.uk

Very few people aren't moved to a wistful nostalgia at the sight and sound of an old locomotive in full steam, and this is one of the most popular places in the country to enjoy the experience. Some, me included, would argue that it is best to not actually be on the train but watching from outside, but there is no doubt that either way everybody seems to enjoy steam trains immensely. Waving is *de rigueur* of course. I once even saw a group of middle-aged travellers all with a handkerchief to flutter at passers-by. 'It's got to be done,' one of them said. 'The nice man in *The Railway Children* did it so we have to keep up the tradition.' Steam travel is somehow very English. Thank goodness for those few passionate and far-sighted enthusiasts back in 1965 who knew that Dr Beeching had made a big mistake in shutting the line. It is them that we have to thank for the continued existence of the railway here because two years later they started a preservation society. In 1972 they took on one full-time paid worker and now they operate a huge business with 135 paid staff and even more eager volunteers helping out.

The scenic route of this railway also adds to its popularity. Most of the journey follows the spectacular valley of Newtondale, a deep and precipitous ravine with the incongruously small Pickering Beck trickling down the middle. This feeble stream is obviously incapable of excavating such a large valley. That job was done 10,000 years ago at the end of the last ice age, when Lake Eskdale overflowed and emptied into Lake Pickering in a raging torrent.

It is 18 miles from Pickering to the official other end of the line at Grosmont, and your journey will call at four stations, each renovated in a different period style. Pickering recreates the 1930s, Levisham has been decorated as it would have been in 1912 and Goathland boasts a 1922-style tea room. Finally, Grosmont has been left how it was in the 1950s just before closure, and also features the fascinating locomotive sheds (page 72). If you want to complete the story and visit a modern station then stay on the train because some of them now continue the extra six miles into Whitby courtesy of Northern Rail. Carriages are wheelchair-accessible and will carry bikes if there is space (phone to check). Trains run on one of four colour-coded timetables; gold at peak times with nine trains a day on the hour, and red, green or silver, each with six trains a day. Note that some services are diesel-hauled.

If just being a passenger is not enough for you and you don't mind getting your hands dirty, then a Footplate Awareness course would be just the ticket. Over the course of one to five days you get the chance to fulfil many a childhood dream, and drive a steam train.

Fares are reasonable and it's only a few extra pounds to Whitby. Make a full day of it by catching the first train out in the morning and the last one back, taking full advantage of the hop-on hop-off nature of your rover ticket. That way you can explore around each of the stations for an hour or so and get the next train that comes along.

3 SINNINGTON

Travel four miles west of Pickering and you will reach a crossing of the River Seven, a fraction of the size of its West Country namesake and a different spelling. A detour off the main road here to the village of **Sinnington** is worth the effort if only to sit and picnic on the green by the old arched bridge, but there are also many more active things to do if you have the inclination. The walking and biking along the river upstream are both good and pony trekking can also be done from here (page 103). If you keep following the river, you will find yourself in **Rosedale** (see opposite), a rural idyll now, but a major ironstone mining valley not so long ago.

¶¶ FOOD & DRINK

Fox and Hounds Main St ♪ 01751 431577 ⊘ thefoxandhoundsinn.co.uk. An old coaching inn in sleepy Sinnington. Expect homely panelled bars with open fires and modern pub food with a European twist. Cask beers are from Yorkshire (Bradfield and Black Sheep) and Lancashire (Thwaites). Luxury accommodation available.

Pearson's Soft Fruits Strawberry Fields YO62 6SL ♪ 01751 433380 ⊘ pearsonssoftfruits. com. Pick your own strawberries, raspberries, gooseberries and blackcurrants, or buy homemade jam of all the above. Just west of Sinnington.

4 CROPTON & 5 LASTINGHAM

The main route out of Rosedale passes through the village of **Cropton**, birthplace of the famous Whitby whaling ships' captain, William Scoresby. His local connection is celebrated in the name of a fine beer made in the village, Scoresby Stout. Cropton Brewery is a rarity, a very successful and long-lasting micro-brewery that has been operating from the New Inn since 1984. It still produces the original 'Two Pints' bitter along with numerous other recipes, including my favourite, 'Blackout Porter'.

A gentle two-mile cycle or walk away from Cropton on quiet country lanes is another village of a similar size. **Lastingham** is another one of those 'pub and church but not much else' places, but the Blacksmith's Arms deserves all the plaudits it receives in many good pub guides, and **St Mary's Church** is very special. It does not look unusual from the outside but venture in and you will find that it is in effect one church on top of another. Steps lead from the aisle down to a huge vaulted Norman crypt, extraordinarily unchanged since it was built as part of an unfinished abbey in the late 11th century; you won't come across a more atmospheric place too often. It is the only example in this country of a crypt with a nave and side aisles.

The lane east from Cropton towards Newton-on-Rawcliffe passes **Cawthorn Roman Camps**. Here an assortment of humpy earthworks are the remains of a temporary camp and forts for training Roman soldiers; the Cawthorn Trail is worth following to bring it all to life.

⫙ FOOD & DRINK

Blacksmith's Arms Anserdale Lane, Lastingham YO62 6TN ✆ 01757 417247
🖥 blacksmithsarmslastingham.co.uk. This is almost how you imagine a country pub to be; rambling and dimly lit, very, very old and with legends of a ghost and a secret tunnel to the church crypt opposite. There are usually four cask beers on – Theakstons Old Peculier and Best Bitter, Saltaire Blond and a guest – and the food is wholesome and traditional. If there is room then eat in the bar, as it is the most atmospheric part of the building by far. B&B available.

New Inn/Cropton Brewery Cropton YO18 8HH ✆ 01751 417330 🖥 newinncropton.co.uk. This is a great beer-drinkers' village inn with its own brewery, know internationally as The Great Yorkshire Brewery, and an annual beer festival in November. Food comes in generous portions and is good value and home cooked. Accommodation is available in the pub or there's camping in a quiet field behind the brewery. Brewery tours are excellent and well worth the entrance fee.

6 ROSEDALE ABBEY & ROSEDALE

Standing on high ground, and casting an appreciative eye over the fields, folds and pastoral corners of Rosedale, you may find it hardly possible to imagine what has gone on here in the past. Today, fewer than 500 people live out a sleepy, rural existence in this valley and it was much the same in 1851. Twenty years later that figure was nearer 5,000 as a Klondike-style rush of miners poured in and turned Rosedale into a loud, smoky, and crime-ridden industrial centre. It wasn't gold they were after but iron: between 1856 and 1926, millions of tons of high-grade ore were extracted and transported to the blast furnaces of County Durham. How they got it there was both dramatic and ingenious: a railway was constructed that stayed almost level, as railways have to do,

ROSEDALE GLASS – ANCIENT & MODERN

Not long ago, archaeologists unearthed a furnace last used 400 years ago by exiled Huguenot French glassmakers who plied their trade using local sand and wood fuel. This ancient local craft is celebrated in a thoroughly modern setting at **Gillies Jones glass-blowing studio** in Rosedale Abbey

($\mathscr{O}$ 01751 417550 $\mathring{\diamond}$ gilliesjonesglass.co.uk). Steven Gillies and Kate Jones, partners in life and art, work together to produce exquisite works inspired by the Rosedale countryside. Stephen is the glassmaker and Kate the sand-carver and painter. Drop into the studio to see them at work.

by contouring right around the head of the valley at about 1,000ft up. It then crossed Blakey Ridge and into the neighbouring valley of Farndale where it did the same, hugging a high-level line round to a point where descent was possible down a steep incline to join the mainline railway system at Battersby. Fortunately for us, the track bed is still there providing a perfect gentle walk or cycle way that is even wheelchair-accessible in places.

The ironstone boom had a major and lasting effect on the only village in the dale: Rosedale Abbey lost its abbey. The ruins of the Cistercian nunnery were dismantled stone by stone to provide building material for mine buildings and houses. Only one small belfry turret survives, but the village boasts two pubs, a café and a glass-blowing studio.

¶¶ FOOD & DRINK

Dale Head Farm Tea Garden YO18 8RL $\mathscr{O}$ 01751 417353 $\mathring{\diamond}$ daleheadfarmteagarden. co.uk. $\odot$ Wed–Sun. A welcoming little oasis up the dale from Rosedale Abbey and a short stroll downhill from the old railway line.

Graze on the Green Rosedale Abbey $\mathscr{O}$ 01751 417468 $\mathring{\diamond}$ grazeonthegreen.co.uk $\odot$ Wed–Sun. A great all-round reputation but particularly for breakfasts and cakes.

White Horse Farm Inn Chimney Bank $\mathscr{O}$ 01751 417239 $\mathring{\diamond}$ whitehorserosedale.co.uk. A 16th-century country inn just off the reputed steepest public road in the country. Black Sheep beer, wholesome pub grub and B&B always available.

7 THORNTON-LE-DALE

⋏ Low Farm Campsite Ellerburn (page 248)

East of Pickering, Thornton Beck, full of lime from the springs of Dalby Forest, flows between the much-photographed limestone buildings of Thornton-le-Dale. This large village is perennially busy with visitors.

On your first visit to Thornton-le-Dale you may well, like me, have a feeling of *déjà vu* with one building in particular seeming very familiar. **Beck Isle cottage** is one of the most photographed buildings in the country so the chances are that you have seen it before on a calendar or jigsaw. It isn't the only photogenic view in the village by any means; the combination of village green with cross and stocks, sparkling beck with 15 bridges and 17th-century almshouses has resulted in Thornton being regularly voted the most beautiful village in Yorkshire. This fame attracts visitors, of course, so if you need any respite from people then take a stroll on the beck-side footpath upstream past Thornton Mill to the sleepy hamlet of **Ellerburn**. A trout hatchery here takes advantage of the clear, cold, limestone spring water.

A tiny church, part Saxon, has had some unwelcome attention recently due to a wildlife controversy. Rare Natterer's bats lived in its roof space, a fact to celebrate you might think, but the bats were not particularly grateful lodgers. Droppings rained down on to the hymn books, sometimes even during the services, and the whiff of bat wee wasn't really conducive to contemplative worship. Thankfully a compromise was reached; the bats' access points to the church interior were blocked, but they still live in the loft.

If you continue on this route up Thornton Beck, you will reach **Dalby Forest visitor centre**, a fine walk in itself.

¶¶ FOOD & DRINK

Both pubs (The New Inn and The Buck) and all the cafés in Thornton le Dale are good, but these two establishments deserve a special mention.

Brandysnap Bistro Whitbygate ✆ 01751 474732 ⬦ brandysnapbistro.co.uk ⏱ Wed–Sat. An excellent evening-only restaurant that has become very popular by word of mouth. Book well in advance to have any chance of a table.
Tea Cosy Tea Room Ellerburn ✆ 01751 477198 ⏱ 10.00–16.00 Tue–Thu. Top-quality teas and coffees, soups and cakes. Popular with cyclists, walkers and their dogs.

8 THE OLD COACH ROAD VILLAGES

Thornton-le-Dale is the largest and busiest of a series of villages strung out along the old York to Scarborough coach road between Pickering and the coast. **Wilton, Allerston, Ebberston, Snainton, Brompton** and **Wykeham** all sit on or around the 50m contour line – above the swampy lowlands but not quite in the hills proper and, handily, on a line of springs that emerge from the limestone beneath. Strangely, the settlements developed historically, not along the main road, but following their respective becks southwards towards what was Lake Pickering. Consequently, they are bigger than they seem at first sight, and quiet. For lovers of peace and quiet they also offer access routes northwards into the least visited side of Dalby and Wykeham forests, most notably the fabulous raptor viewpoint off the Brompton and Sawdon road. A wide variety of accommodation is available and most of the villages boast an old coaching inn.

¶¶ FOOD & DRINK

The Anvil Inn Sawdon YO13 9DY ✆ 01723 850820 ⊘ theanvilinn.co.uk ⊙ Wed–Sun. This welcoming little hostelry is housed in a 200-year-old forge in the back of beyond, with the bar where the blacksmith's workshop was. Traditional and great quality pub grub. Beer is Taylor's Landlord plus two rotating guest ales. A place worth seeking out, off the A170. Self-catering cottage next door.

The Coachman Inn Snainton YO13 9PL ✆ 01723 859231 ⊘ coachmaninn.co.uk. The York–Scarborough mail coach stopped here in Georgian times and it's still old fashioned, with décor now in the 1930s Arts-and-Crafts style. Food features locally sourced meat and fish and is excellent, with some Turkish dishes on offer. Four cask beers are usually available, generally from local breweries. Accommodation available.

Glaves Butchers Cayley Ln, Brompton ✆ 01723 859523 ⊘ glavesbutchers.co.uk. Award-winning pork pies and sausages. All produce comes from its own farm or neighbours.

ARTS & CRAFTS

Ebberston Studios Main St, Ebberston ✆ 01723 859060 ⊘ ebberstonstudios.co.uk. Weekly classes and weekend workshops in a wide variety of arts and crafts – upholstery, painting, mosaics, pottery, book binding, willow weaving and many more. Very professional but also really friendly and welcoming.

DALBY FOREST & LEVISHAM MOOR

The A169 from Pickering to Whitby has been a route for many centuries, and the name Saltergate, literally 'salt street', refers of course to the journey done in the opposite direction, from Whitby and the coast to Pickering and all points inland, transporting a very important and valuable commodity in times past. Only one part of the A169 still bears that old name, where a hairpin bend takes it up to and along the edge of a spectacular crater called the **Hole of Horcum**. As the road makes its gradual descent from here into Pickering, it bypasses the villages of **Lockton** and **Levisham** to the right, and the wooded ridges and dales of **Dalby Forest** to the left.

9 LOCKTON & 10 LEVISHAM

These two neat and tidy moors' villages are like a pair of brothers or sisters – close, but separated by a deep valley, always vying with each other over small things, but jumping to each other's defence over

A walk on Levisham Moor to the Hole of Horcum

✤ OS Explorer map 27. Three possible start points: Hole of Horcum car park (♥ NZ853936), Levisham village (♥ NZ833905) or Newtondale Halt on the North Yorkshire Moors Railway (♥ NZ818910); 5–7 miles; moderate. All are accessible by either bus or train. Refreshment at the pub in Levisham.

Levisham Moor is all open-access land so you can actually walk wherever you like. However, ploughing through deep heather can be tiring so you may want to follow two of the three public rights of way – one out from your start point and another back to it. For the chance of seeing rare flowers, (green-winged orchids in May and dwarf cornel in August) and great views of steam trains follow the Levisham Bottoms path. For dazzling summer carpets of heather and wide

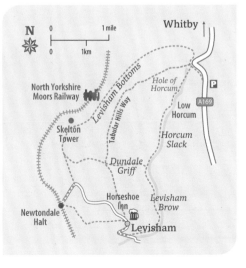

skies go for the moor-top bridleway, and for a close-up view of the enormous natural hollow that is the Hole of Horcum, choose the eastern footpath via Low Horcum and Levisham Brow. The total distance is five to seven miles, depending on which route you choose.

matters of importance. In reality the two places are complementary; Lockton has the church and youth hostel, while Levisham provides a railway station and pub. There was a small village shop in Lockton and a post office in Levisham until recently, but both have gone the way of many rural businesses, and sadly closed.

One resource neither village is short of is ground water: wells and springs are all over the place, because of the porous Jurassic limestone hillsides hereabouts. Near one of these named water sources, Rowl Spring, you will find the most mysterious building in the vicinity. **St Mary's Church**, roofless and derelict, is in neither village, but sits between the two in splendid isolation. Local stories claim that there was a village around the church which was wiped out by the plague in the 14th century, but there is no archaeological evidence for this. Whatever the history, St Mary's Church is an evocative ruin in a memorable setting.

To the north of Lockton and Levisham is a large area of moor and valley, making up the Levisham Estate, which was in private hands until 1985 when the National Park Authority bought it to safeguard its riches. Such is the wealth of archaeological remains there – tumuli, dykes, enclosures

"This is one of the best places in the country to see golden plover and the dashing little falcon, the merlin."

and settlements – that Levisham Moor is the largest scheduled ancient monument in England, though you need to poke around carefully with an OS map in hand to spot its ancient features. It is also designated a Site of Special Scientific Interest, for its rare breeding birds in particular; this is one of the best places in the country to see golden plover and the dashing little falcon, the merlin.

Skelton Tower

There can be few buildings in the North York Moors with as impressive a position and prospect as Skelton Tower. Perched on the lip of Newtondale, a mile north of Levisham Station, it affords magnificent views up and down the gorge, particularly rewarding when a steam locomotive is grunting up the valley hundreds of feet below. In reality the tower was a shooting-lodge-style folly built in 1850 by the Reverend Robert Skelton, vicar of Levisham. The official line is that he retired

◀ The North York Moors Railway at Levisham station.

there for the peace and quiet required to write his sermons, although unofficial local opinion is that it doubled as his secret drinking den. Such is the sinister aura of the ruins now that they were chosen by local author Ian Johnson as home for the murderous goblin Red Cap in his supernatural novel *The Witcher Keys*.

¶| FOOD & DRINK

Fox and Rabbit A169, near Lockton YO18 7NQ ✆ 01751 460213 🖰 foxandrabbit.co.uk. Brothers Charles and Toby Wood have got this pub just about right, very welcoming to travellers to and from the coast with three fine Yorkshire beers (Black Sheep, Theakstons and Timothy Taylor) and a wide selection of wines. The food is simple and traditional. Caravan Club site attached.

The Horseshoe Inn Levisham ✆ 01751 460240 🖰 horseshoelevisham.co.uk. This is a genuine traditional village pub sitting proudly at the top of the green. Food is similar to the Fox and Rabbit (it has the same owners) and the beer is from the Dales (Black Sheep) and Moors (Cropton). B&B available.

Lockton Tea Rooms and Gallery Lockton ✆ 01751 460467 🖰 locktontearooms.co.uk. Not just a great café during the day but also a bistro on some evenings when the Supper Club operates. Also, as the name suggests, a platform for the talents of the Lockton Artists Group. Accommodation is available in the loft apartment.

🛍 SHOPPING

David Stephenson Artist Blacksmith Sunny View, Lockton ✆ 01751 460252 🖰 davidstephenson.org.uk. Hand-forged fireside furniture, frames and weather vanes.

11 THE HOLE OF HORCUM

Levisham Beck starts its life in a series of tributary, spring-fed valleys. In one of these deep dales the springs have eaten back into the hillsides evenly over thousands of years, leaving a dramatic, almost circular, basin. Our ancestors did not have the benefit of our geographical knowledge and assumed that there must be a diabolical explanation for the phenomenon. The Devil, it is said, in his anger scooped out a vast ball of earth and hurled it over the Moors, the resulting hole being that of Horcum, and the mound where the earth landed, the nearby hill of Blakey Topping.

1 The Hole of Horcum. **2** Dalby Forest. **3** Skelton Tower. **4** Dalby Forest offers cycling opportunities for all ages and abilities. ▶

Plainly visible to the north of the Hole of Horcum is a much more recent monument, the pyramid-shaped radar building of **Fylingdales Missile Early Warning Station**. The 'sandcastle', as it is known locally, is a recent replacement for the original and famous three 'golf balls' constructed during the Cold War. Despite regular peace protests here, and with an ironic twist to what we would normally regard as 'heritage', there was actually a suggestion that the golf balls should be made listed buildings and preserved; certainly they are said to have become the subject of the best-selling postcard in the area.

12 DALBY FOREST

Dalby Forest Visitor Centre YO18 7LT ✆ 01751 460295 ⌂ forestry.gov.uk/dalbyforest

This huge area of woodland has become one of the Forestry Commission's beacon leisure forests, so much so that it's easy to forget that it still primarily is a commercial timber production area. The focus of everything here is the purpose-built forestry village of **Low Dalby**, which I am covering in this section with Slow transport and economy in mind. You can drive here, but the nearest village by road is Thornton-le-Dale, and that would involve you paying a hefty toll to drive through the forest. By foot, horse or bike, Lockton is the closest access point, and it's free to arrive under your own muscle power. Once you are here you can hire a bike from the **Dalby Forest Cycle Hub** (page 103).

"Each stone has ended up perched delicately above the heather on an undercut pedestal."

The **visitor centre** at Low Dalby was designed with all things sustainable and recyclable in mind. It is constructed from wood and glass, has toilet doors made from reconstituted mobile phone cases and is powered by a wind turbine and solar panels. Such a shame then that the architect made it the ugliest box of a building I've ever laid eyes on. Inside the visitor centre are exhibitions, a shop, a café, an astronomical observatory and information on the bewildering array of things that you can see and do in the forest itself. Outside are barbecue and picnic areas, two adventure playgrounds, a Go Ape ropes course for adrenaline junkies, and free maps for various waymarked trails. One is a permanent orienteering course, and there are also ten walking trails of varying distance, four of which are accessible to wheelchairs. My favourite of these is the Staindale Lake circuit, which I had the privilege of sharing

CYCLING IN DALBY FOREST

Of everything on offer, off-road biking is Dalby's speciality, and what it is nationally renowned for. Most people's first stop is at the Dalby Forest Cycle Hub in the Courtyard, not far from the main visitor centre car park. And what an absolutely brilliant place this is for everything to do with mountain biking. If you have your own bike there is a well-stocked accessory shop and a superb cleaning, maintenance and emergency repair service. If you haven't got a mountain bike with you, you can hire a really good-quality standard, electric or one of a bewildering range of accessible bikes. Training courses range from a kids 'Learn to Ride your Bike' (1½ hours) to an adults' 'Black Skills Course' and everything else in between. Best of all, the staff are skilled enthusiasts who will go out of their way to give you a great biking experience. Once kitted out, you can head out on one of the graded trails:

Ellerburn cycle trail (green; 2½ miles) A short, relaxing and almost flat route perfect for young families that starts and finishes at the hub, with a gentle skills park for the kids partway round.

Adderstone cycle trail (green; 6 miles) A longer but easy circular route starting at the Adderstone field, itself a five-mile tarmac-road ride from the visitor centre.

Dalby blue trail (blue; 8 miles) A long intermediate circular route starting at the visitor centre. Still easy terrain but one or two steep hills.

Dalby red trail (red; 21½ miles) Very long and difficult; one of the best of its kind in the country and justifiably popular. Don't be tempted on here without decent equipment and skills.

Dalby World Cup Cycle Trail (black; 3 miles) and **Dixon's Hollow Skills Park** – if you are good enough, then you will already know about these, if not, then don't even think about them!

with a group of students from a special school in Scarborough. One of the children, who was using a wheelchair, said, 'This is brilliant. I've seen places like this on telly with explorers going through the trees and mountains. Now it's me, I'm here and I'm the explorer.'

Staindale is also the best start point for another short expedition of less than a mile, this time to just outside the forest, on the adjacent moor. The **Bride Stones** are a series of wonderfully sculpted sandstone blocks and buttresses, which wouldn't look out of place in a Hollywood western movie, such is their desert-style, wind-eroded profile. Each stone has ended up perched delicately above the heather on an undercut pedestal, and they are in the care of the National Trust, manages this area as a nature reserve. There is a full calendar of events throughout the year, from ranger-led nature trails to car rallies and summer rock concerts.

ACTIVITIES

Go Ape ⏟ goape.co.uk. High-adrenalin, high-wire forest adventure or gentle exploration on a segway 'bike'.

ROBIN HOOD'S BAY TO SCARBOROUGH

In the 20 or so miles between Whitby and Scarborough, **Robin Hood's Bay** is the only place of any size on the coast. Such is the ruggedness of this coastline there is not even any road access to the shore anywhere else, and the few small villages that exist are perched on top of the cliffs, like **Ravenscar**, or set back inland, like Cloughton and Burniston. Then suddenly there's big, sprawling, friendly **Scarborough**, very much a different world.

13 ROBIN HOOD'S BAY

⌂ **Boggle Hole YHA** (page 248) & **The Pigsty** Fylingthorpe (page 248)

Let's get one thing straight from the start. Robin Hood, if he ever existed, never had anything to do with this place. Wild theories abound as to the origin of the name, but not one scrap of evidence that he even came here on holiday. Even the locals in a gesture of embarrassed denial have dropped the Sherwood Forester from the name. 'Bay' or 'Baytown' is what they call their home. Confusing names apart, it is certain that there have been outlaws here in fact, in the 17th century it appears that most of the

"It is said that a bale of silk could pass from the dock at the bottom of the village to the top, without seeing the light of day."

population were actively involved in smuggling. There were tunnels linking cellars, secret passages and hidey holes for both people and contraband. It is said that a bale of silk could pass from the dock at the bottom of the village to the top, without seeing the light of day. If you are feeling adventurous it is still possible to scramble up part of this route by following the beck from the beach up into the tunnel a few hundred yards. All you need is a pair of wellies, a torch and a sense of adventure.

READ ALL ABOUT IT!

The residents of Robin Hood's Bay form a close-knit community. There is a real family feel to the place, including 'adoptees' – those repeat visitors that come back year after year to the many guesthouses and holiday cottages. Part of the 'glue' that sticks them all together is the monthly town magazine that almost everybody subscribes to. *Bayfair* can tell you virtually everything you need to know about the place, from tide times and local events lists to nature or history articles and details of over 80 places to stay.

'I took it over in 1995 after finishing work at HM Customs and Excise,' said Jim Foster, the ex-editor/designer/printer. 'It was a great move; I was ready to retire but needed something to keep me busy and interested, and *Bayfair* certainly does that. Bay has a

real magical quality about it, with its history and all the maritime connections. It draws people in and they stay. I suppose with *Bayfair* we're trying to sprinkle a little bit of that magic about – and inform of course – as this is one of the most aware communities on the coast I think. It's time consuming but I try not to do the real hard work; that's the job of the regular contributors who do a great job,' admitted Jim Foster back in 2009 when he was still at the helm. Jim had his second retirement in 2017 when he passed on the editing reins to Matt Crossland who continues the brilliant work today. If you are planning to stay in Robin Hood's Bay then *Bayfair* is an invaluable reference and fantastic value at 50p. You can even order it online (⊘ bayfair.co.uk) before you come.

Modern-day Bay is very different from those times when it was considered a more important place than Whitby. Fishing has all but gone, the railway is closed, and no alum or jet is mined here anymore. Robin Hood's Bay is now entirely dependent on the tourism industry for its livelihood, but it has embraced it with enthusiasm and does it tastefully in the main, celebrating its own history and heritage well. Of course, having the wonderful scenic surroundings and prolific wildlife of a national park on the doorstep helps. The village, or town as some claim it to be, is tucked into an almost sheltered corner of the coast, behind the Ness (Viking for headland) also called North Cheek. South Cheek sits proudly, three miles across the wide, sweeping bay with the village of Ravenscar on top. In between, when the tide is out, lie the limestone scars of the shore. I hesitate to say 'beach' because sand is in short supply; there is some, but nothing to compare with Scarborough or Filey. The silver lining is that this is the best **rock pooling** territory in the region. This whole section of shore is protected as part of the Yorkshire and Cleveland Heritage Coast.

As for the town – and by that I mean the **old village** on the hillside, not the more modern development at the top – my favourite means of exploration is by semi-formal potter. Wandering up and down the many ginnels and alleys on both sides of the main street, seeing which are interconnected and which are dead ends, is the best way to make sure you see everything, and make no mistake, there is lots to see. Among the old cottages at Fisherhead, for instance, you will find in the old mortuary the village's tiny **museum**, a whale's jawbone in a garden and ship's portholes as windows. In the maze of alleyways on the other side of King's Beck, look out for a plaque to mark the spot of John Wesley's sermon, and cottage walls sporting insurance company fire marks, which directed the fire brigade to those houses that had paid to have fires put out, and those unfortunates that hadn't. The abruptly ending King Street is near here, and was the town's main street until its northern end fell into the sea in 1780.

All alleyways and streets lead down to **the Dock**, now the only access to the shore since the 1975 sea wall was built, and still a focal point. On either side of the slipway sits the Bay Hotel, the eastern terminus of celebrated walks writer Alfred Wainwright's Coast to Coast Walk (the other end is St Bees Head in Cumbria), and the Old Coastguard Station, now a National Trust visitor centre. For added spice, do your pottering after dark, from pub to pub maybe, and you will stand a good chance of bumping into some of Bay's other night walkers – badgers. Apparently the population of the local sett has taken to raiding bins; they are very bold about it and quite easy to see. If you are staying in town, don't leave your front door open late in the evening as one local resident did, to later find a badger wandering around in his upstairs bathroom.

"All alleyways and streets lead down to the Dock, now the only access to the shore."

At the top of the bank you are still in Robin Hood's Bay but a part with a completely different feel to it. It is newer in the main, with many of the Victorian buildings springing up when the railway arrived in 1865. There is not much of interest up here, save one or two good

---

1 Robin Hood's Bay. **2** The North York Moors National Park en route to Robin Hood's Bay.
3 Species-rich Forge Valley. **4** Cayton Bay is a super spot for surfing. **5** South Bay, Scarborough.
6 Ravenscar is a great place for seal spotting. **7** Scarborough's Rotunda Museum. ▶

CONSTANTIN STANCIU/S

HELEN HOTSON/S

ANDREW KEARTON/A

HEYMYNAMEISMARK/S

JACK COUSIN/S

JUDITH ANDREWS/S

TONY BARTHOLOMEW

eating houses and the old railway station itself, which is now the home of a few Slow businesses and organisations.

The Bay

Any Cleveland Wayer worth his or her salt, when heading south from Robin Hood's Bay, would choose to walk on the seashore rather than the official clifftop path, if the tide allows. Not only is it the flat alternative, it is also a delight – part sand, part rock-ledge, but always with the tang, noise and excitement of the sea right by your side.

The first half mile to Boggle Hole could be busy, as this is a popular stroll, and not just with those staying in the youth hostel. This imposing building was originally a big Victorian watermill, built to take advantage of the latent power in the beck that spills on to the beach here. Fewer people make it to the next beach stream, another half mile on at Stoupe Beck, but there is a route on to the clifftop back to civilisation and even a nearby road.

You are likely to have the remaining three miles of shoreline to yourself – well, you and the oystercatchers, fulmars and turnstones – as there is no escape up the cliffs until Old Peak. I find it incredible that where the looming cliffs are at their steepest, with waterfalls tumbling over the edge, there was once a harbour. A couple of centuries ago, this was where ships loaded up with alum, a chemical extracted from the shale rock that was quarried from Stoupe Brow, hundreds of feet higher up. The remains of the quarries and works are still there to be seen, owned and ably interpreted by the National Trust, both on-site and in its Peakside Centre (page 128).

¶¶ FOOD & DRINK

The Cove Café Bar Chapel St ✆ 01947 880180 ⌖ thecoverhb.com. An innovative venture in an old chapel, with superb views across the bay from the café balcony. Pizzas a speciality.

Grosvenor Hotel Station Rd ✆ 01947 880320 ⌖ thegrosvenor.info. A hotel with a popular lounge bar, pool table and regular live music; Sunday is quiz night. Bar food includes fish and chips and local lobster. En-suite rooms available.

Hare and Hounds Hawsker ✆ 01947 880453 ⌖ hareandhoundshawsker.co.uk. Two miles out of Baytown on the Whitby road but worth including for the quality of its fare. The beer range is varied and very good and the food is a brilliant mix of traditional English (pie night especially good) and exotic.

Tea, Toast & Post King St ✆ 07880 732115 ⬛ ◷ Tue–Sun. Eclectic little cafe in the old post office with legendary bacon butties. Live music some evenings.

14 RAVENSCAR

🏠 **Worfolk Cottage** Staintondale (page 248)

There is a major crack in the earth's surface here, well known among geologists as the Peak Fault, and it has a lot to answer for. It has indirectly led to Romans and seals taking up residence here and a Victorian property company going out of business. What the fault did was raise the land level to the south 600ft higher than that to the north, where the bay now is, and it brought different, more resistant rocks to the surface (apologies to geologists, I know it's a lot more complicated than that). The Romans consequently had a convenient high vantage point to build one of their chain of coastal signal stations, where the Raven Hall Hotel is now, and the seals got a protective shelf of hard rock to shelter behind (page 128).

As for the property company, this was a group of Yorkshire businessmen who formed the Peak Estate Company in 1885, with the bright idea of creating a seaside resort at Ravenscar to rival Scarborough and Whitby. They spent a small fortune laying out a road system, putting in water mains and digging sewers and then put 1,500 building plots up for sale. Call it naïve, but what they hadn't accounted for was that holidaymakers would not want to walk 600ft down (and more importantly back up) to a beach that was predominantly bedrock and boulders. They sold eight plots and went bankrupt. Details of their ill-fated scheme, and much

A coastal walk from wyke to wyke

❊ OS Explorer map OL27; start: either Wyke, ♥ SE018952; 4 miles; easy.

Between Ravenscar and Scarborough, the walk along the wild section of coast on the Cleveland Way from Hayburn Wyke to Cloughton Wyke, and back along the old railway Cinder Track Cinder Track, is a most rewarding one ('wyke' means 'bay', incidentally). It's two miles each way, and you can start at either end with refreshment at the Hayburn Wyke Inn. Tea/ beer at the end or half way – that is the question. There's good rock pooling at Cloughton Wyke, and at Hayburn Wyke a stream gushes on to a boulder-strewn cove backed by high cliffs.

SEALS

I heard about the seal colony at Ravenscar, near Robin Hood's Bay, back in 2009, so one clear crisp day in March I went to investigate for myself. It was cold enough to see my breath as I picked my way down the steep cliff path but thankfully there was no wind or I would have needed much more than the thin fleece I was wearing. I heard the seals before I saw them, a slightly forlorn-sounding strangled wail every now and again. At least I knew they were here. I headed towards Peak Steel, the rocky outcrop where the noise seemed to be coming from, and found that I wasn't alone. 'Hello there,' said a man who turned out to be Callum Foster, 'have you come to see the seals as well?'

Callum lives in Robin Hood's Bay and was accompanied by 12 schoolchildren from York who were staying at nearby East Barnby Outdoor Education Centre. 'We usually take the children on seashore walks nearer the centre but I thought we'd come here today for a change and see the seals,' Callum explained. 'This colony hasn't been here that long. Five years ago, all we'd see were odd individuals out in the bay now and again. But then a few more came from somewhere and started hauling themselves out on the scars here. One winter we noticed some small pups with white furry coats among the rocks and realised that they had started breeding. Numbers have increased dramatically, to the point now… how many have we counted today kids?''Sixty-five!' piped up the voice of ten-year-old Emma, 'but these are different to the two we saw yesterday. These are grey seals 'cos they've got big noses like Romans, and yesterday's when we were canoeing on the river were common seals 'cos they had faces like dogs.'

Emma was right; the Ravenscar colony are grey or Atlantic seals, *Halichoerus gryphus*,

more about this clifftop village, can be found in the National Trust's little visitor centre (✆ 01723 870423) by the hotel. Retracing the planned road system makes an interesting potter.

ⓘⓘ FOOD & DRINK

Hayburn Wyke Inn Hayburn Wyke YO13 0AU ✆ 01723 870202 ⓐ hayburnwykeinn.co.uk. Well-used by walkers and cyclists on the 'Cinder Track' that goes right past the door and a popular Sunday lunch carvery venue. En-suite accommodation is available and camping by arrangement.

15 SCARBOROUGH

Scarborough has an old provenance: a Roman signal station, a Viking name, a Norman castle and the tourist industry that started in the 17th century. It is also a modern seaside resort, and a 'fast' one at that, with which literally means hooked-nosed sea pig, and they probably came as colonists from the big population on the Farne Islands in Northumberland. The adult bulls, at 10ft long and weighing 300lb, are our biggest wild land animal, if you count lounging on beaches now and again as being terrestrial. They eat 10lb of fish per day which doesn't make them popular with local fishermen – just do the sums, 10 x 65 x 365: that is a lot of fish in a year. Fast forward to 2022 and Ravenscar's grey seals are doing very well; numbers are up to over 300 now and, in the breeding season, the steady stream of visitors are advised and informed by volunteers from the Yorkshire Seal Group (⏚ yorkshireseals.org).

The common or harbour seals that Emma and her friends had seen the day before in the tidal section of the River Esk are much smaller than grey seals. Their nearest breeding colony is 20 miles north on Seal Sands in the Tees estuary, but adventurous individuals often appear along the Yorkshire coast. They are quite happy to venture up rivers, especially when their favourite food of sea trout and salmon are doing the same. Up to five seals take up residence at times, on a grassy bank of the river, halfway between Ruswarp and Whitby. They are visible from the train, so keep your eyes peeled if you are on it, just after Ruswarp Station, or take a riverside walk up from Whitby.

If you want more than a fleeting glimpse from a train, then call in at the Sea Life Centre at Scalby Mills, Scarborough (page 132). It operates a seal rescue centre that takes in sick, orphaned or exhausted seals, and pampers them for a bit before releasing them back into the wild. Sign up for a 'Breakfast with the Seals' experience and you can even help feed them – very entertaining!

many visitors coming for the nightclubs, amusement arcades, lager and speedboat trips. The words 'go slow' and South Bay seafront fit together as comfortably as, well, a square peg and a round hole. It is all relative though – in the loud-brash-tacky stakes it is not in the same league as Blackpool or Margate, and you can still savour its genteel Georgian class in some hidden, serene corners.

A good place to begin is the Spa at the foot of South Cliff, where the original therapeutic spring was discovered in 1626. Behind the elegant **Spa complex**, with its concert hall and café, **South Cliff Gardens** cling to the steep hillside. You could easily spend half a day exploring the three miles of zigzagging path on foot, or by wheelchair or bike (there are no no-cycling signs) and enjoying stunning views over the sea. In summer you can walk down and take the **Spa Cliff Tramway** back up. Even on busy days the gardens are remarkably quiet, especially at the non-town end. For the more intrepid, a walk in this direction does not need to stop at the end of the gardens, but could continue along the shore, on to Black Rocks and around White Nab, tide permitting. South of town, the clifftop is accessible again at **Osgodby Point** and your two-mile return follows the Cleveland Way path. This route crosses debris from the 1993 landslip, when a huge section of cliff suffered a 'rotational slip' taking the Holbeck Hall Hotel with it. You can find out all the details and much more about local geology in the **Rotunda Museum** near the Spa.

If you can brave crossing the seafront (on the beach itself is the most pleasant route) the other end of **South Bay** has Scarborough Castle on the headland. From the top of this promontory you can see down on to Scarborough's other beach in **North Bay**, where you can enjoy more sand and fewer people. Halfway round North Bay, where the road ends, is Peasholm Park, once a huge tourist attraction but now dilapidated and scheduled for redevelopment.

"From the top of this promontory you can see down on to Scarborough's other beach in North Bay."

Two welcome exceptions here are the **Peasholm Glen Tree Trail** (get a map from the tourist information centre) described in the National Tree Register as 'one of the richest and most diverse tree collections of any English town', and the **North Bay Railway**. Scarborough itself is not in the North York Moors National Park but the boundary comes close to the town in the north near Cloughton, and especially the west, where Raincliffe Woods and Forge Valley are very accessible.

The Rotunda Museum

Vernon Rd ✆ 01723 353665 ⬡ scarboroughmuseumstrust.com/visit/rotunda-museum.
☉ Tue–Sun

Historically and architecturally, this is one of the most important small museums in the country, but the Rotunda is a real riches-to-rags-to-riches-again story. It was built in 1829 to the specific design of the remarkable geologist William Smith, who almost single-handedly produced a geological map of England and Wales, the first of its kind in the world. Near the end of his career he wished to celebrate his discoveries, and the rich fossil beds of northeast Yorkshire, by displaying his huge collection in the same vertical layers that they occurred in nature, the youngest on the top floor and the oldest in the basement. This graceful

50ft-high Doric-style building with a viewing spiral staircase was the consequence, and a roaring success in Victorian society.

Simon Winchester lamented in his 2001 biography of Smith, *The Map that Changed the World*, that in recent years the building had become a shadow of its former self and had lost its fossils. To their eternal credit, Scarborough Museums Trust have since done a fantastic job of returning the Rotunda to its former glory. In 2008 it reopened as the William Smith Museum of Geology and has since been re-branded as the Museum of Coastal Heritage and Geology.

Scarborough Castle

Castle Rd ☏ 01723 37245 ⊙ variable, check website for details

On the lofty headland between North Bay and South Bay, this is such a textbook defendable site that it's no surprise there has been a fort here since Iron Age times. The Romans also had a signal station here and finally the Normans built the present building. Actually, to call it a building is stretching a point a bit, because little is left except the barbican, curtain walls, and the tottering remains of the keep. Parliamentarians did most of the damage in the Civil War, and that was added to last century by the Germans – not as you may suspect, World War II aerial bombing, but an artillery attack from a battleship in 1914. What is

"It is a great place for a family picnic though, with plenty of grassy space for the little ones to run around in."

left is a big castle site but not an awful lot to see. It is a great place for a family picnic though, with plenty of grassy space for the little ones to run around in, and English Heritage produces free activity sheets for them to do while you sit and have a cup of tea in the café.

Just outside the castle entrance is another building worth a visit, especially for those with a literary bent. **St Mary's Church** is old, but not remarkable, save for a much visited grave outside. It is a memorial to part of the tragic family history of the Brontës, being the resting place of Anne. She moved to Scarborough in May 1849 to take the restorative sea air and try to avoid the fate of her brother Branwell and her sister Emily who had already died from tuberculosis, or consumption as it was known then. It didn't work; she died of the same disease within the month and was buried in St Mary's graveyard. To add insult to injury, there were five errors on her original gravestone which her surviving sister Charlotte replaced with the present one, but even that has a mistake – she was 29 at her death not 28 as the stonemason's engraving claims.

A seafront tour

The best of what Scarborough has to offer is by the sea, between the Spa and Scalby Mills, but these two are almost three miles apart. That's a little too far to walk there and back, and probably the last thing you would want to do is even attempt to drive through town. Here is a suggested multi-transport tour of the seafront, starting at either of Scarborough's park-and-rides, although it could just as easily start at the Scalby Mills car park.

Pack your bags for the day, and take the **park-and-ride bus** into town, getting off at Aquarium Top. Just around the corner is the Spa where you can catch the **Shoreline Suncruiser bus** (every 15 minutes between March and October) and enjoy the open-top views, weather permitting. This will take you around South Bay, the harbour, the kittiwake colony on the castle headland and North Bay to **Peasholm Park**. Just across the road from the park, in Northstead Manor Gardens is the southern terminus of the **North Bay Railway** (⊘ nbr.org.uk), a narrow gauge line dating from 1931, where you can take a short ride to Scalby Mills. If you have to wait for your train, then there are always the pedal boats nearby, or a cup of tea at the **Sidings Snack Shack**.

Scalby Mills is the end of the seafront, there being cliffs beyond, but two temptations await here – the **Sea Life Centre** (⊘ 01723 373414 ⊘ visitsealife.com) and the Old Scalby Mills pub (see opposite). My

CORNELIAN – A YORKSHIRE GEM

Cornelian, or carnelian, is a semi-precious stone with a deep orange colour, often found on the beaches of North Yorkshire. One beach, between Scarborough and Cayton Bay, is a particularly good hunting ground and has earned itself the name Cornelian Bay. Geologists class cornelian as iron-oxide-stained chalcedony – rusty quartz in other words – but that doesn't stop it polishing up into beautiful jewellery. The cornelian pebbles have had a long and eventful journey to these beaches because they do not originate from the local Jurassic cliffs. They have actually been washed out of the cliff-top boulder clay which was left here by the last North Sea ice sheet 10,000 years ago. The ice must have brought the pebbles from the nearest source of cornelian – Scotland!

distrust of anything resembling a zoo put me off visiting the Sealife Centre for years but I went for the first time recently with my granddaughter and have to say that I loved it almost as much as she did. Being small and intimate you can get very close to some fascinating marine (and other) animals. More importantly, the management is committed to marine conservation ethics and the staff are knowledgeable, enthusiastic and very welcoming.

ⓘ FOOD & DRINK

Cafés

Scarborough probably has more than a hundred cafés, so to find out which were the best, I approached John Savile and Martin Stirling, two locals who drink almost as much tea as they do beer. Here are the best three in the experts' opinion:

The Clock Café The Spa ✆ 01723 500390. Probably the oldest café in town, in a listed building that's just celebrated its centenary. The jury is out over its best feature – the view over South Bay or the scones.

Eat Me Café Hanover Rd ✆ 07445 475328 🖥 eatmecafe.com. ☉ Mon–Sat. This popular venue, just behind the Steven Joseph Theatre and handy for the railway station, does imaginative international cuisine with vegan options. Friendly welcome extended to all customers, including dogs.

Lifeboat Fish Bar Eastborough ✆ 01723 363081 🟦 ☉ very seasonal, check Facebook. Mainly a very popular take-away but with a great little eat-in café round the back. Widely regarded as the best fish and chips in town.

Pubs

Old Scalby Mills Scalby Mills Rd, YO12 6RP ✆ 01723 698445 🖥 oldscalbymills.co.uk. Popular seafront local frequented by Cleveland Way walkers, Sea Life Centre visitors and the odd sea kayaker. The good range of beers includes a house beer named after the pub dog. Not renowned for food, though.

Stumble Inn 59 Westborough ✆ 07837 716774 🖥 stumbleinnmicropub.weebly.com. Scarborough's first micro-pub, a minute's walk from the railway station, proudly provides 'real beer, real cider, real perry and real conversation.' Very welcoming.

Valley Valley Rd ✆ 01723 372593 🖥 valleybar.co.uk. This is first and foremost a drinker's pub but, very unusually for this part of the world, the emphasis here is on cider. The Valley was once voted the best cider pub in the country and still serves eight ciders along with six draught beers and 100 Belgian bottled. Food is homemade and very good value, especially the locally caught fresh fish. Accommodation available.

⚓ BOAT TRIPS

A variety of boats offer sightseeing and/or wildlife trips (seals, whales and seabirds) from the harbour. Sometimes bad weather keeps the smaller boats confined or they may be out on a fishing charter so the best strategy is to peruse the sandwich boards on the harbourside to see what's on offer on any given day.

16 FORGE VALLEY

The River Derwent follows one of the weirdest routes of any river in the country. It rises on Fylingdales Moor near Robin Hood's Bay, a mere two miles from the sea, but then decides to wander inland and south for another 50 miles, finally joining the River Ouse to empty into the Humber. Before the last ice age it was a normal and much shorter river, finding a fairly direct route to the sea at Scalby Mills. All changed when this exit was blocked by the massive North Sea ice sheet and the river was dammed to form a lake in the Hackness Valley. Water always finds a way out and the lake eventually overflowed south, cutting a new channel through the Tabular Hills – the gorge we now know as Forge Valley.

What we are left with is a steep-sided wooded ravine with a flora and fauna rich enough to warrant its designation as a National Nature Reserve, and a crystal-clear trout stream babbling along its centre. Forge Valley really is a delightful place, the only intrusion into its wildness the traffic noise from the road that follows its whole length. Natural England has provided excellent boardwalk paths for walkers and wheelchairs (but not bikes), and riverside picnic areas with feeding stations that attract masses of woodland birds.

Special flowers to look out for are broadleaved helleborine and birds' nest orchids; exciting birds you may see include woodwarblers, redstarts and woodpeckers. The wooded section of Forge Valley is only a mile long, but if you are walking here it is worth extending your route a little to include the remains of Ayton Castle (small but picturesque) and Raincliffe Woods (extensive and quieter than the main valley).

⑪ FOOD & DRINK

Tree Top Press Orchard Suffield YO13 0BJ ✐ 01723 363731 ⊗ treetoppress.co.uk
🕓 09.30–12.30 Wed, 09.30–noon Fri. An old, traditional orchard given a new lease of life to produce artisan ciders and cordials with other local produce for sale in the attached farm shop.

17 CAYTON BAY

This small beach resort has changed dramatically within the past 20 years. Back in the days when Butlins and Pontins were fashionable, Wallis's Holiday Camp at Cayton Bay was very popular and the beach here almost an east coast Blackpool. There is still a large caravan park but a big new road separates it from the beach, which is consequently much quieter. The beach is a classic in the holiday-postcard tradition, a small, almost perfect semi-circle of soft sand, but with a rocky reef in the centre of the bay that makes this one of the best surf spots on the Yorkshire coast. A surfer mate of mine rates it: 'better than Cornwall and, on a good day, rivalling Australia.'

Not having any of your own gear is no excuse for not having a go in the waves, as **Scarborough Surf School** (⊘ scarboroughsurfschool. co.uk) has a base here. The cost of a lesson includes equipment hire, 2½ hours coaching, a shower and a hot drink; it is only a little more than hiring the gear yourself and doing your own thing, so it adds up to fantastic value. Stand-up paddle-boarding and coasteering are also offered.

If the idea of squeezing yourself into a rubber suit and venturing into the cold North Sea fills you with horror, then head to the quiet north end of the beach. You can bask in the sun or rummage among the pebbles for gemstones.

Just inland from Cayton Bay lies the village of Cayton, nice enough but unremarkable – except that is for a small craft business tucked away down the back lane to Killerby. The Stained Glass Centre (⊘ stainedglasscentre.co.uk) is run by Valerie Green, keeping her family tradition going, as her grandfather was a master glass stainer in 19th-century Bradford. Valerie and her team produce stained glass and leaded lights for businesses all over the country, but also sell items in the centre shop and run very popular courses so you can learn to do it for yourself. The tea shop is excellent.

SOUTH FROM SCARBOROUGH: FILEY BAY

Filey Bay is huge, stretching ten miles from **Filey Brigg** in the north to **Flamborough Head** in the south and straddling not just two counties but two geological time zones. The brigg marks the end of the Jurassic

series of rocks, while Flamborough, in East Yorkshire, is the start of the Cretaceous chalk that makes up the foundations of the Yorkshire Wolds. **Filey** itself is the only settlement on the bay at all, and it is tucked away at the northern end. The wide sweep of the rest of the bay is backed by fast-eroding clay cliffs and is not fit for any permanent buildings, so consequently it is capped by a rash of caravan parks and holiday villages – decidedly non-Slow.

18 FILEY

As part of the Yorkshire Riviera, along with Scarborough and Whitby, Filey has been a holiday venue for many years. It was the planned destination of my mother and her friend Ena on a hare-brained tandem trip in the 1940s. They never got there as it turned out (brake failure before even leaving Lancashire, and recuperation in Blackburn Royal Infirmary) but, had they managed it, their first impressions would have been pretty much the same as today. Filey seems to exist in a time warp of sorts and its very old-fashionedness is what many of its visitors like.

'I hope your book won't go bringing more people here,' commented Bella, the elderly lady with whom I shared a park bench, 'We don't want anything changing. It's just right as it is thank you very much.'

Parts of the resort are crowded, like the short seafront, but not on the scale of Scarborough or Whitby, and there is always some deserted tranquillity just around the corner. Between the buildings of Beach Road and the rest of the town are a line of public gardens that make a pleasant walk between two wooded valleys at either end of the town. Martin's Ravine is at the southern end and The Ravine is to the north. The latter was the pre-1974 boundary between the old North and East Ridings with most of the houses on one side and the church and graveyard on the other. This led to the cryptic traditional saying, 'Yon'll straightly be off t' North Riding,' meaning so and so's not in good health and could soon find themselves in the graveyard. The old fishermen's cottage community of Queens Street is nearby, two of which have been converted into **Filey Museum**, a fine local collection (✆ 01723 515013 ⬦ fileymuseum. co.uk ⏱ 11.00–15.30 Sun–Fri). Don't be put off by the motto over

---

◀ **1** The seafront at Filey. **2** Filey Brigg.

the door; 'The fear of God be in you' was a reminder to 17th-century fishermen, not a dire warning to us.

Naturalists may well wish to visit **Filey Dams** (⌀ ywt.org.uk; free entrance), a freshwater marsh nature reserve on the inland edge of town. It is managed by the Yorkshire Wildlife Trust, mainly to protect its rare newts, dragonflies and plants, but it is also a magnet for migrating birds, and a long list of unusual visitors has been seen from the hides.

FOOD & DRINK
Cafés
There are lots of cafés to choose from – these are my best four:

The Coffee Shed Murray St ℰ 07852 879066. ⓕ ⊙ Mon–Sat. Great quality coffee as you would expect, but also fine tea and legendary toasties.
Country Park Café Northcliff ℰ 01723 514881 ⓕ Country Park Cafe Filey. ⊙ Fri–Tue. The toasties, pies and sausage rolls are particularly tasty.
Frothies Union St ℰ 01723 515173 ⌀ frothies.uk. Wide range of teas, barista-quality coffees and good-value snacks.
The Lighthouse Tea Room Belle Vue St ℰ 07891 327075 ⌀ lighthousetearoom.co.uk ⊙ Sat–Thu. Homemade cakes and scones, and great coffee in a traditional tea room. Crab sandwiches also very popular.

Pubs
Good pubs are in short supply in Filey, but this one definitely meets the standard:

Bonhommes Bar Royal Crescent Court ℰ 01723 514054 ⓕ. Named after the ship of the American rebel, John Paul Jones, the *Bonhomme Richard*, which sank in Filey Bay, this hidden-away gem is worth searching out. It is a friendly and lively local with music, quizzes, a rotating range of guest cask beers and basic food.

19 FILEY BRIGG

Filey owes its existence as a fishing settlement to this narrow promontory of hard Jurassic limestone, as it keeps the worst of the North Sea's waves from reaching the town's boat landing areas and essentially converts Filey Bay into a huge harbour. It forms part of North Cliff Country Park where a caravan park with shop and café sits cheek by jowl with a large car park. There is a big green space here for children to be let loose in, but for me the place to head for (with care) is the cliff edge. Unofficial descent points here are used by anglers and youths in wet suits engaged in the dangerous sport of 'tombstoning' – leaping off the cliff into the sea.

You can easily spend hours watching people pursuing their contrasting leisure activities, ships and seabirds passing or just waves thundering into the rock wall below. Or you could amble along this end section of the Cleveland Way but, unfortunately, not down to the wave-wasted rocks of the brigg-end itself. Erosion has caused the steep end path to collapse so access has to be across the beach from the other end of the country park, via the yacht club. It is worth the effort though; it's an exhilarating place to be, especially in heavy seas, and the rock pooling here is excellent. There are some huge tame prawns in the upper shore pools who will investigate a wiggling finger or even take food from your hand. Take binoculars: the strong currents off the end of the brigg attract seals and porpoises.

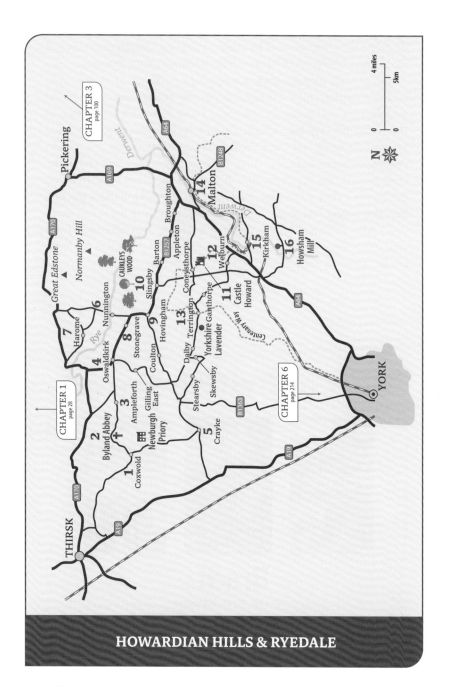

HOWARDIAN HILLS & RYEDALE

4

HOWARDIAN HILLS
& RYEDALE

If Yorkshire is England in miniature, then this is its Cotswolds. The Howardian Hills are gentle, rolling and agricultural, with more than their fair share of trees; no big forests but some sizeable woods and lots of clumps and copses, dark pillows lying on a rumpled patchwork quilt of a landscape. This arable pastoral embroidery hides a scattering of honey-coloured hamlets and villages, one of which was my home for a while. It is no coincidence that the look and feel of the place is so similar to the Cotswolds as it is the same Jurassic limestone that underlies both, prompts a similar land use, and forms the warm, yellow stone walls of the old buildings.

This is archetypal well-off countryside: sleepy, self-contained and quintessentially English, with each village seeming to have its old manor house, very old church and huge vicarage. I can easily imagine Miss Marple taking tea with the Colonel in Bulmer or cycling past the green in Hovingham. The Edwardian landed gentry feel to this area is no illusion. Feudal old England is alive and well here, with a fair proportion of the Howardian Hills still owned and run by three families as their country estates. The Wombwells rule the roost in the west at Newburgh Priory near Coxwold and the Worsleys' family home is Hovingham Hall, but pride of place for pomp, opulence and grandeur must go to the Howards. Not only do they have a castle named after the family, but a range of hills named after their castle; now that is true arrogance – oops, sorry, I mean influence.

Nunnington sits alongside the River Rye just as it leaves the Howardian Hills Area of Outstanding Natural Beauty (AONB) and slides lazily out into the floodplain of its own making, Yorkshire's fenland. Scenically, lower Ryedale is nothing to write home about. Most people would go as far as to say it was boring, unless they had a thing about crop rotation, yields per acre or the relative merits of David Brown tractors

SLOE MOTION

Hedgerows in the Howardian Hills are often full of dazzling white flowers in April, and tiny wild plums in autumn. These are sloes, the fruit of the blackthorn bush, and although they are far too sour to eat as they are, they make a delicious natural flavouring for other foods and drinks.

The Curtoys family and their colleagues have made a business out of the sloe taste. Their company, Sloemotion (✆ 01653 618288 ⌂ sloemotiondistillery.com), is based at Green Farm, Barton le Willows (though not currently open to the public), and collects sloes using an army of local pickers, before making them into a range of rich and fruity products. Traditional sloe gin is the biggest seller, but have you ever tried sloe vodka, sloe brandy, sloe whisky, sloe chutney or sloe truffles? No, I hadn't either and I didn't know what I was missing – they are delicious. There is even a hedgerow version of Pimms called No. 7. Buy online or from farmers' markets, shows and good specialist food stores.

over Massey Fergusons, because this is prime arable farming country. It does have attractions though; its rivers, the Rye and its tributaries, are wonderful linear reserves of nature and tranquillity.

The River Rye empties into the bigger River Derwent. Three miles below this confluence sits the town of Malton, on the north bank, with its twin Norton facing it from the other side of the river. This has always been an important river crossing, even back to Roman times, and Malton is still very much the social hub of this region. When people from **Terrington**, **Hovingham** or **Welburn** say that they are going into town, this is where they mean; likewise, local farmers taking their beasts to market will also head this way. **Malton** is a market town, but a real one that still does what it says on the tin.

Downstream from Malton the River Derwent winds its way south, through Kirkham Gorge and away down the western edge of the Wolds, finally joining the sea at the Humber estuary.

SELF-POWERED TRAVEL

CYCLING

It is mixed news on the two-wheeled front. The good news is that **road biking** in places is superb, mainly because the minor roads around here are so quiet. I once cycled from home in Barton le Street, in the middle of the day on a circular route, through Butterwick, Brawby and Salton.

The sun was out, skylarks and yellowhammers were singing throughout the whole nine miles over minor tarmac roads, and I did not see a single motorised vehicle; come to think of it, I did not see another person at all. Ryedale has the added advantage of being mostly flat as a pancake, so is very forgiving for the less athletic biker.

The Howardian Hills half of the region is not quite so gentle; the clue is in the 'hills' bit of the name. There are still some lovely quiet road circuits like Hovingham to Stonegrave to Gilling East to Coulton and back to Hovingham, or west from Terrington along Bonnie Gates Lane and back via Stearsby and Skewsby, but some of the hills on the way are killers. Dalby Bank, up from the beck to the hamlet, is my nemesis, but what the heck, there is no shame in getting off and pushing every now and again.

Off-road biking is less promising. The areas of the OS map devoid of bridleways suspiciously correspond to the biggest estate lands. Gilling Castle and Newburgh Priory estates seem to have been particularly good at keeping peasants off their land in the past, which is reflected in the lack of rights of way today. A decent network exists elsewhere, with Castle Howard lands being surprisingly rich. One of my particular favourites is a circuit linking Hovingham and Coneysthorpe, with much of the northern leg following the Centenary Way, and the parallel southern return on the Ebor Way. This is a lovely nine-mile ridge route predominantly under trees and with lots of alternative options to shorten or lengthen the ride. Wildlife encounters are likely, with hares lolloping away from you across every field you pass and buzzards soaring on the up-draught at any point on the ridges. If you are early or late in the day you have an excellent chance of seeing badgers bumbling along the track side, roe deer melting into the trees or barn owls drifting along hedgerows. Other recommended off-road hill routes are Caulkleys ridge from Nunnington and a circumnavigation of Welburn.

Down on the flats of Ryedale, off-road biking is not recommended unless you can see from the OS map that the bridleway follows a farm track. The chances are that those marked in bold green across the fields, or along riverbanks, do not in reality exist on the ground, or are complete quagmires. I have had some nightmare walks-with-a-bike in swampy fields between Butterwick and South Holme and, worse still, had my bike gears completely destroyed by wheat stalks that had been planted over a bridleway, jamming in the mechanism.

CYCLE SHOPS

Northern Ride Saville St, Malton ✆ 01653 699070 🖰 northernride.com ⊙ Tue–Sat. Shop with accessories.
R Yates and Sons Railway St, Malton ✆ 01653 605400 🖰 yatescycles.co.uk. Shop with accessories and a repair service.

HORSERIDING

Sadly, and surprisingly for such a horsey area, there is a dearth of facilities for riders here. **White Rose Riding School** at Park House Farm near Coxwold (✆ 07764 575249) is the only one offering horses, hacking and lessons, although there are four not so far away in bordering regions. These are at Sinnington (page 103) and Hawnby and Boltby (page 30). It is good riding country though, so if you can bring your own horse you will have a field day. Grazing, feed and a secure tack room are available at Manor Farm, Old Byland (✆ 01439 798247) and other horse accommodation can be found in neighbouring areas at Boltby, Gillamoor, Hawnby, Helmsley, Pockley and Sproxton (*Chapter 1*) and Appleton le Moors, Cropton, Ebberston and Sinnington (*Chapter 3*).

WALKING

Although the options for walks are more limited here than in the neighbouring North York Moors, the quality is high. Because the Howardian Hills are so compact and small-scale, one walk can visit a variety of landscapes in a short distance. The brief section of the Centenary Way north of Welburn is a good case in point. Within two miles it crosses arable farmland, follows a small beck through ancient deciduous woodland containing a fen nature reserve, visits classically managed parkland, cattle and sheep pasture and finally dark conifer plantations. The drawback is that this is the whole list of what the area has to offer; you won't find proper hilltops or fast flowing rivers, and

---

 TOURIST INFORMATION

Howardian Hills AONB Office Shared with the North York Moors National Park in Helmsley ✆ 01439 772700 🖰 howardianhills.org.uk. The website is a great source of information and useful downloads like walks leaflets (see opposite).
Malton Tourist Information Centre Malton Library, St Michael St ✆ 01653 600048

the only open access land is a small area of woodland near Yearsley voluntarily opened by the Forestry Commission.

Three **long-distance footpaths** visit the area in passing, the Ebor Way en route from Helmsley to Ilkley, the Centenary Way from York to Filey and the Foss Walk, briefly, through Crayke.

As for shorter and more practically achievable ventures, the Howardian Hills AONB authority has produced a range of excellent leaflets with suggested representative **circular walks**. The start points are Hovingham, Welburn, Nunnington, Slingsby, Barton, Castle Howard and Terrington, with the walks ranging from three to nine miles. Even shorter routes are available for the country lane rambler. All these routes are downloadable for free from ⌀ howardianhills.org.uk.

"The Rye, with its tributaries, is a lovely river, so it is worth trying to search out the few footpaths that follow them."

Point-to-point walks using public transport are possible, but require a bit of forward planning because buses are so few and far between. The simplest strategy is to catch a bus from Malton to Welburn, Castle Howard, Terrington or Hovingham and walk back. It is best done this way round with unreliable buses, to avoid being marooned in the sticks. For shorter walks, the 'Street' bus can be caught for a few stops, and the return made along the Centenary Way ridge, Hovingham to Barton (five miles) for instance, or Slingsby to Appleton (four miles).

The **Rye**, with its tributaries, is a lovely river, so it is worth trying to search out the few footpaths that follow them. Pickering Beck south towards Kirbymisperton is a delightful stroll, as is the mile along the River Seven from Marton to Normanby, or vice versa, but the longest and best stretch is the Rye itself from Helmsley to Nunnington via Harome. This convoluted five miles can be extended by one more to West Ness, or two more to Salton.

The **River Derwent** suffers the same problem of pathlessness, especially upstream of Malton, but there are places where you can stroll along the banks. My favourite of these is the three mile stretch from Kirkham Priory to Howsham Bridge, an added benefit being the choice of return routes. One is via the quiet country lane through Crambe village while the other samples the sylvan delights of Howsham Woods where the display of bluebells in May has to be one of the best in the country.

AN ABBEY ROAD – FROM COXWOLD TO OSWALDKIRK

Where the northern edge of the Howardian Hills butts against the southern slopes of the Hambleton Hills, the village of Gilling East sits astride a narrow gap often called the Gilling Gap. Its centuries-old use as a transport route is not surprising: as well as having a road and disused railway line, it is a known Roman route. What is not quite so clear is why it was such an ecclesiastical magnet, as within six short miles, from **Oswaldkirk** to **Coxwold**, are two abbeys (**Ampleforth** and **Byland**), two very old churches (Oswaldkirk and Coxwold), and a priory at **Newburgh**. This little corner's pulling power does seem to have waned though, as it never seems anywhere near as busy as nearby Helmsley, Sutton Bank or Nunnington. For us lovers of undisturbed walks or traffic-free cycling this is no bad thing of course.

To the south of Coxwold lies the quietest corner of the Howardian Hills, with the hilltop village of **Crayke** perched at its edge.

1 COXWOLD

🏠 **Newburgh House** (page 248)

'I am as happy as a prince in Coxwold, and I wish you could see in how princely a manner I live. Tis a land of plenty.' So wrote Laurence Sterne, vicar of Coxwold in the 1760s. This small village is undoubtedly a highly desirable place to live but, more importantly for us, it's also a really interesting place to visit. At first sight it seems like just another Cotswoldy village typical of this corner of the Howardian Hills but beneath the surface lies a rich vein of quirky eccentricity. **Shandy Hall** at the top of the village is the best example; a singular building that was lived in by a very singular man, Laurence Sterne himself. As vicar of the village he spent a good deal of time, though not as much as he should have spent apparently, in **St Michael's Church**, the next large building down the main street. He almost certainly spent too much time in a building opposite the church, the Fauconberg Arms, although it was not called that then. The pub name has followed the family name of the residents of nearby **Newburgh Priory**, being

---

1 Nunnington Hall. **2** Byland Abbey. **3** Daubenton's bats can be seen at Nunnington after dusk. **4** Ampleforth Abbey is famous for its cider. **5** Coxwold. ▶

SS

AC RIDER/S

RUDMER ZWERVER/S

FLPA/A

KEVIN EAVES/S

the Bellasis Arms in Sterne's time, although it has not so far changed to the Wombwell Arms in honour of the present family name. Two lines of honey-coloured stone buildings lead down the broad main street with an ancient crossroads at the bottom. Wakendale Beck crosses the road by the old schoolhouse, changes its name to Green Beck and passes the old mill it used to power. The Old Schoolhouse is now the Schoolhouse Tearooms.

Shandy Hall

⌕ 01347 868465 ⌂ laurencesternetrust.org.uk ⊙ gardens: May–Sep 11.00–16.30 Tue–Sun; house (tours only): May–Sep 11.30 & 14.30 Sat, Sun & bank hol Mon

Shandy Hall is the oldest building in Coxwold, and looks it. A wonderfully rickety maze of a place, it would merit preservation in its own right, but the reason it is a museum is not for what it is but

"A wonderfully rickety maze of a place, it would merit preservation in its own right."

for who lived here. In 1760 this was the Parsonage, and the new parson, Laurence Sterne, was part-way through writing what would become his most famous novel, *Tristram Shandy*. He finished it in this house along with *Sentimental Journey*, both books written in a surreal comedic style way ahead of their time and a touch ribald for a country vicar. Sterne enjoyed eight years of fame, and a little controversy, before succumbing to ill health and dying in 1768. After Sterne's death the renamed Shandy Hall became a place of literary pilgrimage and in the 1960s was bought by the newly formed Laurence Sterne Trust, which has looked after the house and gardens ever since. The present curator Patrick Wildgust lives in the house with his wife Chris. 'My job is to celebrate the life of this great writer and introduce other people to his work, but there are things here to appeal to all sorts. Sterne was never a dedicated gardener, as he said himself he would sometimes "weed, hack up old roots or wheel away rubbish", but the gardens he has left us are lovely. Much like the man really, a complex contradiction; two acres of old-fashioned roses, formal walled garden, and semi-wild old quarry'.

St Michael's Church

The Pope wrote to the King of Northumbria in AD757 instructing him to repair Coxwold Minster so we know this is a very old church site – in fact there was probably a pagan temple here before then. The present building is not that old (1430) but some really unusual features inside and out justify an exploration. As you would expect, there are lots of connections with the Bellasis/Fauconberg/Wombwell family – monuments, memorials, tombs and the like – but Laurence Sterne has also left his mark. He installed a three-decker pulpit (now reduced to two) and box pews, and his gravestone sits just by the porch outside. In a bizarre chain of events typical of Sterne, he was buried three times: firstly in Westminster Abbey, then again after his body was stolen for medical research but reclaimed, and finally in 1960 when the London graveyard he lay in was built on. The Laurence Sterne Trust obtained permission to bring his head up to Coxwold and its final resting place near his beloved Shandy Hall.

Newburgh Priory

☏ 01347 868372 ⊘ newburghpriory.co.uk ⊙ gardens: Apr–Jun 14.00–18.00 (last entry 17.00) Wed & Sun; house tours available

Just south of Coxwold, this house is one of those places whose brilliance lies in its differentness. For a start, it is not a priory but a stately home, and a refreshingly un-heritage one at that. The building is a hotchpotch of styles with some of it derelict and roofless, and the grounds are very randomly set out with no apparent plan, but the whole place has a serene, informal air about it.

> "The building is a hotchpotch of styles with some of it derelict and roofless."

It is a special place for me because I so much savoured a sense of discovery, chancing upon it with no pre-knowledge of its existence, and just turning in off the road on spec. I was lucky as opening times are very singular; and it was late afternoon on a Sunday when I was greeted at the entrance shed by a dapper, elderly gentleman dressed in slacks, shirt and straw trilby. He listed the attractions, each with a vague directional point. 'There's the lake of course, but you can see that. The walled garden is splendid at the moment (it was). The basin pond and water garden are over there (vague point), and should you feel like you can tackle the hill behind the house, you will find a view over to the Hambleton Hills (cursory wave) absolutely marvellous.'

'Is there a map or guidebook at all?' I asked. 'Oh no – it's very much a go and find it for yourself experience here,' was the reply. So I went and

NOT ALL MONKS ARE NICE

Byland Abbey has boasted many colourful characters over the years, too many to mention, but one story in particular deserves to be told. The 'most audacious acts and merited misfortunes' of Wimund the Blind Monk were recorded by William of Newburgh.

Although of humble origins, Wimund learnt to write and became a monk at Furness Abbey. His 'ardent temper, retentive memory and competent eloquence' resulted in quick promotion (sounds like a few politicians I can think of). After a meteoric rise he became bishop of the Isle of Man but still yearned for greater acclaim and more power (definitely a politician, then). He announced that he was the rightful heir to the earldom of Mowbray and that the King of Scotland was depriving him of his inheritance. Gathering an army of followers he invaded Scotland, 'wasting all before him with rapine and slaughter'. Sensing military defeat, the King of the Scots decided on a more subtle strategy that would use Wimund's own arrogance against him. He granted large areas of land, including Furness, to the rebel knowing that Wimund would not be accepted by those who once knew him as a low-born monk. Sure enough, as he was parading his army around the area, a trap was set and he was captured. His punishment was to be blinded, castrated and sent to Byland Abbey as a lowly monk once more (politicians take note). He remained

searched, and in the walled garden I found leeks growing in tubes, new potatoes part-harvested, a pink climbing rose with an overpowering perfume, a lily pond with dancing blue damselflies and newt tadpoles just below the surface. At the side of the house, a series of 'Royal Trees' were planted by visiting monarchs, and a small fenced-off area near the water garden contains the graves of family dogs.

Inside the house is just as quirky and interesting. The compulsory tea shop visit at the end was, as expected, very non-National Trust. The handwritten sign 'Tea Shop' directed us through the old servants' quarters and into the dining room with its faint smell of lavender and mothballs. Old paintings lined the walls; each small table had a single rose in a small vase and the clock on the wall tick-tocked slowly. Such was the peaceful atmosphere in the room, the two people already there were actually whispering.

The rest of the house has the usual lines of family portraits, wood panels and Chippendale-esque furniture, but then suddenly you come face-to-face with the death mask of Oliver Cromwell on an attic vault door. Unsubstantiated rumours claim that Cromwell's headless corpse is also here, hidden by his daughter Mary when she lived at Newburgh.

there, humiliated but unrepentant until his death, moaning to all who would listen of his woes: 'Had I the eye of the sparrow, my enemies should have little occasion to rejoice at what they have done to me.'

The fact that the abbey was built here at all is down to a strange series of 12th-century events and a long journey by 13 Savignac monks. Amazingly, we know all their names; they were: Gerold the Abbott, Robert, Tocka, John, Theodore, Hormi, Roger, Alan, Wido, William, Peter, Ulfus and Bertram (an interesting study in which names survive nearly 1,000 years and which don't – I certainly don't know any Widos or Hormis). The 13 were sent out from Furness Abbey in Lancashire to found a new abbey, and tried four sites before ending up here. Their penultimate choice was five miles due north of the present abbey at a place still called Old Byland. The apocryphal reason for them leaving there after only four years was that they were too close to Rievaulx Abbey and their church bells clashed with those of the established Cistercian community. The monks finally settled near the village of Wass, converted to Cistercianism and, in 1170, started to build their magnificent monument. During the next 370 years Byland prospered and became a very rich and powerful organisation/landowner until the catastrophic Dissolution in 1538.

⊬⊦ FOOD & DRINK

The Fauconberg ⊘ 01347 868214 ⊘ fauconbergarms.com. On Coxwold's main street, this ancient inn manages to be a great pub, a fine restaurant and a four-star hotel all at the same time. Food is locally sourced and the traditional meals come in very generous portions. There is a family connection to the Isaac Poad Brewery so their IPA is a regular, and there's two other guest cask beers.

Rumah Home Tea Room The School House ⊘ 01347 868138 🅵 Rumah Home Tearoom & B&B ☉ Wed–Sun. Basic, cosy café handily placed at the bottom of the village near the craft workshops. Also does its own arts and crafts and B&B accommodation.

2 BYLAND ABBEY

Byland YO61 4BD ⊘ 01347 868614; English Heritage

Two things catch your attention on first sighting the ruins of Byland Abbey. The first, from a distance, is the amazing rose window (the first of its kind to appear in England), or rather half rose window, and the question of what is keeping it up, as it looks so precarious. The second, with a closer view, is likely to be the size of the place; the site is huge with the abbey church alone as big as some cathedrals. Other features to look for are the 13th-century ceramic mosaic floor tiles, still in their

AMPLEFORTH CIDER

Ampleforth Abbey has a historic five-acre organic orchard with more than 40 varieties of apple trees, which until the last couple of decades was largely unloved and untended; most of the apples went to feed autumn wasps and blackbirds. Father Rainer Verborg had other ideas, first producing apple juice to sell at local farmers' markets, and then moving on to cider-making as well. The production plant, in old abbey farm buildings, now makes over 25,000 litres a year, but could sell twice that amount, such is the popularity of this pale, dry tipple.

Tours of the orchard and cider mill are available from about £20 per person (✆01439766000 ⌂ ampleforthabbeydrinks.org.uk for details) from April to November. Ampleforth Abbey cider is available in the abbey shop, various pubs, cafés and delis locally and over a hundred other outlets countywide. Its website has an exhaustive list of stockists. Look out also for the excellent Ampleforth cider brandy, apple liqueur and Belgian Trappist-style beer , made using a Benedictine recipe developed in the early 18th century.

original position and made on site, and said to be of World Heritage significance as far as ceramics go; and a medieval doodle of the rose window scratched into the wall beneath the window itself, on the left as you come in (not at all easy to spot without some expert guidance).

3 AMPLEFORTH

Ampleforth is an unusual and not overly attractive place, or should I say, two places. There is a village, but mention the name of 'Ampleforth' and most people will think of the abbey and associated private college. These two are tenuously attached to the village but very definitely culturally separate. The whole lot is strung out along two miles of busy and often congested road. Surprisingly, the village is much older than the abbey and college, it being mentioned in the Domesday Book while the latter was only founded in the 19th century.

Ampleforth Abbey is one of the few living and active Benedictine monasteries in the country, and certainly the largest. Until recently, the monastic community kept its slow and peaceful lifestyle pretty much to itself and the students of the college. But, times have changed, and an outreach venture that has really taken off in recent years has been the sale of abbey produce. At the heart of this has been cider-making, started by Father Rainer in 2008 (when it made the columns of the national press), and now a team effort led by Tim Saxby.

FOOD & DRINK

Hearts of Ampleforth West End ✐ 01439 788166 ⬛ ⊙ Fri–Mon. A very welcoming, family-run cafe which is justifiably very popular. Breakfasts and cakes especially good.
The White Horse Inn West End ✐ 01439 788378 ⬙ whitehorseinnampleforth.co.uk. All a village pub should be – cosy, cheerful staff, great food, fine local beer from down the road in Helmsley, comfortable accommodation and dogs welcome.

4 OSWALDKIRK

This tiny village clings precariously on to the hillside known, not too flatteringly, as Oswaldkirk Hag. Most of the village buildings sit on the slightly less steep south side of the road and fall within the jurisdiction of the Howardian Hills AONB, whereas those on the other side lie within the North York Moors National Park.

Oswaldkirk has two buildings of note and these are, as is so often the case, the church and the pub. I suppose for decency's sake I ought to deal with the **church** first, especially as the village was named after it. It is a lovely, peaceful little building, especially the side away from the road where the sloping graveyard allows panoramic views across the vale. There was probably a wooden Saxon church here originally but the present building is a humble mixture of Norman and more modern stonework.

There are no prizes for working out that the church is dedicated to St Oswald but the story of the man himself is much more obscure. He was a Saxon king of Northumbria in the 7th century, and one of the original 'Christian soldiers'. It was he who invited St Aidan to establish the original monastery at Lindisfarne. In the year AD642 King Oswald was killed in battle against the heathen King

"The present building is a humble mixture of Norman and more modern stonework."

Penda and he was sainted soon afterwards. A cult surrounding him developed, resulting in many St Oswald's churches in the Saxon areas of eastern England. His head, as a prized relic, was taken to Lindisfarne and, when the Viking raids threatened, was put into St Cuthbert's coffin for safekeeping. It is still in the coffin now, buried in the foundations of Durham Cathedral.

I like old churches, but I love good pubs and the **Malt Shovel** was one of my favourites – I say 'was' because it's currently closed, with its owners (Sam Smith's Brewery) unsure as to when it will reopen. The front of this remarkable building, on the roadside, has two dark, low-ceilinged rooms, one a cosy bar and the other a flag-floored pool room and, during many visits to the Sunday quiz, this is all I saw. It was only when my neighbour, on a sunny day, suggested a pint from the back bar to be drunk in the beer garden, that I saw the original front of the building – and it is magnificent. From here its origins as a manor house are obvious, a storey higher than the back because it is lower down the hill, and with stunning views over the terraced gardens and patchwork of fields and woods in the vale.

The Malt Shovel looks as if it should be haunted, and apparently is. The official ghost is of a five-year-old boy, Thomas Bamber, who died in the house in the 1890s and whose mother, unable to accept the death, kept his body for weeks. He is still said to be there, in his bedroom – now the ladies' toilets. 'I've never seen Tom,' said the landlady as we chatted in the lounge bar on my last visit, 'but I have seen a bloke in here. No idea who he was but he drifted across the room and through the wall there. It doesn't bother me – they can't hurt you can they? That only happens in films.'

¶¶ FOOD & DRINK

I'm eagerly looking forward to the reopening of The Malt Shovel, whenever it happens, but in the meantime here's an able stand-in just a mile down the road.

The Fairfax Arms Gilling East ✆ 01439 788212 🖉 thefairfaxarms.co.uk. The emphasis in this 17th-century coaching inn is high-end accommodation and fine dining, but the bar is cosy and welcoming as well, with four Yorkshire cask beers on offer.

5 CRAYKE

The charming village of Crayke sits on top of a little eminence with staggering views across the Vale of York. This isolated Howardian Hill, cast adrift from the rest, is thought to be the one that the Grand Old Duke of York famously marched his 10,000 men up and down.

Crayke has very strong ties with County Durham; in fact until 1844 it was still officially a remote enclave of the county. St Cuthbert founded a monastery here, giving his name to the church, and the Prince Bishops built the original castle, which is now a private house. It is said that the saint's body was hidden from marauding Vikings here before its final burial in Durham Cathedral.

¶¶ FOOD & DRINK

Durham Ox Westway ☏ 01347 821506 ◈ thedurhamox.com ☉ Wed–Sun. This is an unashamedly high-quality food and wine establishment and it does it brilliantly, with seafood and local game specialities. However, it is proper pub as well, supplying customers with four cask Yorkshire ales, board games and live music.

LOWER RYEDALE

Part of what is now called the Vale of Pickering, Lower Ryedale a few thousand years ago was Lake Pickering which stretched some 20 miles from Ampleforth in the west to Scarborough in the east, making it probably the biggest lake in Britain at the time. Lake sediments make fabulously rich farming soils and agriculture here is productive and very lucrative. Stand atop one of Lake Pickering's old islands, now small hillocks, like Great Edstone or Normanby Hill, and turn through 360°; all you will see is a flat carpet with a repeating pattern of wheat, barley, spuds, hay, wheat, beans and barley – thank heaven for a break in this monotony. The saving grace is the River Rye itself, and its tributaries the Dove, Seven and Costa Beck. They are ribbons of oasis in the desert, willow-fringed and hidden away behind flood banks. Wherever footpaths and bridleways meet them it is a joy, especially so to float down in a kayak or canoe in the few places not policed by landowners or fishermen. In summer they're bejewelled by iridescent blue and green damselflies, and in winter, when they burst their banks to temporarily re-form Lake Pickering, they're alive with cackling and honking flocks of ducks and geese.

"They are ribbons of oasis in the desert, willow-fringed and hidden away behind flood banks."

6 NUNNINGTON

All most visitors see of Nunnington is its stately home. Granted, Nunnington Hall is well worth a visit, but there is more to explore here. The hillside village is bigger than it seems: you could spend a pleasant hour pottering up and down its two lanes. The **church of All Saints and St James** at the top of the village is unremarkable except for two stories recorded in the porch; one of a local St George-style dragon slaying and the other a framed piece of writing that I found particularly

NUNNINGTON'S WATER BATS

The hall is closed, the car park is empty and the crowds have gone: this is the best time to enjoy the River Rye, a balmy summer evening with the last yellowing of the sky reflected in the water under the old bridge arches. Wait a few minutes longer, if you can bear the attention of the dusk midges and mosquitoes, because these insects will soon tempt out some of Nunnington's special residents. In crevices and crannies in the stonework of the bridge lives a healthy population of bats, and not any old flitter-mice either; these are **Daubenton's bats**, a species that loves to live near, and hunt over, water. When they appear they are unmistakable, whizzing around in circles and figures of eight, inches above the river, sometimes setting off ripples as they grab a hapless insect from the water's surface. You will get about half an hour's watching in before the light goes; the bats will carry on hunting of course, but you can retreat to the pub to enjoy a glass of wine or beer and scratch your new midge bites.

moving. It was a 'thank you' note to the villagers, and his guardians in particular, from a war-time evacuee (or 'vaccy', as they were known), with an accompanying drawing of the church that he did himself as a child in the 1940s.

The River Rye winds its way lazily around the bottom of Nunnington. I have seen it cold, brown and uninviting after winter rain, but in summer it is delightful. Leaning over one of the village's three bridges and gazing into the gin-clear water, with its long slowly waving tresses of water crowfoot and hanging trout shadows, can be an hypnotic experience.

Nunnington Hall

Nunnington YO62 5UY ✆ 01439 748283 ☺ Apr–Oct Tue–Sun; Nov–Mar variable. Entry to the tea shop & tea gardens is free & if you're not visiting the hall there's a reduced fee for the garden; National Trust

By the standard of its near neighbours, this is not an exceptional stately home. Hovingham Hall is bigger, Castle Howard is more spectacular and Newburgh Priory is older. What Nunnington Hall has though, is a just-rightness and great charm, with everything that a stately home should have – stone-flagged floors, oak panelling, old paintings and tapestries, a giant, creaky staircase and a haunted bedroom. The restored walled garden, with a local-variety apple orchard and flower beds, is a balanced mix of practical and ornamental and the hall's location, tucked into a bend of the River Rye, is serene.

So it is not surprising that the National Trust accepted the hall and gardens from the Fife family in 1952, or that it is one of its most popular properties with visitors. Many come here specifically for what is in the attic, the old servants' quarters, which houses a permanent exhibition of miniature rooms and buildings (the Carlisle Collection), that has nothing to do with Nunnington; it is just a convenient place for the National Trust to store it. Other attic rooms house constantly changing exhibitions from rock musicians' photographs to Victorian cartoons and more besides.

It can get very busy here, especially early afternoon with folk calling in en route from Castle Howard to Helmsley, or vice versa. Being such a small place, crowds can spoil the experience here so my advice would be to go midweek if you can, or if not, be first at the door when it opens in the morning.

¶↑ FOOD & DRINK

Nunnington Hall tea room This was originally a dining room and it has been restored with the original dark décor, which makes it a bit dingy, and service is quite formal. In good weather, the tea garden by the river is much the better choice. Usual National Trust good quality and value, locally sourced produce.

The Old Yard Coffee Shop Low St ☏ 01439 748572 ⬛ ☉ Sat & Sun. Peaceful setting by the river where both people and dogs are made welcome. Proper tea and coffee, and snacks are fresh, homemade and tasty

7 HAROME

This must be one of the most mispronounced place names in the country. I have heard 'Ha-rowm', 'Ha-rom' and 'Har-rowm', to name but three, but the correct one apparently is 'Hair-um'. One of the village's claims to fame is its seven thatched cottages, the most of any place in Yorkshire, giving it more of a West- rather than North-country feel. What brings most people to Harome is not its chocolate-box look but the gastronomic delights available in the Star Inn, Pheasant Hotel and shop.

¶↑ FOOD & DRINK

Pheasant Hotel Mill St ☏ 01439 771241 ⬥ thepheasanthotel.com. A country hotel in buildings that were once barns and a blacksmith's workshop. This is part of the Pern family stable (page 158) so high-quality service and food are both guaranteed; they're also open for morning coffee and afternoon tea. Luxury accommodation available, some dog friendly.

THE STAR INN

For a little backwater village, Harome is very well known, even beyond the bounds of Yorkshire. This fame is almost solely down to one man, Andrew Pern, and his now ex-wife Jacquie. They took over the quaint, thatched village pub and turned The Star Inn into a top-quality catering business that has significantly influenced and inspired chefs and owners of other restaurants and gastropubs in this corner of Yorkshire.

It all started in 1996 when the pub came up the sale and the newly wedded Perns, working for another nearby pub, had their offer accepted. It was a brave move, as Andrew remembers. 'It was knee-high in weeds and ridden with mice. We left the Milburn Arms on 10 June, 1996, and were faced with opening our new venture just ten days later. There was just me in the kitchen, Jacquie out front and her mum behind the bar. We were serving off plates that were our wedding presents, and washing them at once to serve the next customer. On the first day we ran out of food, beer and change as an avalanche of people fell into the place. The encouraging thing was that the avalanche never stopped. We worked 18-hour days for 20 months virtually without a break, until our first child, Daisy, was born.'

Their hard work paid off in 2001 when the Star Inn was awarded a coveted Michelin star with more to come in 2006 when it was rated the best gastropub in the country by Egon Ronay, and again in 2017 on the Estrella Damm list.

Star Inn Main St ✆ 01439 770397 ⬥ thestaratharome.co.uk. Possibly the best food anywhere in Yorkshire (see above), in a low, rambling building with a nicely old-fashioned bar as well as a sleek dining room and plenty of space to sit outside; decent beer too. Gastronomic Michelin-starred heaven, but meal prices reflect the quality so save it for a special occasion, like a birthday, anniversary or holiday.

THE 'STREET' VILLAGES

The Romans were famously good road builders. Contrary to popular belief though, their roads did not always follow the straightest route, but they did invariably choose the easiest course. Consequently, when they decided to link the garrison town of Malton (Derventium) with Aldborough (Isurium) near Boroughbridge, they avoided the direct line across the steep ups and downs of the Howardian Hills. Instead they followed the flat land to the north, through Lower Ryedale and the Gilling Gap, but just uphill enough to avoid the swamps. This is the course of the present B1257, known locally as the 'Street' in

Andrew is very aware of the importance of his local roots, and values not just the quality but the 'localness' of his supplies. 'Taste and smell are potent in their ability to evoke faces and places, times and events. Looking back to my childhood on a farm, I can instantly recall the waft of bacon frying, the aroma of roasting beef, the gamey scent of partridge in the oven, and the tang of blackberries as I plucked them, purple-fingered, from the hedgerows. The North York Moors was an idyllic place to live and learn about nature's larder: seafood from the North Sea, lamb, beef and pork reared by people with pride in their produce, game from the rough shoots alongside the Esk Valley and especially grouse from the purple-cloaked moors of Egton, Rosedale and Danbydale. The food you were eating was teaching you about the seasons'.

The success of Andrew and Jacquie's business allowed them to expand to include Cross House Lodge, a 13-bed hotel across the road and their most recent acquisition was the village hotel, The Pheasant, which Jacquie now runs on her own. Further afield, the 'Star Inn' brand has spread to York (Star Inn The City) and Whitby (Star Inn The Harbour) where, not surprisingly, the emphasis is on seafood.

All was going swimmingly until November 2021 when a catastrophic fire badly damaged The Star Inn. At the time of writing, almost a year later, renovations are still not complete but the restaurant is open and The Star should be back to its best in 2023.

recognition of its antiquity. A string of old **villages** punctuates this road, from **Broughton** in the east to **Hovingham** in the west, with two of them, **Appleton** and **Barton**, even having 'le Street' tacked on to their name to distinguish them from nearby Appleton le Moors and Barton le Willows.

8 STONEGRAVE

I have a rule: any place that I pass through on a busy road thinking 'Ooh, this looks nice', by definition isn't, and what spoils it is the very busy-ness of that road. Stonegrave suffers from this phenomenon unfortunately as the whole hamlet is strung out along the well-used Malton–Helmsley road, the B1257. There are three consolations though: a lovely short circular walk nearby, a truly ancient church, and the rarest native tree in England (page 160).

The walk is a tour of **Caukleys Wood** east of the hamlet; go clockwise if you prefer your uphill bit first, along the top of the wood, with panoramic views of the moors to the north, then down Caukleys Bank to return under the trees at the bottom of the wood. Do it in reverse if you need a warm-up before any ascent.

Any church with Minster as part of its name is usually very old or has been very important at one time; **Stonegrave Minster** is both. Sadly, the building has suffered many 'modernisations' over the years so only part of the tower is original Saxon, but you can see fragments of intricately carved 9th-century crosses on display just inside the porch.

9 HOVINGHAM

This is arguably the prettiest village in the Howardian Hills, and certainly one of the most popular with visitors. Hovingham is a sunny-Sunday sort of place, somewhere to lounge and stroll, because to be honest there is not an awful lot else here to do. It has more than enough to be a living, working village – a hotel, a pub, two shops, two cafés and a bakery – but for me its biggest attractions are the buildings themselves. It does 'grand', notably **Hovingham Hall** itself which dominates the village green, and **All Saints' Church** with its impressive Saxon tower, but it is the little buildings that make Hovingham special for me, especially some of the tiny cottages hidden away behind the church and the strangely Gothic primary school. Historically, the hall and church were the epicentres of the community, but now on most days, and especially weekends, the focus is the **Rolling Pin Café** and adjacent beck. Everybody seems to gravitate there, grown-ups to sit with a cup of tea and children to paddle and fish for bullheads in the limey waters of the brook.

THE BLACK POPLAR

I will be honest; I was not overawed when I first saw the Howardian Hills' only surviving black poplar tree. It is a handful of feeble re-growing shoots sprouting from an old dead stump of the original tree that blew over in 1996. But, such is its value as a sole survivor that cuttings were taken and pampered lovingly in local nurseries, and are now being replanted in hedgerows around the region. Black poplars need this helping hand because they have lost the ability to germinate from seed and are very fussy about the soil they grow in – it has to be silt over gravel. So if you are walking in the Yearsley, Brandsby or Hovingham areas and see a ditch-side sapling with a protective mesh guard, then the chances are it's one of the VIP baby poplars.

The parent tree is in a hedgerow just south of Stonegrave village on the Cawton road, with an AONB information board telling you all about it.

Hovingham Hall

YO62 4LX ✆ 01653 628771 ⌖ hovingham.co.uk ☺ Guided tours by appointment only

Most stately homes are extravagant status symbols, built to be viewed as much as to view from. To this end almost all of them sit in splendid isolation, with a definite front on display to the world.

Hovingham Hall is an exception. It is right in the middle of the village, presenting a not very imposing façade to the main road, but neither is the other side particularly impressive. The odd reason for this is that Hovingham Hall was never built as a house at all, but comprises a huge, ornate riding school and stables with the living quarters tacked on as an afterthought. The man responsible, back in the 1750s, was Thomas Worsley, known as Thomas the Builder to differentiate him from the other five Thomases. The Worsley family, incidentally, are an amateur genealogist's nightmare, specialising as they do in duplicate names. Since 1563 there have been six Thomases, six Williams, six Roberts and we are now on a run of Marcuses in the present day.

Thomas the Builder is regarded as an eccentric today, but when he was alive he was considered completely disreputable by his fellow aristocrats, for two reasons. Firstly, he married a servant, his half-sister's governess, but more seriously, his riding school did not teach proper riding for hunting, but strange prancing about that Thomas had seen on his travels – dressage to you and me. Two generations after Thomas, in the 1800s, one of the Williams changed the layout of the building to make it more habitable for humans, but its equine origins are still very obvious.

The next obsession to shape the house and grounds was cricket. Sir William number five was a cricketer of note, captaining the Yorkshire county team in 1928 and 1929. He had the field behind the house made into a cricket pitch and converted one of the rear stables into a pavilion. An indication of Sir William's priorities can be seen in his proclamation that, if a batsman broke a window in the house with a strike for six, then five pounds was payable, not by the player to cover the damage, but to him as a reward for such a good shot. This area in the hall's history is commemorated by one of the village pubs. In the Worsley Arms, facing the hall on the main street, the Cricketers' Bar has old photos of famous visiting teams, signed bats and other memorabilia.

Like Newburgh Priory, Hovingham Hall has a pleasant family-home feel to it, basically because it still is. On my last visit, the guided tour had reached one of the staircases just on the hour, and we were listening to

an antique grandfather clock playing an intricate Baroque tune which echoed around the domed stairwell. As we stood there we were joined by the baronet Sir Marcus himself, just passing through. He offered a prize for anyone who could recognise the tune, and breezed off again.

All Saints' Church

'There is a church and a priest here' said the Domesday Book of Hovingham in 1080, and there still is, although the priest is now a vicar shared with the other three 'Street' parishes. Most of All Saints' Church is a Victorian rebuild, but a very sensitive one that has incorporated many of the original medieval features and, thankfully, left the fantastic Saxon tower completely untouched. With a bit of searching inside and out you should find other even older relics that show that the Saxon church was itself a replacement of a still more ancient church. Here is your tick list: an Anglican cross above the west doorway, a Danish wheel cross over the South Belfry opening, and a Viking carved cross on the altar.

The Worsley family obviously had a strong influence on All Saints' from the 1500s onwards, paying for the Victorian rebuild for instance, so it is no surprise to see memorials aplenty, of various baronets and ladies, and the family mausoleum in the churchyard.

𝅘𝅥 FOOD & DRINK

Rolling Pin Cafe High St ✆ 01653 628898 ⊘ hovinghambakery.co.uk ⊙ Wed–Sun. A very welcoming and popular café with bakery attached. Victoria and Simon, the husband and wife team of bakers, do everything well, but the bread and pastries are particularly good, as you would expect. Victoria is Swedish so there is a distinct Scandinavian influence at work.
Worsley Arms Hotel High St ✆ 01653 628234 ⊘ worsleyarms.co.uk. There is a restaurant but I much prefer the atmosphere in the Cricketers' Bar for eating and drinking. Food is very good, beer is well-kept local Hambleton Ales and the owners are justifiably proud of their well-stocked wine cellar.

10 SLINGSBY

This is the largest village in the Howardian Hills but also one of the least well known. Even temporary residents on its two caravan sites tend to use the place as a base from which to go and visit more entertaining places, but its castle and its maypole make it worth a look.

◀ **1** Stonegrave Minster. **2** Hovingham.

Slingsby has a tradition of impressive **maypoles** which probably goes back over a thousand years, but the first one to be documented was in 1799. The tallest, at 91ft high, was erected in 1895 but the villagers are just as proud of the current 41-footer, which stands on the village green right in front of the primary school entrance. If you want to see the pole in action, then go on May Day Bank Holiday Monday. You will see Slingsby completely out of character, in a frenzy of fertility-rite excitement, with the maypole the central attraction of a bustling village fete. With a summer fair in early July being the only other exception, Slingsby soon settles down after May Day to its normal, quiet existence with life just ticking along.

I find **Slingsby Castle** fascinating because it is a ruin; not just in the sense of having no roof and not being lived in, but in its state of utter dilapidation. There are no mown lawns or interpretive signs here, but a series of completely overgrown and dangerously teetering walls and tall towers. Underlying these is a series of interconnecting, vaulted, basement chambers and the whole lot is surrounded by an intact but dry moat. At twilight, with owls hooting and bats emerging from the cellars, it is like a scene from a Gothic novel – a hugely memorable place.

The castle is owned by the Castle Howard Estate, and unfortunately has no public access, but public footpaths pass close enough for you to get a distant glimpse.

¶¶ FOOD & DRINK

The Grapes Railway St *⌀* 01653 628076 *⌀* thegrapesinnslingsby.co.uk ◔ Wed–Sun.
I was drawn to this pub by the sign outside: 'Flat beer, poor food and rude staff – but still great.' The lighthearted atmosphere continued inside with Guinness memorabilia and a stuffed wild boar's head wearing a fez. Despite the sign, it is serious about its food and drink, with good wholesome pub grub and four cask Yorkshire beers on offer. Dog friendly, and swifts nest outside under the eaves in summer.

CASTLE HOWARD & AROUND

11 CASTLE HOWARD

YO60 7DA *⌀* 01653 648333 *⌀* castlehoward.co.uk

Castle Howard still does what it was always designed to do – dominate and impress. What is in effect one building is the focal point of the whole area, having for instance more attached shops than the nearby villages of Terrington, Welburn, Bulmer, Crambe, Whitwell and Coneysthorpe put together. As for its origin, well I like to imagine the scene. It is 1699 and Charles Howard, the third Earl of Carlisle, is in London and sitting in the Trumpet Tavern with other members of the Kit Kat Club. Drinking brandy with him is a chancer, ex-soldier and playwright John Vanbrugh, and they are discussing the Earl's intention to build a house on his Yorkshire estate.

> Vanbrugh: So Charles, who is going to design this big house of yours?
> Charles: I don't know. None of the chaps I have so far have come up with anything I like.
> Vanbrugh: Really... now that is interesting. Charles, I'll do it for you.
> Charles: Would you? Splendid! How many similar projects have you done before, John?
> Vanbrugh: Erm... not many, but what say, how difficult can it be?
> Charles: John, exactly how many buildings have you ever designed?
> Vanbrugh: Well, none – but I am a quick learner...

It reads like a *Blackadder* script, with Rowan Atkinson as Vanbrugh, Hugh Laurie as the Earl, and Mrs Miggins hovering nearby with pies, but astonishingly it is more or less true. Quite how Vanbrugh managed to convince Charles Howard he was the right man for the job is anyone's guess but he did, and over the next ten years their joint dream became a magnificent reality, probably with more than a little help from a lowly clerk of works who happened to be Nicholas Hawksmoor, one of Christopher Wren's apprentices.

Oddly, the iconic great dome, such a signature feature of Castle Howard today, was not part of the original design, but added almost as an afterthought well after the building work had begun, and was reconstructed after World War II. Vanbrugh died in 1726 and the third Earl followed in 1738, but their work was continued by two subsequent earls and various architects and landscape gardeners during the rest of the 18th

"Public rights of way thread through the wider estate, allowing you to get some choice glimpses of the house."

century. Castle Howard in its entirety, that is the mansion, park, lakes, temples, mausoleum, road and monuments, was complete by the start of the 19th century.

All that has happened since then has been tinkering really, and a massive repair project after a fire in the main building in 1940. World

War II nearly saw the end of Castle Howard. First the disastrous fire reduced the mansion house itself to a burnt-out shell and the dome was destroyed, then the heirs to the title began to drop like flies in the war in Europe. Mark, the eldest son, died on the Normandy beaches and the next in line, Christopher, was killed flying with the Dambusters. Things were looking so bad for the estate that the trustees began to sell off the mansion's contents, assuming that it would never be lived in again. Enter a hero; George, the third son, returned wounded from the war and turned everything around. He moved into the house and set about the mammoth task of repairing the damage and restoring the building to its former glory, dome and all. The house and gardens were opened to the public in 1952 and the estate has not looked back since. The palatial grandeur of the house, inside and out, is instantly familiar to anyone who has seen the filmed version of Evelyn Waugh's novel *Brideshead Revisited*, either the wonderful 1981 TV 11-hour adaptation or the 2008 movie.

Today, Castle Howard is a multi-million-pound business run by a private company, of which two of George Howard's sons, Nicholas and Simon, are the directors – and business it very definitely is. At the stable courtyard, your first port of call if arriving by car or bus, you'll find a café and five castle shops selling books, gifts, local farm produce, plants and chocolate. Tours and talks, constantly changing exhibitions, events and outdoor concerts are on offer throughout the year; in fact no end of expensive things to do with lots of other people.

The **grounds** are big enough to escape the crowds and get lost in. Public rights of way thread through the wider estate, allowing you to get some choice glimpses for free of the house, the majestic 20-column mausoleum, and the Palladian splendour of Temple of the Four Winds from a distance. The hamlet of **Coneysthorpe**, built for estate workers around an oblong green, makes a handy starting point for walks, with scope for getting close up to the house and lake to the south and a fine section of the Ebor Way to the north, which offers choice views of the Vale of Pickering.

There is **wildlife** here, especially around the lakes where there are breeding flocks of greylag and Canada geese all year. The Great Lake is

◄ **1** The Yorkshire Lavender Farm. **2** Castle Howard. **3** The Yorkshire Arboretum at Castle Howard.

even more of a magnet for birdwatchers in winter when large numbers of migrant waterfowl arrive; pochards, wigeon, goosander and goldeneye brightening up the chilly season. For those interested in furry, as well as feathery, flyers, some of Castle Howard's ancient hollow oak trees are important roost sites for noctule bats.

Castle Howard has a high season (Mar–Oct & Dec) when the house is open, while in other months just the gardens are available. There is no getting around it, entrance fees are very high so consequently many people don't get past the free café and shop area, making do with distant views of the house. Fortunately, those wanting more affordable parkland walking can find it in the nearby arboretum at a fraction of the price.

The Yorkshire Arboretum

Castle Howard YO60 7BY ✐ 01653 648598 ♦ yorkshirearboretum.org ◷ Feb–Nov 10.00–16.00 daily

This delightful rural escape is always a lot less crowded than the big house next door, but it is rapidly being discovered by more and more people. Although it is sited on the Castle Howard estate and was set up by the Royal Botanic Gardens at Kew, the arboretum trust is independent of both. It exists to manage the huge collection of trees planted here in 1975, and to entertain and educate visitors in all things woody. There is lots to do here, especially for families, with the most obvious being a walk to see the trees, either on the one mile short trail or on the long trail of 2½ miles into the wild corners for the more energetic. For keeping children entertained, the treasure hunt, leaf bingo and orienteering course work really well. I overheard one lad, running past me with a map, say to his mate in a broad Leeds accent, 'This is mint, innit? Much better than that castle place wi t'fountains over t'road.'

The trust have worked hard to make everyone welcome – those with an artistic bent can enjoy a community sculpture trail, visitors with limited mobility can hire a motorised buggy, and dogs and their walkers are actively encouraged.

¶¶ FOOD & DRINK

Arboretum Café The Yorkshire Arboretum ✐ 01653 648767 ♦ Feb–Nov daily. Very welcoming and cheaper than the nearby Castle Howard Stables Courtyard Café. More importantly, it is much quieter, with seating inside and out and wide, green views over the arboretum park.

12 WELBURN

🏠 **Cherry Tree Lodge** (page 248)

What a difference a pub and a shop make. Bulmer has neither and Welburn has both, and consequently the latter is very much the livelier and busier of these two neighbouring villages. There was a time though when the balance of power was reversed, when the church was the focus of village life and Bulmer's old St Martin's served both villages as a joint parish. Welburn got its own church in 1865 thanks to monies from the then Earl of Carlisle: its recent resurgence is almost solely due to its proximity to Castle Howard. Two routes to the 'big house' passed through Welburn, the present public road being originally for aristocracy only, as it took them from the private Castle Howard railway station at Crambeck. This now sadly defunct station was built for one visit of Queen Victoria to the castle in 1850. The proletariat's route by road from the main York road, now the A64, to Welburn was from near Whitwell village (♀ SE725665) along what is now a green lane

> *"The now sadly defunct station was built for one visit of Queen Victoria to the castle in 1850."*

and a very pleasant cycle or walkway. As it broaches the ridgetop above Welburn you get your first view of Castle Howard. Such was the impact of this first sight that a gateway was built for extra emphasis and the posts of the 'Exclamation Gate' are still there for you to lean on and frame your photos of the castle.

Welburn is the base for another series of excellent AONB 'History and Habitats' walks (page 145), although the selection of three by no means exhausts the wide choice of others nearby. A particularly nice two-miler circles the village keeping your walk's-end refreshment venue in sight most of the way round, whether at the Leaf and Loaf café or in the Crown and Cushion pub.

🍴 FOOD & DRINK

Crown and Cushion Main St ✆ 01653 618777 ⌖ thecrownandcushionwelburn.com. Originally called the Ship Inn, the pub was given its current name in 1850 as this was the emblem on Queen Victoria's train when she visited nearby Castle Howard that year. In 2013 the Crown joined the fine North Yorkshire Provenance Inn stable and has been serving excellent locally sourced food and drink ever since. Dog-friendly.

Dogh Bakery Deli & Cafe Main St ✆ 01653 618352 ⌖ dogh.co.uk. Artisan café and bakery; homemade breads particularly good.

13 TERRINGTON & AROUND

🏠 **Secret View Cottage** (page 248)

On the face of it Terrington seems much like other nearby villages of a similar size, with neat limestone houses set back on the wide main street, a relatively modern looking church on an old site, a big Victorian rectory building and one central pub.

What is different here is the modern bustle about a place that has had a very slow and uneventful past. As one local historian put it, 'History has its place in Terrington, but nothing big ever happened here.' It has never had a castle or an abbey and the Victorian railways were always too far away to have any influence. Other villages have had, and lost, these exciting things and feel as if they are having a well-earned rest; Terrington gives the impression of waking up after a big sleep. Much of this new life is centred on the shop, **Terrington Village General Stores**, the only proper shop for five miles in any direction and consequently one of those admirable sell-a-bit–of-everything sort of places. It also has a café attached and a little art gallery around the back with the no-nonsense name Back o' the Shop Art Gallery.

The road west out of Terrington runs along one of the Howardian Hills ridges, giving spectacular views to Sheriff Hutton and the Vale of York beyond. The best place to enjoy this vista is just on the edge of the village at the **Yorkshire Lavender Farm**, or you can carry on for a couple of miles to the hamlet of **Dalby** and the church of St Peter. This has to be one of the most serene little buildings anywhere; plain, unassuming and so quiet you will feel obliged to whisper. The view from the porch, through the trees and down the hillside, could grace any calendar.

If you travel east on Terrington's only road you will first pass the enormous rectory that later became Terrington Hall, and since 1920 has been a private preparatory school. A mile down the road is the hamlet of Ganthorpe, birthplace of Richard Spruce, an apt name for an eminent Victorian botanist, who is buried in All Saints' churchyard.

THE CITY OF TROY

Eight ancient turf mazes survive in England, and this one, the smallest in the whole of Europe, sits by the roadside near the hamlet of Dalby. It is a seven-ringed puzzle based on the classical labyrinth of Crete, and named after the walls of the Trojan city. Why it is here, when it was made and by whom, is a mystery.

My preferred choice for exploring around Terrington, though, is on foot rather than by car, and Howardian Hills AONB authority have obliged by producing two **walks** leaflets (page 145).

Yorkshire Lavender Farm

Terrington YO60 7PB ℘ 01653 648008 ♁ yorkshirelavender.com ⊙ mid-Apr–late Sep 10.00–17.00 daily

What started off as a plant nursery specialising in herbs has evolved over the years into an award-winning celebration of all things lavender. Everything in the café and shop is either coloured or flavoured lavender, including the walls, the chairs, the cake, the tea and even the custard! I found it all a bit death-by-mauve but loved the outside, wandering around the gardens, watching the children feed the deer and admiring the 'Spirit of Yorkshire' cricket game sculptures – all with the heady scent of fresh lavender in the warm summer air.

⍧ FOOD & DRINK

EJ's Tea Room Yorkshire Lavender Farm YO60 6PB ℘ 01653 648008 ⊙ mid-Apr–late Sep 10.00–16.30 daily. You could just have a coffee and a biscuit, but where else is it possible to have lavender cake, lavender and blueberry cheesecake, and a lavender scone washed down with lavender tea? It wouldn't be quite right not to try at least one.

MALTON & THE DERWENT VALLEY

When asked where I live, my reply of, 'Near Malton', usually prompts the response, 'Isn't that the place that flooded? Where exactly is it?' Malton is not a well-known place outside of northeast Yorkshire, even though tens of thousands of holiday visitors pass close by every weekend on the A64 or railway on their way to Whitby, Scarborough and Filey. This is not a place geared to mass tourism and that, I think, is where its attraction lies. **Malton** is very much a small workaday, rural market town serving the people of Ryedale and the Wolds.

14 MALTON

⌂ **The Old Lodge** (page 248) ⋀ **Hobground Campsite** (page 248)

Getting to know Malton takes time because of its very strange and confusing layout; it took me months to get my bearings when I first moved here.

What most people describe as Malton town is actually three separate places welded together, Old Malton, Malton and Norton. Even Malton proper is confusing as it has no one obvious centre but a scattering of focal points that reflect areas of shifting importance through history. The County Bridge over the River Derwent and adjacent fort was the Roman town centre, but emphasis shifted in medieval times to Castlegate where the Old Lodge Hotel now stands on the old motte and the roads from York, Beverley and Helmsley all meet at the old crossroads. The marketplace was the hub in days past, and still is on Saturdays, but the cattle market is now a shadow of its glory days. Like most towns of its size Malton has its fair share of necessary but not very welcome 'new', like 1950s housing estates, high-street chain shops and the Ryedale Borough Council offices, but it is slow and sleepy enough to have retained some genuinely old-fashioned traditional shops and businesses.

A town trail

Malton has a great little volunteer-run museum in the old Subscription Rooms on Yorkersgate (✆ 01653 691262 🖰 maltonmuseum.co.uk). It has two rooms, one dealing with prehistoric and Roman Malton and the other with more recent social history. Entry to the museum is free but spend £1 and you can take away a town trail booklet called the Malton Heritage Walk and, armed with this, see the best of what the rest of the town has to offer. It visits both of Malton's old parish churches and five historic pubs, including one with a medieval hospice crypt (the Cross Keys). It will also lead you up two alleyways; Chancery Lane, downhill from the marketplace, has Charles Dickens connections. Also here is the fabulous small, traditional, **Palace Cinema**, a very informal, family-run establishment where you can relax with a glass of wine or cup of tea while watching your film – very civilised.

"It is slow and sleepy enough to have retained some genuinely old-fashioned traditional shops."

Uphill from the market is **The Shambles**; like its more famous namesake in York, an historic site of butchers' shops. There are none there today, but just around the corner is the acclaimed Derek Fox's, a traditional butchers, and supplier of the extraordinary Yorkshire Pot. This is a local delicacy produced at Christmas and by order only,

TWO ARTISTS IN WOOD

An old stable building next to the Orchard Fields in Malton is, quite literally, the shop window for the art of **Mark Bennett**, working under the name of Woodlark (✆ 07985 276439 ⌖ thewoodlark.com). Mark is a genius at producing (he would say 'finding') the beauty in wood. In his workshop he works in many different timbers, sometimes inlaying metals and gemstones, and combining several different types of wood. No matter what the finished product, whether it be a functional ash and yew jewellery box with gold inlay, a bog-oak toilet seat or just a hand-carved ornamental spiral, they are all beautiful.

In complete contrast, another 'master whittler', **Nick Nixon** (✆ 01653 695525 ⌖ nixoncricket.com), in his workshop up near the old cattle market, works with two sorts of wood only, willow and cane, and makes just one finished product – cricket bats. These aren't just any bats though, they are handcrafted, bespoke items, shaped by an ex-player who loves the game and knows his stuff. Nick makes over 600 bats a year, and though they are only used for whacking a lump of leather around, each one is a work of art. As Nick says, 'There are only two ways of making a bat worthy of the great game, the wrong way and the right way'.

comprising four boned birds, one inside the other in order of size, and ready for roasting. One Christmas I shelled out £60 for a partridge in a pheasant in a duck in a turkey; it was delicious and lasted for weeks.

The trail crosses Railway Street Bridge, takes you along a short section of the River Derwent (officially Norton on this side, not Malton) and back over the County Bridge. From here you can then access the sites of Malton's old **fortifications**, first the Roman legionary camp of Derventio followed by Malton Castle. Don't get too excited – there are no buildings left to see at either place, just mounds, banks and ditches. Having said that, Orchard Fields, where the Roman fort was, and Castle Gardens are very pleasant and peaceful green areas and the nearest Malton has to a park. Information boards are on hand explaining the strategic importance and huge size (22 acres) of the Roman fort, and the turbulent history of the castle.

An optional extension from Orchard Fields follows the river through **Lady Spring Wood** to Old Malton. Boardwalks keep your feet dry as you visit the limestone springs and marshes, and a mosaic trail marks the route. Take care in wet weather; the water meadows here become lakes when the river gets very full and even the boardwalks won't stop your feet getting wet.

Old Malton

A confusing name this, because it is in fact younger than 'new' Malton's Roman settlement, but presumably this was the bigger of the two places in Saxon times when the new non-Latin names were given. It was certainly a very important place in the 1150s when the large **priory of St Mary** was built here on the site of an earlier church. What was unusual was the monks that occupied it; they were Gilbertines, an exclusively English order that had 26 priories or churches across the country. All are now complete ruins except St Mary's; it is considerably reduced in size from its original but it is the only Gilbertine church in the world still in use, and incidentally the only church that I know of with a medieval barn-owl nest box built into the tower wall (page 200).

"The only church that I know of with a medieval barn-owl nest box built into the tower wall."

Such was its importance in its heyday that it spawned two chapels of ease in 'new' Malton, which later became the joint parish churches of St Michael's and St Leonard's. In 1971 the Church of England had a rush of ecumenicalism and donated, or should that be returned, St Leonard's to the Roman Catholic Church.

The remainder of Old Malton village consists of the main road into Malton (from the A64) with two pubs positioned almost next door to each other, and some rather attractive, old stone buildings, two of which are thatched.

Just outside the village though, and on the other side of the A64 dual carriageway, squats a very singular museum. I say 'squats' because the buildings of **Eden Camp** (01653 697777 edencamp.co.uk) are all low, single-storey Nissen huts, which would be very inconspicuous were it not for the banking spitfire suspended above the entrance. This excellent World War II museum is housed in an old prisoner-of-war camp from that very conflict.

¶¶ FOOD & DRINK

Cafés & restaurants

Grapes Inn Great Habton YO17 6TU 01653 669166 thegrapes-inn.co.uk 18.00–23.00 Tue–Fri, noon–14.00 & 18.00–23.00 Sat, Sun noon–23.00. Northwest of Malton,

◀ **1** Malton town centre. **2** Howsham Mill. **3** Kirkham Priory. **4** Malton's thriving market.

YORKSHIRE'S FOOD CAPITAL

Like many old market towns, Malton has quite a feudal past, with an influential local family estate owning property and land in and around the town. That family is the Fitzwilliams and the estate is the Fitzwilliam Malton Estate, but here comes the deviation from the norm. Landed gentry are so often a drain on a community's economy, but many would say that the Fitzwilliam Estate, or more specifically, Tom Naylor-Leyland, heir to the estate, has been the town's champion in recent years as he is credited with being the driving force behind Malton's 'Food Town' status.

After working in London in high-end catering trade and noticing the amount of Yorkshire produce that was finding its way down to the capital, Tom decided to come back to Malton and get the town more involved. There have always been great, traditional food shops here – butchers, greengrocers, bakers and the like, and a very popular monthly farmers' market so it wasn't a giant step to host a week-long food festival in 2009. It was at the 2012 festival that celebrity chef Antonio Carluccio first described Malton as 'Yorkshire's food capital' and the term stuck. The three-day festival, involving artisan stalls, street food, talks, tastings, celebrity chefs and live music, has happened every non-Covid year since, usually in May.

On the back of the food festival, cafés and restaurants began to pop up in town with the Fitzwilliam Estate itself opening one in 2012 at the Talbot hotel, with TV chef James Martin at the helm. Tom has always been convinced though that food producers were the key to stability and longevity, so he set out to attract food and drink artisans and many of them set up shop in Talbot Yard, off Yorkersgate. The town now boasts five bakeries, three butchers, a brewery, gin distillery, ice-cream parlour and coffee roastery – all of which supply the ever-increasing list of cafés and restaurants. To find out where everything is and what's going on see ⟨⟩ visitmalton.com.

this is not the most inviting of buildings or villages, but there's always a warm welcome and excellent food here. Very good value as well, with lots of thoughtful extras for the price.
Leoni the Coffee House Wheelgate ✆ 01653 691321. A fabulous place, once voted best coffee shop in Britain and still run by award-winning barista Simon Robertson. 'I want good coffee to be seen in the same light as good food,' said Simon. 'Just like food, the difference between good coffee and bad coffee is passion. Like a chef I am passionate about creating something beautiful.' Leoni also does food with an Italian slant, snacks and lunches made from listed local sources.
Malton Relish Market Pl ✆ 01653 699389 ⟨⟩ maltonrelish.co.uk ⟨⟩ 09.00–16.00 Tue–Sat. This delicatessen sells specialist foods from Yorkshire and beyond. Sit at one of the small tables in the corner with whatever takes your fancy from the shop and wash it down with a brew from behind the counter.

The New Malton Market Pl ✆ 01653 693998 ⌂ thenewmalton.co.uk ◷ noon–21.00 Thu–Sat, noon–20.00 Sun. Possibly the most popular eating place in town. Sophisticated but unfussy food at very reasonable prices. Dog and beer drinker-friendly.

Pubs

Malton's pub story is a sad but familiar one. Twenty-five years ago the town was regarded as a haven for the traditional inn lover, with a string of heritage town pubs to rival York. Most of these have now gone night-clubby, downhill or out of business, save for a couple of oases in the desert, notably:

Rose and Crown Hotel Wheelgate, Malton ✆ 01653 698252 ⌂ roseandcrownmalton. co.uk. Still unofficially known locally as Suddaby's (but don't say it within earshot of the current landlord), after the family that ran it for 138 years. This Grade-II listed coaching inn has had long-overdue renovations without losing its lively-town-boozer personality – Wednesday is quiz night and there is regular live music. Draft beer quality is as high as it always was and an attached shop sells over 200 bottled beers and some wines.

Spotted Cow Cattle Market ✆ 01653 692100. As befits a pub in the middle of the cattle market, this has a country farmers' inn feel to it. Excellent beer, and bustling on market days. Limited food.

THE DERWENT VALLEY:
15 KIRKHAM & 16 HOWSHAM

Not long after leaving Malton, the River Derwent enters Kirkham Gorge and reverts to its wild state after the last 20 or so miles of agricultural straightening and urban encroachment. This is the start of the river as a linear nature reserve of national importance, because the wildlife here is so rich. The Derwent was one of the few rivers where otters never died out in the 1970s and they are now thriving, sustained by more than 20 species of fish that swim in these clean waters – including salmon, which are making a comeback (page 236). Although this is an historical navigation route all the way up to Malton from the sea, no boats use the river now as it has been designated a Site of Special Scientific Interest and the right of navigation removed.

The only way to see the delights of this waterway is on foot or by train; the Malton–York line accompanies the river through the gorge. **Walking**, it's almost possible to hug the riverbank all the way from Malton to Howsham by following the Centenary Way for five miles to Kirkham on the left bank, then swapping to the right bank for the remaining three miles. No buses run to either of these places and, sadly, the train no longer stops anywhere between Malton and York, so a point-to-point walk is awkward.

Kirkham is best known for its Augustinian Priory ($\mathcal{J}$ 01653 618768 $\odot$ Apr–Oct variable; English Heritage), its riverside situation as glorious the building itself.

The OS map does not indicate much of interest in **Howsham** but that is misleading. The small village is quiet and pretty and the Old Hall was a private school until recently, but the real interest is down by the river. Canoeists and kayakers have long known about the weir here as a play spot, but since 2004 it has been the mill it serves next door that has hit the headlines (see below). Once the river water has done its job at Howsham Mill it slides downstream towards the fantastic floodplains of the Lower Derwent, but out of our area.

Howsham Mill

$\mathcal{J}$ 01653 619712 $\mathcal{E}$ howshammill.org.uk $\odot$ Island usually accessible, building only 1st & 3rd Sun of the month: check in advance

Howsham Mill was built in 1755 in the Gothic revival style and was operational until 1947 when it was abandoned. In 2004 it was taken over by the Renewable Heritage Trust. 'This is a wonderful Grade II listed building that desperately needed rescuing back then,' explained Dave Lister, one of the volunteer restorers. 'Our plan was not just to restore it but to put it back to work harnessing energy from the river. This time it would generate "green" electricity via the waterwheel, plus two modern Archimedean screw turbines, enough for the whole thing to be completely self-sustaining. The building could then be given used for educational visits and a wide range of events. We got enough support for the idea to win the Northern England round of the BBC's *Restoration Village* programme in 2006 – that was a massive boost. Since then it's just been a lot of hard graft by a few dedicated volunteers'.

"Our plan was not just to restore it but to put it back to work harnessing energy from the river."

The first screw and waterwheel were connected to the grid in 2010 and a second screw started generating in 2018; together, over 24 hours, they can produce enough electricity for up to 120 houses. The income from electricity sales funds the educational work and subsidises other events. Restoration of the building was completed in 2013 with a Heritage Lottery Fund grant, and its quality has been recognised with national awards from English Heritage and the Heritage Alliance. There have been ups and downs (largely vandalism and several floods) but the project has been a success.

To visit the mill, cross to the east side of the Derwent bridge at Howsham, follow the path under the bridge and then upstream along the boardwalk. After a few hundred yards of pleasant riverside walking, you will cross a small footbridge to the mill on its own little island.

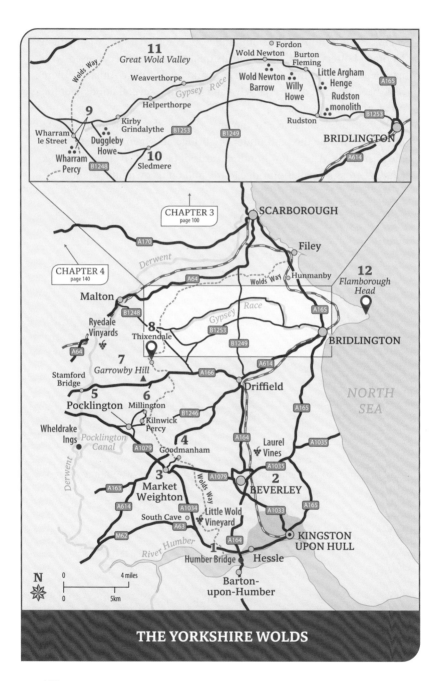

THE YORKSHIRE WOLDS

5

THE YORKSHIRE WOLDS

'Wold' is an Anglo-Saxon word meaning wooded hill, which is odd because this is an area noticeably lacking in woods, especially on higher ground. The Yorkshire Downs would be a better name perhaps, as these rolling uplands bear a distinct similarity to the hills of Sussex, Hampshire and Berkshire.

Bedrock is the key. The Yorkshire Wolds are rooted on an extension of the same chalk that is found under the North and South Downs, the most northerly chalk in Britain, in fact. An arc of these chalk hills extends from the Humber estuary in the south to a precipitous terminus in the northeast where **Flamborough Head** meets the North Sea. To the east lies the plain of Holderness and to the west the Vale of York, with the River Derwent a handy boundary on that side.

These are not the hills that a hardened Dales fell walker would recognise. The summits, in fact, are where the least interest lies. The rich, limey soil here has been ploughed and planted for millennia, resulting in the tame, rolling landscape familiar from David Hockney's paintings. There is a wildness here, but it hides away in the deep flood-cut valleys – land too steep to cultivate and left to harbour native woodland or rough grazing for sheep.

SELF-POWERED TRAVEL

CYCLING

Big skies and quiet roads. These two attributes of a good Hockney painting are also what makes the Wolds such a desirable venue for **road biking**. Perhaps it's no coincidence that the young painter himself spent two childhood summers cycling up and down the deserted lanes around the village of Huggate. The serious cycling fraternity has long known of the potential here, and their secrets are now shared with the rest of us on the Big Skies Bike Rides section of the Visit East Yorkshire website (⌀ visiteastyorkshire.co.uk): the 146-mile circular Yorkshire Wolds Cycle Route is the jewel in the crown. The southern section of this route, from Pocklington to Bridlington, also corresponds with the final leg of an increasingly popular coast-to-coast route, the Way of the Roses ride.

For us lesser mortals who prefer to be in the saddle for a few hours or a day at the most, the Wolds bike people have also produced ten short (20 miles or so) circular routes starting from Bridlington, Hunmanby, Malton, Sledmere, Pocklington, Market Weighton, Beverley, Driffield, Stamford Bridge and Hessle. Excellent little route maps are downloadable from ⌀ visithullandeastyorkshire.com.

Off-road biking here is a lot less rewarding, but not impossible. Arable farming country is often poor in bridleways, so you will have to search hard for a completely off-road circular route – there's usually some tarmac to put up with to get back to your start point. Having said that, areas with the greatest scope for mountain bikers are between the top end of Millington Dale and Huggate, and the network of green lanes encircling Wetwang and Garton on the Wolds.

 ## BIKE SHOPS

In addition to the bike hire listed here, Hull also has a plethora of bike shops (see Hull Cycle Map and Guide on ⌀ hull.gov.uk).

Eastgate Cycles Eastgate North, Driffield ☏ 01377 253274 ⌀ eastgatecycles.com. Accessories and repairs.
Hull Trinity Backpackers Market Place ☏ 01482 223229 ⌀ hulltrinitybackpackers.com. Also cheap accommodation and coffee shop.
Minster Cycles Norwood, Beverley ☏ 01482 867950 ⌀ minstercycles.co.uk. E-bike specialists.
Wilson's Wheels Grovehill Rd, Beverley ☏ 01482 882881 ⌀ wilsonswheels.co.uk. Accessories and repairs.

HORSERIDING

With such an equestrian tradition hereabouts, you would expect there to be lots of hacking and trekking opportunities in the Wolds – not so unfortunately. You may well see thoroughbreds on the gallops near Malton and Norton or even witness the famous race at Kiplingcotes

TOURIST INFORMATION

Beverley 34 Butcher Row ✆ 01482 391672
Bridlington 48 Promenade ✆ 01482 391634

(page 192), but centres or stables where you can ride yourself are few and far between and all on the periphery of our area.

 RIDING CENTRES

Woldgate Trekking Centre Bridlington YO16 4XE ✆ 01262 673086 ⬧ woldgatetrekking. co.uk. Pony trekking for beginners through to experienced riders on a variety of rural routes. Campsite attached.

WALKING

Wolds walking is very different to hiking in the Dales or in the Lake District. It's usually gentle, tending towards a potter or a ramble, rather than a scramble or clamber. What the area may lack in excitement it more than makes up for in its peace and quiet quotient. It's very easy to have a day's walk in the Wolds and not see another soul, especially if you wander off the paths in open access areas – 'wild' patches of land, not on the hilltops as you might expect, but in the deep, dry valleys in between. What isn't so easy is finding enough public rights of way to link into convenient circular walks. For much of the area, the best option is to follow sections of the 79-mile **Wolds Way**, a National Trail from the Humber Bridge at Hessle to Filey Brigg. Two other well-used long-distance trails are the 50-mile long **Minster Way** (linking the two minsters of Beverley and York) and the **Wilberforce Way** (a 60-mile route from Hull to York, named after the anti-slavery campaigner William Wilberforce) – see ⬧ ldwa.org.uk for details of both. In places, open access land can link footpaths and bridleways to create a rewarding **loop-walk**. Three good examples (all on OS Explorer map 294) are:

- From Huggate (♀ SE882554) – a three-mile walk using Horse Dale to the north.
- From Fridaythorpe (♀ SE874592 – a two-mile walk using West Dale to the west.
- From Warter (♀ SE868504) – a two-mile circuit of Great Dug Dale.

THE SOUTHERN FOOTHILLS

On its completion in 1981, the Humber Bridge became the longest single-span suspension bridge in the world, linking Lincolnshire's Barton-upon-Humber to Hessle in Yorkshire. I have it on the good authority of an engineer friend of mine that this is the only place that the bridge could possibly have been built as the north tower needed the solid rock here as foundation; anywhere else it would have sunk into mud and clay. This rock happens to be our first chunk of Yorkshire Wolds chalk. As the Humber Bridge road heads north towards **Beverley**, the Yorkshire Wolds Way footpath veers to the west following the chalk. On its journey inland it gains altitude and interest, especially near the **villages** of Brantingham, South Cave and the Newbald twins (North and South). By the time it reaches **Market Weighton** we are in the Wolds proper, and the deep valleys are turning wilder – at their most beautiful near Millington, east of Pocklington town.

1 HUMBER BRIDGE

From Hessle you get a terrific view of this vast structure, with its main span of 7,283ft (nearly 1.4 miles) that held the title of the world's longest single-span suspension bridge until 1998. Its opening in 1981 was the culmination of more than a century's campaigning by Hull businesses after a road tunnel in 1872 came to nothing. It replaced a 20-minute ferry crossing and was the very first suspension bridge to have concrete towers, standing to a height of 510ft. It went massively over budget, partly because of interest rates and spiralling inflation, and the construction loans are not expected to be paid off till around 2032.

National Cycle Route 1 crosses the bridge on its journey from Hull to Fakenham (Norfolk), giving cyclists and walkers the chance to appreciate the views as they cross via the cycle path, happily separated from traffic. Hull, incidentally, is a 5-mile riverside pedal or stroll away east of the bridge and well worth the diversion.

¶¶ FOOD & DRINK

Since the visitor centre closed there is nothing at the Humber Bridge Country Park; the following are nearby:

The Hase Swinegate, Hessle ✆ 01482 648559 ⌂ thehase.co.uk. The oldest, and in my opinion, by far the best pub in Hessle. The staff are welcoming to both people and dogs and there is always good-quality beer available; traditional home-cooked pub grub served Fri–Sun.

Little Wold Vineyard South Cave ⚭ littlewoldvineyard.co.uk. A relatively new vineyard producing a range of wines and offering tasting tours

Villa Natura Prestongate ☏ 07447 410240 ⚭ villanatura.uk. Great coffee, soups and sourdough bread sandwiches.

2 BEVERLEY

The chapter has barely started, and I've wandered out of the Wolds again. It's forgivable I think, because Beverley is such a delightful place, bursting with history, tradition and culture, and as 'Slow' a town as you'll find anywhere in Yorkshire.

Beverley's coat of arms gives a clue that this is a lowland town – a beaver over three wavy blue lines representing water. The nearby River Hull once formed a vast area of lake and marsh, thriving with beavers, hence the town's name since medieval times.

What turned Beverley from being a bustling market town into a nationally important settlement (the town was the tenth largest in England, at one stage) was the foundation of the monastery of Inderawuda, later to become **Beverley Minster**, one of the largest parish churches in the country. The less visited **St Mary's Church**, on the north side of the town centre, has a feast of medieval carving on its bosses and misericords, and a gregarious painted panelled ceiling with depictions of English kings.

With its medieval fortified bar, snickelways, and ancient pubs, the town is very much like a mini-York. It even has a quaint racecourse, about half the size of the one by the River Ouse at Knavesmire.

"With its medieval fortified bar, snickelways, and ancient pubs, the town is very much like a mini-York."

Much of the appeal of Beverley is derived from wandering around at will and enjoying its numerous, mostly Georgian, terraces. **The North Bar**, the sole survivor of five gateways in the long-vanished town wall, is a handsome specimen of medieval brickwork, beyond which 18th-century shop frontages line Saturday Market, as the marketplace is known, with its elaborate market cross. In Register Square, the imposing classical Grade 1 listed **Guildhall** (free entrance) is worth a look for its magnificent courtroom with intricate stucco work by Giuseppe Cortese.

HULL – UK CITY OF CULTURE

There's a lot more to Hull than Rugby League, fishing and North Sea Ferries. I was one of the many people made more aware of what else this great city has to offer in 2017, when it took on the mantle of UK City of Culture. During that year, much was made of the city's literary and performing arts heritage with numerous live events going on. I went to see a play at the excellent Hull Truck Theatre, and while I was in the city I chanced upon what I now regard as Hull's crowning glory – the Old Town, which was there long before 2017 of course.

Strictly speaking, Hull is the name of a small river that joins the Humber at this point – the town which was founded here in the 12th century is Kingston upon Hull. Almost all of the places in the city worth visiting are clustered into a tiny medieval enclave a mere few hundred square yards in area. Holy Trinity Church is here, now officially Hull Minster after it was granted cathedral status in 2017.

There are also five excellent museums (the Maritime Museum, the Streetlife Museum of Transport, the Hull and East Riding Museum, Wilberforce House and the Arctic Corsair trawler) as well as the Ferens Art Gallery – all free of charge (hcandl.co.uk/museums-and-galleries). It's not just the big buildings that are worth seeing; a brilliant collection of heritage pubs are tucked away down roads like Scale Lane, Silver Street and the wonderfully named Land of Green Ginger.

Trails are available to guide you around the Old Town, such as the Blitz Trail and the Blue Plaque Trail, but my favourite is the Fish Trail (visithull.org/to-do/fish-trail), marked by 41 fish sculptures. Ironically, the Fish Trail does not venture over the footbridge to the other side of the River Hull where The Deep (thedeep.co.uk) can be found. This spectacular, award-winning aquarium houses over 3,000 marine creatures and has to be seen to be believed.

⫚ FOOD & DRINK

The Lion and Key High St ✆ 01482 210253 ⊞ ⊙ Tue–Sun. One of the area's many very old and characterful pubs, this former CAMRA city pub of the year is very much a beer drinkers' establishment but the food is also very good – the fish and chips is legendary.

Beverley Westwood certainly contributed to the town being voted the 'Best place to live in England' in the past. Sounding more like a Hollywood film star, this is actually a lovely area of parkland complete with meadows and a windmill, and easily walkable from the town centre.

Beverley also has a lively cultural scene, with annual festivals for food, real ale, early and folk music, and literature. The poet Philip Larkin features prominently in the last of these. His home city of Hull is only eight miles down the road, and he regularly called in on Beverley.

Beverley Minster

Minster Yard North ⊘ beverleyminster.org.uk

Although officially only the parish church of St John and St Martin, Beverley Minster is larger than many cathedrals and a masterpiece of Gothic architecture, renowned above all for the quality of its medieval stonework. The present building is uncannily like a smaller scale version of York Minster.

The building owes its existence to an East Yorkshire cleric named John, who is still here incidentally, buried under the nave. He was a contemporary of Abbess Hilda of Whitby, and rose through church ranks to become Bishop of York in AD706. When he died in 721 his remains were buried in the monastery that he had founded in Beverley, then known as Inderawuda. Supposed miracles associated with his remains caused a cult to develop and Bishop John was canonised in 1037. The present church was built over his tomb, starting in 1220 but with the construction work spanning 200 years. Much of Beverley's subsequent prosperity has been a consequence of St John's fame and popular pilgrimages to venerate his bones.

Besides the magnificent aura of the space inside the Minster, other things to see are the 68 ornate misericord seats dating from the 16th century, the extraordinarily delicately carved Percy tomb canopy and the Saxon Sanctuary Chair or frith stool (one of only three in England), which entitled anyone who sat on it to sanctuary from the law for 30 days.

¶¶ FOOD & DRINK

Cafe Velo North Bar Within ⊘ 01482 679270 **f**. There is a bewildering array of good cafés in Beverly but I like this one best. Fry ups, bacon butties, cakes and proper coffee are specialities. Bikes and dogs welcome.

Laurel Vines Aike YO25 9BG ⊘ 07513 012708 ⊘ laurel-vines.co.uk. A family-run vineyard and winery established in 2009. Wines available online and in many local outlets. Tours are offered on occasional summer Thursdays, with a picnic included; page 191.

The Pipe and Glass Inn West End, South Dalton HU17 7PN ⊘ 01430 810246 ⊘ pipeandglass.co.uk ⊙ Tue–Sun. Not actually in Beverley but a village six miles to the northwest. What tempts most travellers out to this isolated 15th-century inn is its Michelin star (enough said). Also offers accommodation.

The White Horse Inn Hengate ⊘ 01482 861973 ⊘ nellies.co.uk. Known to its many fans as 'Nellies', after a long-serving previous landlady, this pub serves very cheap and drinkable

Sam Smith's beers. What makes it an exceptional place is the quite astonishing building itself. Sitting in one of the pokey gaslit rooms or navigating the warren of rickety wooden corridors and staircases is like stepping back in time. This is no mock-up though, the interior of the White Horse has remained virtually unchanged for nearly a century.

Whites Restaurant and Patisserie North Bar Without ✆ 01482 866121 ♂ whitesrestaurant.co.uk. Good enough to feature in the Michelin Guide. Patron/chef John Robinson offers two tasting menus, a nine-course one from Wed to Sat and a four-course one on Wed and Thu.

3 MARKET WEIGHTON

In 1251, Henry III granted Wicstun a Royal Charter, allowing it to have a market. The locals were presumably so proud of the accolade that they added 'Market' to their town's name and one operated here for the following 700 years, finally closing in the late 1900s. There was an attempt to restart it in 2015, but sadly it came to nothing.

Most of the town centre is made up of humble brick buildings dating from Georgian times, with the Norman All Saints Church a notable exception. All-in-all, nice

"Most of the town centre is made up of humble brick buildings dating from Georgian times."

but nothing special. If that was it I suspect that few folk would have heard of the town, but one man put paid to that. He was born in 1787 and became known as the Market Weighton Giant. By the age of 20 **William Bradley** stood at 7ft 8ins tall and weighed 27 stone. A bit of a celebrity in his own lifetime, William made a living touring the country as part of a travelling show. Before he died, aged 30 from tuberculosis exacerbated by his medical condition, he met George III, who presented him with a gold chain. A **Giant Bradley Heritage Trail** around the town starts at William's specially adapted house on York Street (big doorways!) and includes his grave in the church. This was originally in the graveyard, but was moved into the church after worries that his skeleton may be stolen. One of his boots is in the York Castle Museum.

During the rail heyday, Market Weighton sat at the junction of two routes, the York–Beverley line and the Selby–Driffield line. Sadly, both are now gone and Market Weighton is rail-less, but one of the old track beds (eastwards towards Beverley) doubles as a **public footpath** and

◀ **1** The Humber Bridge. **2** Aerial view over Beverley. **3** Streetlife Museum of Transport, Hull.

YORKSHIRE WOLDS WINE

Yorkshire? Wine? I know, it's hard to believe but there are now eight commercial vineyards/ wineries in the old county, three of which operate in the Yorkshire Wolds. Though England is now firmly on the map when it comes to producing wines of internationally recognised quality, most of the commercially viable vineyards tend to hug the southernmost regions of the country. **Ryedale Vineyards** (✆ 01653 658035 ⌀ ryedalevineyards. co.uk) crossed that north–south divide by becoming the most northerly commercial vineyard in Britain when it opened in 2006. Close to the village of Westow, the vineyards were originally planted by Stuart and Elizabeth Smith, an established name in the commercial world of grape growing as they had been running a vine-supply business for over 20 years previously.

'Before we bought the land,' Elizabeth told me, 'we made regular trips over the course of 12 months to see the plot in all different weathers – to see if it sat in a frost pocket in early morning for example, which could be extremely damaging to the vines. But the vineyard is on a south-facing slope, the ideal orientation.'

A selection of modern, disease-resistant red and white grape varieties are grown at the vineyard, in addition to some small test plantings of the more familiar French Pinot Noir and Chardonnay grapes, in the hope of producing some delicious sparkling wine in the future.

At least one of Ryedale's wines won a national award every year during the Smith's tenure and they passed the business on to Jon and Michelle Fletcher in 2016 who have carried on the good work since, with the business also diversifying into apple juice, cider and small-scale beer production. As well as vineyard tours there are regular

permissive bridleway. The full ten-mile trip to Beverley completes the Hudson Way, named after the Victorian railway entrepreneur who built the original line. This fine day's excursion takes you past the historic village of Goodmanham and two excellent little nature reserves owned by the Yorkshire Wildlife Trust. Rifle Butts Quarry is famed for its geological features and Kiplingcotes Chalk Pit boasts many rare meadow flowers and ants. Whichever direction you choose to do the walk, the regular X46 bus can take you back to your starting point. Cycling the Hudson Way doesn't give you the bus-back option but there is an excellent quiet minor-road return route.

¶¶ FOOD & DRINK

Sadly, Market Weighton is not a gourmet's paradise so it is probably worth travelling out of town to eat and drink, to Sancton or Goodmanham.

live music and theatre events, and B&B is available on-site.

Laurel Vines (📞 07513 012708 🌐 laurel-vines.co.uk) started production at an isolated farm in the hamlet of Aike, just north of Beverley, in 2013. It is owned and operated by the Sargent family who annually produce at least one white wine, usually using Solaris grapes, a rosé and a full-bodied red using Rondo and Pinot Noir grapes. Tours are part of the vineyard's Thursday Picnic (page 187) and occasional English Heritage open days occur, with food, a wine bar and tours available.

Little Wold Vineyard (📞 17956 773533 🌐 littlewoldvineyard.co.uk) is another family-run affair, this time by three generations of the Wilsons. They are based at Market Place Farm in South Cave, a village ten miles southwest of Beverley, but the vineyard is atop a south-facing chalk hillside called Littlewold. Planting of vines began in 2012, following advice and encouragement from the Ryedale Vineyards team, with the first winemaking harvest in 2016. Since then, production has expanded to a range of whites, rosés and reds, and an on-site Tasting Room was built in 2019 where a variety of events and tours take place. There's also an on-site shop and cafe.

The idea for the **Yorkshire Wine Trail** (🌐 yorkshirewinetrail.co.uk), a guide to visiting all of the county's vineyards, came from Ian Sergant of Laurel Vines; 'We wanted to show people that there is more to English wine than the "sparklers" of the southern counties,' he said, 'and we've had enough of pseudo-experts telling us what we should be smelling and tasting. When people ask me what our wines are like I say, "It's like wine; try it and tell me what you think."' Spoken like a true Yorkshireman. The trail starts at Leeds and finishes at York, visiting all six of Yorkshire's vineyards en route.

The Star Sancton YO43 4QP 📞 01430 827269 🌐 thestaratsancton.co.uk 🕐 Tue–Sun. A fine village pub, two miles from Market Weighton on the main road to Hull. Yorkshire beer from Wold Top Brewery and food even more local – much of the fruit and veg is grown in the pub's own garden and village allotments. The meals aren't cheap but are top quality.

4 GOODMANHAM

Market Weighton is an old town, but the nearby village of Goodmanham is not just very old, it's ancient. It was probably the natural springs emanating from the chalk here that drew the first Stone Age or Bronze Age settlers, who left behind their burial mounds on Howes Hill. To the Celts that followed this became a religious site, with two holy springs, now known as Lady's Well and St Helen's Well, and a temple on the hill where **All Hallows Church** now stands. The name of the village originates from *godo* (temple) and *mynnydd* (hill).

ENGLAND'S OLDEST HORSE RACE

The 17 March 2022 was not a particularly notable day weather-wise – cloudy with a bit of an icy chill in the air. However, the fact that this was the third Thursday of the month made it very special because, in this neck of the woods, it could only mean one thing – the Kiplingcotes Derby.

This race has been run over the same course on the same day for 498 consecutive years, making it the oldest flat race in the country. The starting post is an old stone marker near Kiplingcotes railway station, with the wooden finishing post at Londesborough Wold Farm. The intervening course is a relatively straight four miles of minor road verge and farm track.

So far so odd, and there are further quirks. The prize money for the winner is £50, but the second placed horse wins the sum total of all the £4 race entrance fees, which can in theory be more than the winner's prize money. This all depends on how many entrants there are and no-one knows for sure what this figure will be until the start of the race, as any horse and rider turning up before 11.00 can enter.

For the record, in 2022, race day coincided with St Patrick's Day and was aptly won by a horse called Paddy, ridden by Sally Hill (née Ireland!) and breaking the course record. The horse in second place was called Jasper and, as there were 19 riders that year, Jasper's mount, Tom Cowlam, did indeed take home more prize money than the winner – not bad for a first-time entrant.

The historian Bede recounts that this pagan shrine, later dedicated by the Anglo-Saxons to their god Woden, became a church in AD627 during the reign of King Edwin of Northumbria, the high priest Coifi starting the demolition personally using an axe. A wooden bench near St Helen's well carries an inscribed verse inspired by this conversion, starting with the evocative line: 'From dark to dark through fire-lit hall flies the axe that strikes the shrine.'

That first Saxon church was wooden but the Normans, as was often their want, rebuilt it in stone, and most of their work survives as the present Grade I listed building.

FOOD & DRINK

Goodmanham Arms Main St ✆ 01430 873849 ⬛. From the outside of what looks like a small, boring brick house, you would never guess how good this place is. Going inside is a trip back in time – tile floors, wood fire, home-cooked food and very reasonably priced beer from its own brewery. The landlord's passion for vintage motorbikes is obvious and there are plans for a museum behind the pub. Not surprisingly this is a regular winner of the CAMRA Best Village Pub of East Yorkshire.

5 POCKLINGTON & AROUND

🏠 **The Wolds Retreat** Kilnwick Percy (page 248); ☎ **Skipwith Station** North Duffield (page 248)

Pocklington may be one of the largest of the Wold-foot towns but in terms of regional importance it is a shadow of its former self. When the Romans arrived here 2,000 years ago they found the capital of the kingdom of the Parsii tribe, and by Norman times it was still the second largest town in Yorkshire after York. Now it's just a pleasant market town that benefits from not being particularly on the way from anywhere to anywhere else. Pocklington Beck flows right through the middle of town, but you wouldn't know it as for most of its route as it's hidden in culverts beneath the buildings. It reappears to the south and becomes a feeder for the **Pocklington Canal**, once an industrial boon to the town – now a great place to walk and cycle, and a linear nature reserve.

Burnby Hall Gardens

Pocklington YO42 2QF 🔗 01759 307125 🌐 burnbyhallgardens.com ⊙ daily

What Pocklington does possess that is definitely out of the ordinary is Burnby Hall Gardens, a floral gem on the edge of the town centre. Major Percy Stewart was an extraordinary man, although he didn't think so himself. 'We are terribly dull people', he said to his wife. 'Let us travel around the world so we shall have something to talk about.' They did, and he became one of those Victorian polymaths – traveller, adventurer, collector, scholar and philanthropist but, most important of all, a gardener par excellence.

The major and his wife Katherine bought the Burnby Hall Estate in 1904 and, in between their world tours, set about creating the luscious gardens seen today. They include an aviary, formal Victorian garden, and exotic woodland, but without doubt the centrepiece is the pair of lakes with a national collection of water lilies from around the world. Midsummer is the best time to see them in their full glory.

The Stewarts never had children and left the estate to the people of Pocklington in their will. The hall was never anything special and has become council offices, but the gardens have given pleasure to thousands of people over the years.

Give yourself at least half a day if you come here – time to visit the interesting little **museum** (featuring artefacts collected by the major on his adventures) and to have a brew and a snack in the café.

Pocklington Canal

⊘ pocklingtoncanalsociety.org

Although it wanders out of the Wolds and into the Vale of York, the Pocklington Canal has such special qualities that I feel I must mention it. Like most English canals it was dug in the early 1800s to link Pocklington with the rest of the national waterway system via the River Derwent, 9½ miles away. Competition with the railways led to its gradual decline and complete abandonment in 1932.

My first experience of the Pocklington Canal was on a glorious sunny day's canoe exploration, upstream from the River Derwent, and what a revelation it was. Where the river water was brown and silty the chalk stream-fed canal was crystal clear and teeming with fish – that is, where we could see the water. Most of the canal's surface was draped with a blanket of water lilies whose yellow and white flowers were in full bloom at the time. Dragonflies and damselflies dashed and hovered everywhere, and swans drifted serenely by.

"Dragonflies and damselflies dashed and hovered everywhere, and swans drifted serenely by."

Back in the 1960s, all this could have been lost if a proposal to dump industrial waste into the canal had been approved. Hurrah for the Pocklington Canal Amenity Society (PCAS) that blocked the idea and has looked after this delightful waterway ever since. The main aim of the PCAS is to restore the canal back to fully navigable along its complete length. At present it has managed about half, from Melbourne to the Derwent, and offers 30-minute trips on its narrowboat *New Horizons* (payment by donation). You can explore the rest of the canal on foot along the well-maintained towpath, all of which is part of the Wilberforce Way long-distance footpath (page 183), and bikes are allowed along the first two miles at the Pocklington end.

Madhyamaka Kadampa Meditation Centre

Kilnwick Percy ⊘ madhyamaka.org

One of Pocklington's more dubious claims to fame is that it was the site of the last burning at the stake of a witch in Britain. Thankfully the locals

◀ **1** Ryedale Vineyard. **2** Burnby Hall Gardens. **3** England's oldest horse race: Kiplingcotes Derby. **4** A barge on the Pocklington Canal.

are much more tolerant of other religions these days, and the village of Kilnwick Percy just up the road is home to one of the largest Buddhist meditation centres in the country.

Tiny Kilnwick Percy itself comprises merely a church, a stately home and the estate farm that served it in the past. The oldest part of **Kilnwick Percy Hall** dates from Elizabethan times but most of this graceful brick building is Georgian. An uneventful history was livened up during World War II, when the hall was requisitioned as a military mail sorting-office, but it was 30 years ago that its most unexpected reinvention occurred. In 1986, Kilnwick Percy was bought by a branch of the Kadampa Buddhist movement and has operated as the Madhyamaka Kadampa Meditation Centre ever since.

This is very definitely not a closed community and the centre actively welcomes visitors to the hall and landscaped grounds. It runs the World Peace Café, day and residential classes in meditation, and regular community events. Various forms of accommodation are also on offer.

¶¶ FOOD & DRINK

Of the dozen or so places to eat and drink in Pocklington, here are my favourites in each type of establishment.

The Fresh Food Deli Market Pl ✆ 01759 307370 ♐ freshfooddeli.com ◷ Tue–Sat. Houses a café upstairs, but what makes this place special is the food shop downstairs, which stocks a wide range of specialty, luxury and obscure comestibles.
Railway Street Fisheries Railway St ✆ 01759 302231 ◷ Tue–Sat. Chippies with a sit-in-to-eat bit are becoming a rarity. This is a classic of the genre.
The Wolds Cafe & Coffee House Waterloo Ln ✆ 01759 304868 **f**. Welcoming, traditional café with a good atmosphere.

6 MILLINGTON

This is a delightful little village, boasting the best pub for miles, a classic tea shop and characterful little church. I have to admit though, as much as I love my pint of Everards Tiger Beer in the Gait Inn or tea and toasted bloomer from the Ramblers Rest Tearoom, what brings me to this place time and time again is not the village but the valley that it sits in. Millington Dale is actually a series of dry chalk vales – with names like Pasture Dale, Nettle Dale and Sylvan Dale they could hardly be anything less than idyllic. Most of the dales are open access, meaning that you are free to wander among the grazing highland cattle and meadow flora. One of these little side valleys (Lily Dale) contains an ancient ashwood, such a rarity in these parts it has been designated as a local nature reserve. The **walk** round the wood of just over a mile is highly recommended.

FOOD & DRINK

The Gait Inn Millington ✆ 01759 302045 ⌂ thegaitinn.co.uk ◷ Tue–Sun. This has been an excellent pub for years so many fans were worried when it changed hands in 2021 – fortunately, fears have proved unfounded. The needed renovations have not spoiled the character of the old building and the home-cooked food is still delicious and good value. Black Sheep, Theakstons and three rotating guest beers on offer.

Rambler's Rest Tea Room Millington ✆ 01759 305220 ⌂ ramblersrestmillington.co.uk ◷ Wed–Mon. A watering hole beloved of cyclists for years, in an old village-centre farm cottage. It now also operates in the evening as a restaurant (private group bookings only). B&B accommodation attached.

THE HIGH WOLDS

The old Roman road from York to Bridlington roughly follows the route of the modern A166 up Garrowby Hill to the highest point on the Wolds. Many valleys snake northwards from this summit plateau, some joining up at the village of **Thixendale**. North from here the hills rise again around **Wharram Percy**, an ancient village nestling between the two country estates of Birdsall and Sledmere.

7 GARROWBY HILL

There is very little up here except a stupendous view westwards over the Vale of York and a couple of memorials. The vista has always been well known but in recent years it has been gazed on by many more pairs of eyes, albeit in an unusual colour scheme. David Hockney's 1998 landscape *Garrowby Hill*, featuring his trademark lurid purples, reds and greens, was painted from here.

The memorials are both marked on the OS map, the most visible being a large wooden crucifix on the edge of the Garrowby Hall woodland. It was erected in 1956 by Lord Halifax who lived in the hall, in memory of his friend George VI. The other memorial is further up the hill by the summit and is a much more poignant affair. It commemorates the deaths of eight men when a Halifax bomber crashed here in fog during World War II. Seven of them were flying in the plane but the eighth was incredibly unlucky as he was actually on the road when the Halifax landed on the milk truck he was driving at the time. His ghost is said to haunt the hilltop.

8 THIXENDALE

⛰ Country Huts on the Wolds (page 248)

Most people share the view that this is a very special place, but no-one can seem to agree on where the name came from. Some say that six dales feed into the main valley; others count the smaller dale-lets and reckon on 16, whereas Viking history scholars are sure that this was the home of a Norseman called Sigstein. It's still an open debate.

What's not in doubt is that for hundreds of years this has been one of the country's most isolated and least explored corners. Recently though Thixendale has begun to be discovered, mainly by walkers, art lovers and seekers of solitude.

Thixendale's most obvious connection with the art world is an arresting landscape sculpture by Chris Drury. *Time and Flow* can be found just south of the village (♀ SE841598) and is one of a series of sculptures commissioned by the Arts Council to accompany the Yorkshire Wolds Way along its whole route. Sadly, funding ran out before the other nine intended sculptures could be constructed. More traditional paint-on-paper art can be found a mile up the Fotherdale Road, at Fotherdale Farm. This is the home, studio and gallery of wildlife artist Robert Fuller (⊘ robertefuller.com; page 200). Robert has always taken photographs of animals to base his paintings on and he has a big following on YouTube for his trail-cam footage and owl nest-box films. Thixendale also features as a subject in paintings by the most famous local artist of all. David Hockney's *Three Trees in the Proximity of Thixendale* , a series of four paintings depicting each of the seasons, was exhibited at the Royal Academy in 2009.

> *"Most people share the view that this is a very special place, but no-one can seem to agree on where the name came from."*

---

1 Millington Dale valley. **2** Wharram Percy is perhaps the country's most famous deserted medieval village. **3** The interior of Sledmere country house. **4** Thixendale village. ▶

BARN OWLS

A white owl bounces over the hedge top,
As if on puppeteer's strings
So bright and alive it
illuminates the dusk
So buoyant, it seems its wings are stretched
To keep the Earth from losing it
What heart this bird must have
To fill so slight a body with
such energy...

Mike Bagshaw

Barn owls have inspired poets and artists since ink and paint existed. They provoke conflicting feelings of love and fear, being the nation's official favourite farmland bird but also a traditional omen of death. In living memory they were skinned and nailed to doors to ward off lightning storms. These eclectic birds are in trouble though. Nationally, their numbers have dropped by 75% since the 1930s, yet I see more of them annually in Ryedale than in the rest of my 40-odd years of birdwatching elsewhere in the country. What is it about this part of Yorkshire that suits **Tyto alba**? The obvious person to ask is Robert Fuller. Robert is one of Britain's leading wildlife artists, but also a passionate conservationist with a special interest in barn owls. He directs operations from his home at Thixendale on the Wolds side of the Derwent Valley.

'I set up the Wolds Barn Owls Group with friends a few years ago. It's a real hands-on project where we make and put up barn owl boxes on farms on the Yorkshire Wolds. We're an enthusiastic team and have great support from the local community.

Barn owls have had problems from all angles. A lot of their habitats have changed because there are bigger fields these days and different farming methods. And the old traditional brick farm buildings they liked to nest in are no longer used... a lot of them have been converted, knocked down or have fallen down, so it is important to provide them with an alternative nesting site. Dutch elm disease has been a big problem as well. The elm trees were often important as they had good hollows for owls to nest in, but now all those trees have fallen down and rotted away.

I've designed my own nest box for the project. Normally the male barn owl has to find a new home once the chicks are born and people tend to put out two boxes. My boxes have two compartments with a little penthouse area for the male to live after the chicks arrive. We've put up nearly 200 boxes across our area and about half are occupied – that's a healthy population of owls. It is good to know that, despite the pressures of habitat loss and harsh weather limiting hunting, at least the barn owls won't be short of a place to nest. I've always had a particular affinity for barn owls and they often feature in my paintings – it's nice now to give something back.'

9 WHARRAM & WHARRAM PERCY

🏠 Burythorpe House (page 248)

Almost all the present residents of Wharram live in the village of Wharram le Street, up on the hilltop where the old Roman road ran through – hence the 'Street' tag. This wasn't the case back in the 13th and 14th centuries when the local population farmed a couple of miles away in a village at the bottom of Deep Dale, called **Wharram Percy**. This medieval settlement was abandoned around the year 1500 and is now perhaps the country's most famous deserted medieval village. The church was always fairly obvious being as it was a fairly intact, if roofless, building but what Professor Maurice Beresford and his team

"It's well worth the short detour to marvel at the hundreds of butterflies feeding on carpets of thyme."

of archaeologists managed to do was find the rest of the village. Over a period of 40 years they excavated and mapped the foundations of scores of buildings, the grassy outlines of which you can still make out on the ground.

English Heritage, which manages Wharram Percy, has placed useful information boards around the site to explain all the humps and bumps and answer questions like my 'Why was it abandoned?' The answer was a surprising one – nothing to do with the Black Death but an early example of economic land clearance. In the 16th century, sheep became more profitable than crops so the landlord (not the original Baron de Percy but a certain Mr Hilton) turfed out his tenants, replaced them with sheep and demolished the village.

If you enjoy poking around old churches you should find the ruins of St Martin's interesting, but don't neglect the current, intact church in **Wharram le Street** as it is even older. Most of St Mary's is Norman with medieval additions but the tower dates back to Anglo-Saxon times. The churches are a mere two miles apart and the very pleasant stroll between them takes you briefly on the bed of an old railway that was built to take out stone from the big chalk quarry midway between the two villages. Like many disused quarries this is a haven for wildlife; if you are here in early summer it's well worth the short detour to marvel at the hundreds of butterflies feeding on carpets of thyme, rest harrow and orchids (details from the Yorkshire Wildlife Trust ⬚ ywt.org.uk).

A walk from Thixendale to Wharram Percy

✳ OS Explorer map 300; start: the Cross Keys pub in Thixendale ♀ SE845610; 9 miles; moderate

- -

There are a few circular walks described on the village website (⟨ thixendale.org. uk) and in walking guidebooks but my particular favourite is this nine-miler linking Thixendale and Wharram Percy (page 201). The walking is typical Wolds fare, brilliant in places – where the path follows the bottom of narrow, steep-sided valleys – and tedious when you end up on the flat, arable tops.

With the Cross Keys pub on your left, walk along to the main village street and turn right along it through the village, turning right after the last building on to the Wolds Way footpath. After 1½ miles, where the path meets a farm track and the Centenary Way footpath, turn left. Follow the Centenary Way down a steep hill until you join a tarmac road near the village of Birdsall. Turn right here and follow this minor road for 2½ miles until you reach a row of cottages near a hairpin bend. The Wolds Way joins the road here, but before you turn right to follow

10 SLEDMERE

YO25 3XG ☎ 01377 236637 ⟨ sledmerehouse.com ⊙ gardens: year round Tue–Sun; house: Apr–Oct variable days

There is no genuine village of Sledmere, just a country house and estate belonging to the Sykes family – the old village and medieval hall were demolished in the 18th century by successive 'Lordies' to make way for the big, new house and gardens designed by Capability Brown. Like many country estates it is run as a business, with house and gardens open to the public, and grounds available for weddings and events.

Sledmere does seem to reflect some of the modest and unassuming nature of the Wolds, though, and that's where it differs from big, brash places like Castle Howard. Not that the house is unimpressive; with 30 rooms this is a big building displaying quite a range of architectural styles, partly because of a troubled history. The original early Georgian interior was extended and redecorated 50 years later but then almost completely destroyed by fire in 1911. Fortunately, much of the house contents and the original plans were saved (allegedly by the villagers and staff as Sir Tatton Sykes finished his pudding in the dining room). The inside of Sledmere was reconstructed to the Georgian plans but with an Edwardian twist.

the disused railway line, check out the nature reserve in the quarry nearby. The Wolds Way will take you through the deserted medieval village of Wharram Percy and up the valley of Deepdale. Continue up the side of the valley until you reach another junction with the Centenary Way. Turn left and follow the Centenary Way for a last downhill mile back to Thixendale.

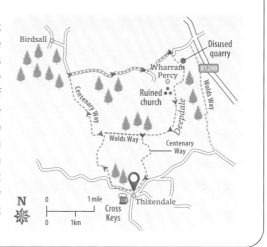

Fourteen rooms are open to the public, including the celebrated Long Library, the drawing and music rooms with Joseph Rose plasterwork and the Chinese Bedroom with a Chippendale bed. The quirkiest room is probably the one inspired by the Sultan's apartments in the Yeni Mosque of Istanbul and called (not surprisingly) the Turkish Room.

The entrance charge for the house is not exorbitant and includes access to the gardens. These are arguably more impressive than the house itself, especially the formal patterns of the Parterre and the Georgian walled rose garden. There are parts of the estate accessible free of charge; these are the shop, café, entrance exhibition and **Waggoners Museum**. This last building commemorates the work of Sir Mark, the sixth Baronet, during World War I – ironically he survived the trenches but died during the 1918 flu pandemic. His body was exhumed from its lead-lined coffin in 2008 to extract DNA for research into flu treatment.

⫶ FOOD & DRINK

The Triton Inn Sledmere ✆ 01377 236078 ⌖ thetritoninn.co.uk ⏱ Wed–Sun. Local Wold Top beers and traditional pub food – nothing fancy, but good quality. The bar also stocks an unusually large collection of gins from around the world. B&B accommodation available.

EAST TO THE COAST

At their northern edge, the Wolds loom out over Ryedale and the Vale of Pickering as a long escarpment, heading east to finally reach the sea at **Flamborough Head**. Behind this high land lies a long dale sometimes known as the **Great Wold Valley**, down which flows the famous Gypsey Race, through the **villages** of Weaverthorpe, Wold Newton, Burton Fleming and Rudston.

11 THE GREAT WOLD VALLEY

⌂ **Wold Cottage** Wold Newton (page 248)

My first visit here was a puzzling one. I was armed with my OS map, which had on it a distinct wiggly, blue line – a stream at Kirby Grindalythe that I intended to follow. When I navigated myself to the right place though, there was nothing there, just a dry ditch in a field. The name **Gypsey Race** should have given me a clue really; gypsy –

"Chalk hills like the Wolds behave as giant sponges, soaking up millions of tons of water a year."

itinerant, wandering, often arriving in spring and then disappearing. This is one of those intermittent streams, often associated with chalk country.

Chalk is no more than a pure form of limestone, and a crucial property of this rock is its permeability, that is it allows water to pass through it. Chalk hills like the Wolds behave as giant sponges, soaking up millions of tons of water a year, which is why we see very little surface water in streams, ponds or lakes. It is only when this water reaches an impermeable layer of rock below, or the underground reservoirs are full to overflowing, that it bubbles out on to the surface from springs. This often happens after heavy rain, but also sometimes mysteriously during dry weather when it is least expected.

Whatever the geological cause, the significance of the Gypsey Race on past human societies here has been enormous historically, and especially prehistorically. Another glance at the OS map reveals a concentration of ancient monuments, clustered along the length of my wiggly, blue line, starting up near the stream's source at Wharram le Street. **Duggleby**

---

1 Weaverthorpe in the Great Wold Valley. **2** The Rudston Monolith. **3** The interior of St Andrew's Church, Kirby Grindalythe. ▶

Howe (⚲ SE881669), one of the largest Neolithic burial mounds in Britain, is the first. Travelling downstream, you pass **Wold Newton Barrow** (⚲ TA048726), **Willy Howe** (⚲ TA062723), **Little Argham Henge** (⚲ TA096706) and finally the remarkable **Rudston Monolith** (see opposite). Current thinking considers the Stone and Bronze Age veneration of springs (page 191); historians reckon that our ancestors probably regarded unpredictable groundwater appearance on this scale, a river appearing overnight, as magical – in other words, Gypsey Race was a major religious site.

THE FALLING STONE OF WOLD NEWTON

A man (me) walks into a pub and orders a pint of the local bitter. 'Why the strange name?' he asks the landlord, pointing to the *Wold Top Falling Stone Bitter* pump-clip. 'Oh, that's to do with what happened in a field near the brewery donkey's years ago,' was the barman's reply. 'Tell me more,' the man said, and joking apart, this is the story he heard.

In the middle of a December afternoon in 1795, farmhands working in the fields behind Wold Cottage Farm watched aghast as a dark object flashed diagonally across the sky and struck the ground near where they were. The explosion of the impact was heard for miles around, and John Shipley, the nearest worker, was showered with soil. The 56lb rock, still hot and smoking from its supersonic flight, lay buried seven inches into the chalk bedrock.

What these men, and others from the village, had witnessed was the final seconds of the journey of the second largest meteorite ever to land on English soil. Or 'an extraordinary stone that fell from the atmosphere,' as it was reported at the time – and boy was it reported. By pure chance,

the Falling Stone of Wold Newton had happened to land in fields belonging to Major Edward Topham, a farmer, writer and magistrate who also owned a newspaper. The stone became a celebrity, so much so that Major Topham put it on display in Piccadilly in London, charging a shilling a time to view. Eventually, what was left of the stone after souvenirs had been chipped off was donated to the national Natural History Museum, where it resides today.

The Falling Stone of Wold Newton remains the only meteorite landing that has ever been observed by reliable witnesses, thus giving the astronomers of the time vital evidence for the cosmic origin of meteorites. Cue top scientific fact of the day – a meteoroid is the rock in flight, a meteor is its visible burning tail and a meteorite is what it becomes when it lands. The landing site is marked by a brick memorial monument erected by Major Topham. Unfortunately, the obelisk sits on private land. However, the current owners of Major Topham's old house, Wold Cottage, offer accommodation (page 248) and any paying guests are able to visit the memorial.

'Race' folklore continued into historical times, with floods in particular said to be the harbingers of doom or disaster. A roaring race, or 'woe-waters' as they were known, preceded the Black Death, the beheading of King Charles I, the attack by William of Orange and the Wold Newton meteorite (see opposite). The last big flood was in December 2012, just before a meteorite shower injured hundreds of people in Russia… a coincidence, of course – or was it?

Most of the time the Great Wold Valley is a sleepy backwater with not much going on besides farming and local people getting on with their lives. Few visitors come here, which means that those who do will be able to enjoy a lot of peace and quiet to themselves. Footpaths and bridleways are virtually deserted and road cycling on the very quiet country lanes is a joy.

There are no tourist attractions to see in the string of villages along the valley bottom. Most have small and interesting **churches**, many rebuilt or restored by the Victorian Sir Tatton Sykes of Sledmere House. Particularly worth visiting are St Andrew's in **Kirby Grindalythe**, St Andrew's in **Weaverthorpe**, St Peter's in **Helperthorpe** and the lovely little St James's at **Fordon** (the smallest active church in Yorkshire).

The Rudston Monolith

Frankly, I can't understand why this place isn't a major tourist attraction, for it is the tallest prehistoric standing stone anywhere in Britain. At 25ft, the Rudston Monolith stands higher than any of the acclaimed Stonehenge stones or menhirs on Orkney, and here it is, hiding down the side of an unremarkable church in a small Wolds village.

"I find it difficult to imagine the effort it must have taken our ancestors 3,000 years ago to move such a block of stone here."

Closer examination of the details makes the stone's presence here even more astonishing. For a 25ft block to stand without falling over it must have a further 15ft underground, and therefore weigh at least 30 tons. What's more, the stone is not local; it is composed of sandstone, the nearest outcrop of which is ten miles away in Cayton Bay near Scarborough. I find it difficult to imagine the effort it must have taken our ancestors 3,000 years ago to move such a block of stone here, armed only with boats, logs, ropes and ingenuity. I don't think that the religious importance of Rudston can be overestimated.

When Christianity arrived on our shores, churches were built on existing holy sites so there is every likelihood that a church has existed here for 1,500 years even though the oldest part of the present building is Norman. Incidentally, the village name is Saxon: not the usual 'ton' for town, but 'ston' for stone, with the prefix rood, meaning cross. It probably commemorates a time when this pagan symbol was converted to Christianity by the addition of a cross on top.

¶¶ FOOD & DRINK

Some of the valley villages have never had a pub in living memory and some have lost them in the last 15 years; those currently with a place to eat and drink are Weaverthorpe (two), Wold Newton, Rudston and Burton Fleming.

Anvil Arms Bridlington Rd, Wold Newton YO25 3YL ✐ 01262 470279. A justifiably very popular pub for both eating and drinking. Food is traditional English and comes in large portions (steak and ale pie world famous). Beers from Theakstons and Wold Top.
Bluebell Country Inn Main St, Weaverthorpe YO17 8EX ✐ 01944 738204 ☌ bluebellweaverthorpe.com. The Bluebell has always been an excellent beer drinkers' venue (Tetleys and Timothy Taylor), but the emphasis is now on high-quality food. B&B and self-catering accommodation also available.
Bosville Arms High St, Rudston ✐ 01262 321645 ☌ bosvillearms.co.uk ☉ Tue–Sun. The region's only community-owned pub, saved from demolition and opened in 2021. Lunches and evening meals are very good, while the beer range includes some from the local Wold Top Brewery, as you would expect. Family and dog friendly.
Spirit of Yorkshire Distillery Hunmanby Industrial Estate, YO14 0PH ✐ 01723 891758 ☌ spiritofyorkshire.com. A Scottish friend of mine was appalled when I gave him some Filey Bay single malt whiskey to taste. 'Wow, that's one of the best whiskies I've ever tasted... but it shouldn't be allowed!' You can buy online but I would recommend a visit as you can book a distillery tour and have a brew and a snack in the Pot Still Coffee Shop.

12 FLAMBOROUGH HEAD

Flamborough Cliffs Nature Reserve ☌ ywt.org.uk. **Bempton Cliffs Nature Reserve** ✐ 01262 422212 ☌ rspb.org.uk

Pedantically speaking, only the relatively low cliff at the very end of the headland qualifies for the name but when most people talk of

---

1 Flamborough Head. **2** & **3** Atlantic puffins and gannets can be seen at RSPB Bempton Cliffs. **4** View across RSPB Bempton Cliffs. ▶

DANIEL J. RAO/S

GIEDRIIUS/S

CHRIS GOMERSALL RSPB IMAGES

ANNA MOORES

SEABIRD CITIES

This is almost a sensory overload experience I am going through. There is deafening cackling all around and the constant pattering of feet on water, so many individuals are coming and going carrying fish that I cannot keep up, and an overpowering fishy smell pervades everything. Where am I? A busy Scarborough chip shop on a Friday night perhaps? No, I am bobbing on the swell in a small boat at the foot of Flamborough Head cliffs, taking in one of the most spectacular wildlife experiences that Britain, never mind Yorkshire, has to offer. Most of the pattering fish-carriers are members of the auk family; puffins mainly, but also guillemots and razorbills that have surfaced with a beak full of sand eels to feed their young. They manage to get themselves airborne with a whirring of their small wings and a frantic leg-sprint over the sea surface before banking over to their cliff-top nest. As they leave, the next shift arrives and plops beneath the surface. I lean over the side and watch enthralled as one puffin flaps its way under our boat (they swim by flying underwater), its progress through the clear water visible because of a silver layer of air clinging to its waterproof feathers.

What sound like two sharp gunshots pull my attention to the other side of the boat, just in time to see the cause of the noise as a gannet folds its wings back at the end of its 30ft dive and 'thunks' into the water at breakneck speed. Two others surface, both with a wriggling mackerel that they wolf down headfirst – what gannets! There is so much going on it is tiring; a seal's head in the water to port, was that a porpoise fin on the starboard side? Yes, there it is again – two of them! After a while though, childish excitement slackens enough to observe and see order in the apparent chaos. Seven or eight species of bird breed on the chalk cliffs of Flamborough and Bempton, 200,000 in total, most feeding on small fish, sand eels and sprats. Kittiwakes and guillemots are the most numerous and nest on ledges high

Flamborough Head they are referring to the whole area of land between Bridlington and the sands of Filey Bay. This enormous chunk of chalk, an extension of the Wolds, sticks out a good six miles into the North Sea, with its highest cliffs an awesome, vertical 400ft at Bempton on its northern side.

Flamborough has always been a very separate place. Indeed the Bronze Age people here completely cut themselves off from the rest of the country by constructing a massive earth wall and ditch now mistakenly known as 'Danes' Dyke'. There is a strong Scandinavian connection here though, with many colloquial terms, stories and traditions dating from Viking times. The annual sword dance that is still performed, even if on the most vertical sections of cliff with gannets and razorbills preferring the lower sloping sections. The puffins here are unusual – elsewhere in the country, such as the Farne Islands in Northumberland, they raise their young in soil burrows at the clifftop. At Flamborough, natural cavities in the rock face do the job and puffins have the unusual experience of tenement living with fulmars as neighbours.

In the past, the vast numbers of birds here were seen as a harvestable resource by locals. Gangs of 'climmers' would make a hair-raising descent by rope from the top of the cliffs to collect both eggs and young birds for food. This sustainable harvesting worked fine until Victorian times when things got out of hand. Shooting birds from boats as holiday sport caught on and many more eggs were collected to supply private collections, but the activity that caused a change in the law was kittiwake collecting. Thousands were massacred to provide feathers for fashion hat accessories and to stuff mattresses. So to prevent their complete wipeout, the first Bird Protection Act of 1869 was introduced to the statute book and today the birds are very well protected.

As my boat chugs back to North Landing at Flamborough I marvel at what a special place of superlatives this is. It is the most northerly outcrop of chalk in the country, England's biggest seabird colony, and the only mainland gannet colony in Britain. Most of all, it provides one of the most exhilarating wildlife experiences to be found anywhere.

If you fancy a boat trip to see, hear and smell the birds of Flamborough Head, there are a few options (page 213), but being afloat is not the only way to experience the birds of course. You can see them with a good pair of binoculars from the beaches at North Landing and South Landing or from the clifftop path looking down. The RSPB has some excellent viewing points at the top of Bempton cliff.

only by local village schoolchildren, is probably the most famous of these old traditions.

Flamborough Head's exposed position has always been a hazard to shipping; over 50 recorded shipwrecks in the vicinity are testimony to that. It should come as no surprise, therefore, to find a lighthouse here but not many people expect two. The present working one was built in 1806 while its predecessor, a wonderful chalk edifice, dates from 1674 making it the oldest standing lighthouse in the country.

Other attractions apart, what draws most people to Flamborough Head are its birds. Two nature reserves are dedicated to the protection of

Walks round Flamborough Head

❋ OS Explorer 301; start: South Landing ⚲ SE231692; 7 miles; easy

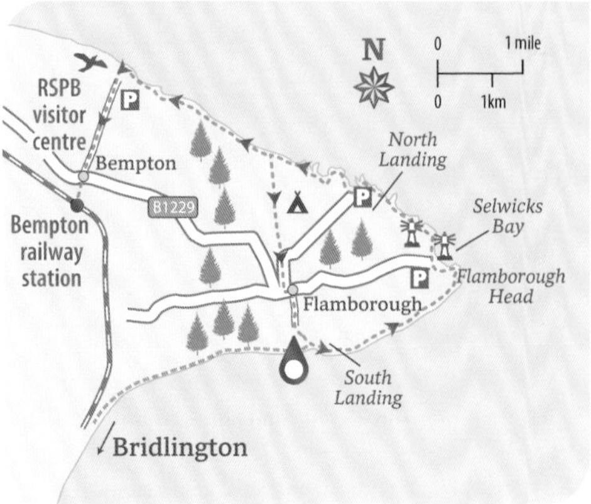

The obvious walk to do here is one that takes you right around the end of the promontory, and just for a change public transport is on your side if you choose to use it. My choice would be to start on the gentler south coast and finish at the spectacular cliffs further north. The walk begins at **South Landing**, which you can drive to, but its only just over half a mile's stroll from Flamborough village where the Bridlington bus (510) stops hourly. Facing the sea at South Landing, turn left and follow the coastal path for two miles to **Flamborough Head** itself. After admiring an historic pair of lighthouses overlooking Selwicks Bay, continue along the steadily rising cliffs of the northern shore for two further miles to **North Landing**. While you could catch the bus back from here, the cliff scenery will probably tempt you on for a further mile to where a public footpath leads across the fields and back to Flamborough village. If you did use the bus from Bridlington to get here, then this seven-mile circuit can be extended by another two miles by continuing along the coast to the RSPB visitor centre perched atop the stunning cliffs of **Bempton** (free entry if you arrive on foot). From here, an amble downhill for a further 1½ miles will take you to Bempton railway station, where you can catch one of the nine trains a day back to Bridlington.

the huge seabird colonies here, Bempton Cliffs Nature Reserve (RSPB) and Flamborough Head Nature Reserve (Yorkshire Wildlife Trust).

FOOD & DRINK

Scrumdiddlyumptious High St, Flamborough ✆ 07761 100083 ⓕ ⏲ Mon–Sat. A proper café – very welcoming staff serving bread and cakes baked on the premises and excellent all-day breakfasts.

Ship Inn Post Office St, Flamborough ✆ 01262 850454 ⬛f. The name is apt, as you will feel as if you have walked into the captain's cabin when you enter the varnished, wood-panelled bar. This traditional local has darts, pool, dominoes and cards available to play, and John Smith's and guest cask ales to drink. The grub is wholesome and very good value, especially the seafood.

White Horse Bempton ✆ 01262 850266 ⬛f. This is the only place to eat in the village and very popular with visitors to the famous nearby bird reserve and locals alike. The beer is fine and the food nourishing, but what most people remember about this place is its amazing multi-shades-of-blue tiled roof.

⚓ BOAT TRIPS

North Landing Boat Tours Flamborough (North Landing) ✆ 01262 850905 ⬛f ☉ summer only. Boat trips to see the birds and caves of Flamborough Head.
Yorkshire Belle From Bridlington Harbour ✆ 01262 850959 ♂ yorkshire-belle.co.uk ☉ May–Jul Sat & Sun. Gannet and puffin cruises on the *Yorkshire Belle*.

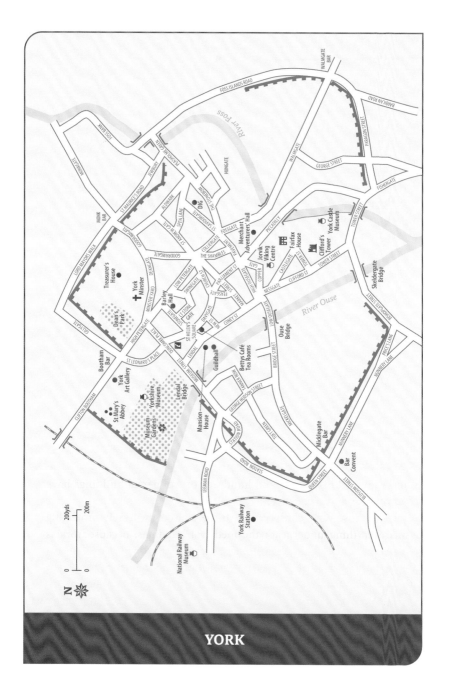

YORK

6
YORK

With Caroline Mills

🏠 **The Bar Convent** & **Grays Court** (page 248); 🏠 **Baille Hill House** (page 248),
The Little House (page 248)

York is, quite simply, a national treasure. It is by far the best-preserved medieval city in the country, a place drooled over by anyone interested in history and consequently always in the top three most visited places in the UK. What I love about it is its compactness – so much of interest packed into such a small area. The magnificence of the Minster, the tranquillity of the Museum Gardens and riverside, the bustle of the Shambles and markets, fantastic old pubs and artisan shops, highbrow culture and secret, pokey alleyways… all within a stone's throw of each other and contained by the old city walls.

Amazingly, the survival of these ancient walls, streets and buildings is not accidental but down to the people of York themselves. In late 18th-century England, many towns and cities were being ruthlessly modernised and the Corporation of York planned to follow suit by applying for an act of Parliament to rubber-stamp a massive demolition program. Thankfully, they were thwarted by the great and the good of the city and hundreds of wonderful buildings have survived as a consequence.

What those early conservationists were also unwittingly protecting was everything underneath the medieval buildings, because York is not just one city but a series of settlements built one on top of each other over a period of 2,000 years. Some necessary modernity has crept into the city centre since, but generally a good balance has been struck between preservation and progress. There is, of course, a 21st-century city of York outside the walls, with hospitals, council offices, railways, ring roads and factories, but 99% of what most visitors want to see is within the city walls. These stone ramparts are themselves an added bonus, providing an excellent raised viewing platform for the city.

THE YORK PASS

If you plan to visit lots of fee-paying attractions, and you're in town for more than a day, it's worthwhile purchasing a York Pass. The pass is a smart card allowing discounted or free entry into more than 30 places of interest, including several outside York mentioned elsewhere in this book. Used well it is fantastic value. Passes can be purchased for one, two, three or six consecutive days from ⊘ yorkpass.com.

My first experience of York was on a junior school trip back in the 1960s. We were dragged around various museums, but – as is the way with childhood memories – two other very disparate incidents have lasted the test of time. One was being pushed into the River Foss by a classmate (I haven't forgotten, John Foster) and the other was being told a ghost story. It was the oft-quoted one about a garrison of Roman soldiers marching through solid walls in the cellars of the Treasurers House.

"York's most famous old inhabitants are probably the Vikings – another bunch of overseas invaders."

Two facts stuck in my young mind – first that there were real Italian people here 2,000 years ago, and second that lots of Roman York is still here, underneath the floors of the medieval buildings. The remains of seven Roman roads converge on York, showing that this was a major city of the empire, originally one of the ten Legionary fortresses the Romans built in Britain. The Legio Sextra Victrix (Victorious 6th legion) had its headquarters on land currently occupied by York Minster, with 6,000 soldiers living in a fortified camp between there and the River Ouse. All that remains above ground is a column from the Roman headquarters in Minster Yard, the **Multangular Tower** – a part of the old Roman bastion – in the Museum Gardens and odd bits of Roman building stone incorporated into later structures.

A modern addition to the cityscape close to the column, by the steps of the Minster, reminds us of a momentous historical event that took place here and went on to shape not just the history of Britain, but that of the whole of the Western World. It is a statue of Constantine the Great who proclaimed himself Emperor of Rome on the death of his father Constantius while they were both in York in the year 306.

Despite all this, York's most famous old inhabitants are probably the Vikings – another bunch of overseas invaders. This lot took possession by sailing up the River Ouse in longships and made the place the capital of their fledgling kingdom. York's Scandinavian heritage is celebrated in the Jorvik Viking Centre (page 241).

First Millennium invasions were only the start of York's story though; they have been followed by medieval merchants profiteering from get-rich-quick schemes, in-fighting royals, people loyal to the royals and those not so loyal to the royals, highwaymen, railwaymen, chocolate makers, fires and floods… all contributing to the very particular personality of the city today.

Dividing the centre of York into segments is somewhat arbitrary for there are really only two relevant parts – inside or outside the walls. In honour of the city's chocolate heritage I've broken the chapter into three bite-sized chunks that are more easily digestible by the visitor on foot; these are Around the Minster, Traders' and Debtors' York, and South of the River Ouse.

GETTING AROUND

Much of the beating heart of York is pedestrianised so the very best way – indeed the only way – to see the main proportion of the city within the walls is on foot, or at least by bicycle. Public transport only helps when crossing the city or getting from the outskirts to the centre.

BY BUS

Buses from the suburbs to the city centre are run by **First Bus** (⊘ firstbus.co.uk). These are colour-coded routes for ease of use, with the main terminus at Station Road outside the railway station and Rougier Street, a five-minute walk from the railway station. They won't particularly help you to see the sights but they will help if you are staying in accommodation away from the city centre.

However, one way to reach some of the attractions is by taking one of the open-topped, sightseeing bus tours. **City Sightseeing** (⊘ yorkcitysightseeing.com) and **Golden Tours** (⊘ goldentours.com) both run hop-on hop-off buses, starting at Exhibition Square and

---

𝑖 TOURIST INFORMATION

Visit York Information Centre Museum St ✆ 01904 555670 ⊘ visityork.org

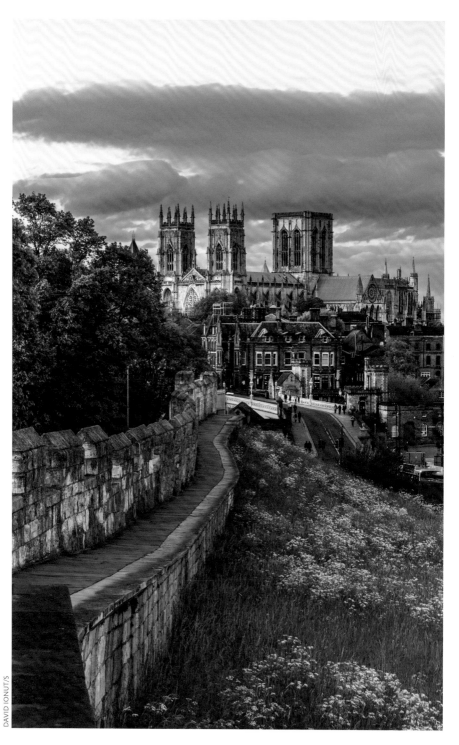

stopping at 20 points of interest. With tickets valid for 24 hours, the tour skirts the city walls and is useful for gathering your bearings, or for those with mobility problems (the buses are wheelchair and pushchair 'friendly'), but it can't replace stomping through the streets.

BY TAXI

Taxis are readily available directly outside the railway station but there are also licensed taxi ranks in various locations around the city centre, including St Saviourgate, Minster Yard and St Leonard's Place (useful for evening performances at the Theatre Royal).

BY CAR

Frankly, this is not a good idea. By far the easiest and most cost-effective thing to do with your car if visiting for the day is to use the convenient park-and-ride scheme (city centre car parks are expensive). With free parking in five locations, all well-signposted around the city ring road, the bus, with a reasonable fare, then transports you right into the centre, stopping at several points around the city.

CYCLING

To get to York, the National Cycle Network Route 65 (The White Rose Cycle Route) has much off-road cycling from Selby to York on the now-official branch of the trans-Pennine route from Manchester to York.

York was one of the first places in the country to embrace urban cycling and it is still without doubt the most bike-friendly city in the north of England. There are many traffic-free **cycleways** to keep you off the busy streets, with bike parking facilities in the city centre. **Bike hire** is available from **Cycle Heaven** at the Station (⌀ 01904 622701 ⌀ cycle-heaven.co.uk) at the railway station and from **Get Cycling** (⌀ 01904 636812 ⌀ getcycling.org.uk) in Hospital Fields Road.

As for **maps**, pick up a free copy of York's Cycle Route Map from visitor information centres and local libraries or download it from ⌀ itravelyork.info/cycle-routes. This details all cycle routes throughout the city as well as off-road tracks for safer cycling.

◀ View across York's walls to the Minster.

YORK'S SNICKELWAYS

Snickelway seems such a lovely word, one that you will not find in any dictionary – yet. Mark Jones created the word by taking certain syllables from three other words – snicket, ginnel and alleyway. A long-time York resident, Mark is very specific about what a snickelway should be but, in essence, they are described as narrow, medieval passageways.

There are dozens of snickelways within York – tiny routes that squeeze between buildings, darting about across the city, linking better-known grander streets and squares; it is not difficult to imagine the hustle and bustle of noisy medieval life while wandering these routes, even though they remain peaceful in modern times. Mark has devised a fantastic walk using many of the snickelways in what could be described as a very enjoyable game – totally disorientating even for those who know the city well. If you follow the route exactly, it uncovers all kinds of hidden gems that cannot be found simply by strolling along the main streets. Time is essential to really appreciate the walk and to accept a fair amount of distractions in the form of nosing into yards, window-shopping and stopping off en route for a coffee or a leisurely pint in a pleasant looking pub. I'd recommend that you get to know York a little via its main

WALKING

The very heart of York, enclosed by the **city walls**, is compact and easily manageable on foot. With your head down, you could cross the centre from wall to wall in approximately 20 minutes, though in reality you'll take far longer because there is so much to see. It is by far the best way to see York, and many of the main streets are pedestrianised. Rather than cross the heart of the city, you can circle it with a walk along the city walls, providing one of the best vantage points from which to view the centre, particularly as an introduction before tackling the core. Originally built by the Romans and beefed-up with stone in the 13th century to keep out the Scots, the castellated walls include an inner parapet-like walkway that is approximately three miles long. They are a significant feature of the York landscape and can make a good shortcut in places. My favourite section to start at is **Micklegate Bar**, considered to be the royal entrance to York as it's the gate through which all members of the royal family have passed on state visits to the city, and walk towards **St Leonard's Place**. Besides the superb golden glow of trumpeting daffodils hugging the banks in springtime, there are fabulous views, when walking this part of the walls, of the curving Victorian arches at the railway station, the beautiful Dutch-looking streets before attempting the snickelways – that way you'll really appreciate them.

The snickelway walk can be disorienting because, despite being 3½ miles long, it is confined to an area within a quarter of a mile of The Shambles, one of York's most famous streets (and deemed a snickelway), so the route of the walk twists and turns every few paces. The game, however, is that you do not recross the path from whence you came or retrace your steps, although you do occasionally need to walk on the opposite side of the street to avoid this. Like The Shambles, there are some fascinating street names that crop up as you pass through, each with a historical narrative all of their own such as Honeypot Lane, Lady Peckett's Yard, Mother Alice Lane and Hornby's Passage. Some professional walking tour guides cover all or part of this walk within their selection of themed tours (see opposite). However, if you would prefer to amble along at your own pace, Mark Jones has produced a fascinating guide entitled *A Walk Around the Snickelways of York*, available online at ⟡ snickelways. co.uk. Try the walk with children; they will love searching for the names of the various snickelways and are usually sticklers (or is that snicklers) for keeping to the rules of the game.

former headquarters of the North Eastern Railway Company, and one of the most magnificent views of the Minster. It's the West Front of the Minster that you see from this particular section of the walls and on sunny afternoons the stone from the façade glows with such vigour as to bring it to life.

York has built a tourist industry around walking and, for visitors who prefer to be guided by a knowledgeable local, there are any number of themed walks provided by various organisations. One of the most notable is **White Rose York** (⟡ 07792 207679 ⟡ whiteroseyork.com) which begins its tours from the main (west) entrance of York Minster every day at 11.00, with an extra 15.00 tour in Summer. This three-hour tour of all the most interesting bits within the city walls is officially free, with customers just asked to leave what they feel is a realistic donation.

"On sunny afternoons the stone from the façade glows with such vigour as to bring it to life."

For **self-guided trips**, following the route suggested by Mark Jones in his book *A Walk around the Snickelways of York* is hard to beat (page 220), and the Rowntree Society has designed five chocolate-themed walks (page 242).

FOOD & DRINK

As York's a cosmopolitan city, you can grab a sandwich or a pasty for pavement food, dine in any number of international restaurants or sink a pint of regional brew in one of the many city centre pubs and bars. But this is Yorkshire, and the city has not forgotten its roots, with a plethora of cafés and tea rooms serving a traditional afternoon tea. With such a compact centre you could eat all day, moving from breakfast to brunch, lunch to tea and evening drinks to dinner without leaving a street.

The area around Newgate and Parliament Street is the place to pick up goodies in the open air. Newgate hosts a daily **market** while St Sampson's Square is the scene for **York Farmers' Market** (first Friday of every month) and several **Continental markets** held throughout the year, including a large one around Christmas. The busiest event of the year is the annual **food festival** during the last week of September (⌂ yorkfoodfestival.com).

DAYTIME CAFÉS

The Bar Convent 17 Blossom St ✆ 01904 643238 ⌂ bar-convent.org.uk. Quiet café, serving delicious homemade food throughout the day in relaxed surroundings. Best experienced on a warm, sunny day when you can eat out in the lovely garden.

Grays Court Chapter House St ✆ 01904 612613 ⌂ grayscourtyork.com. Next door to the Treasurer's House, this is an extra special place to eat for a relaxing mid-morning coffee, lunch or afternoon tea. The entrance to this magnificent historic building is through a peaceful cobbled courtyard. You can relax on sofas or private window seats in the oak-panelled Jacobean long gallery, or find a table overlooking the garden, itself overlooked by the city walls. My pick of daytime places to eat throughout the whole of York. Also open evenings.

Mannion & Co 1 Blake St ✆ 01904 631030 ⌂ mannionandco.co.uk ⊙ Wed–Mon. The Mannion family greengrocer shop took a change of direction in 2011 with the arrival of chef Andrew Burton into the family. It is now a much-lauded 'kitchen, eatery and café' serving fantastic Mediterranean-style food to eat in or take-away. Also open evenings.

The Perky Peacock Coffee Shop Lendal Bridge ✆ 01904 689778 ⌂ perkypeacock.co.uk. Its location is the best thing about this tiny café as it's in the Postern Tower of the bridge itself, with fantastic views over the river. That said, food is of a very high quality and coffees are amongst the best in town. Finding a free table can be a challenge.

Treasurer's House Chapter House St ✆ 01904 624247 ⊙ Sat–Wed. This National Trust tea room (known as The Below Stairs Café) occupies the house's old Servants' Hall and is open to all (not just those visiting the house). A French theme to the food celebrates Monsieur Viande, resident Master Chef in Edwardian times.

York Cocoa House 10 Castlegate 🖉 01904 675787 🖑 yorkcocoahouse.co.uk. An artisan chocolate-making premises keeping alive this traditional York activity. You can eat (and drink) the chocolate in the café, take some home from the shop or even sign up to a workshop and learn how to make your own.

EVENING DINING

Le Cochon Aveugle Walmgate 🖉 01904 640222 🖑 lecochonaveugle.uk ⊙ Wed–Sun. This restaurant's name means 'blind pig' in French, giving a clue to the dining experience expected. The six-course menu is a blind-tasting one with no choice and all guests eating at the same time. An unusual arrangement but worth it because the food is spectacularly good.

Roots Marygate 🖑 rootsyork.com ⊙ Wed–Sat. 'Black Swan in the City' could be an alternative name for this place because this is the metropolitan annex of Michelin-starred chef Tommy Banks's famous Oldstead restaurant (page 45). The quality and price tag of the tasting menu are both at the high level you would expect.

Skosh Micklegate 🖉 01904 634849 🖑 skoshyork.co.uk ⊙ Wed–Sat. A sort of Japanese (and other influences) tapas bar. You need three or four of the dishes to make a decent meal but the quality is extraordinary.

PUBS

If there is a better collection of pubs in any town or city centre in the country, I've yet to see it. Here is the cream of the crop:

Blue Bell Fossgate 🖉 01904 654904 🖑 bluebellyork.com. Small, poky and brilliant. With an interior unchanged since 1903 this is one of CAMRA's elite heritage pubs. Always a good range of Yorkshire beers on sale, but no food, except pork pies over the bar.

Guy Fawkes Inn High Petergate 🖉 01904 466674 🖑 guyfawkesinnyork.com. One of the reputed birthplaces of Guy Fawkes, in the shadow of the Minster and with a suitably dark and atmospheric interior. Black Sheep and a range of guest beers are available in the tiny bar while good food is served in the adjoining restaurant. B&B available.

House of the Trembling Madness Stonegate 🖉 01904 640001 🖑 tremblingmadness. co.uk. This very popular place is, in real life, almost as wacky as its name. It consists of a genuine medieval drinking hall above a bottled beer and spirits shop. Draught beer and good food are served upstairs with holiday apartments in the courtyard behind. There is a sister pub with the same name on Lendal.

Kings Arms Ouse Bridge 🖉 01904 659435. Famous as a flood victim. Not the best beer in town but worth visiting if only to see past flood levels marked on the wall.

Minster Inn Marygate ✆ 01904 849240 ▯. Not where you might expect it with a name like that, but tucked down the side of the Museum Gardens. This was always one of my favourite York pubs, then in 2016 came those dreaded words 'refurbished' and 'under new management'. The refurbishment has, however, been done in keeping with the pub's Edwardian origins and the new management has managed to keep the old, peaceful ambience of the place and added delicious homemade pizzas to the mix.

Roman Bath Sampson's Sq ✆ 01904 620455. A single-roomed locals' pub with nice beer, good-value food and regular live music. What merits its entry here though is the incredible contents of the cellar – not beer barrels but a complete, genuine Roman bathhouse (which operates as a separate museum). Its discovery in the 1930s prompted the pub's name change from the Mail Coach Inn. Accommodation available.

Snickleway Inn Goodramgate ✆ 01904 656138. A friendly and welcoming traditional boozer serving well-kept beer and basic, but wholesome, food (pies and sandwiches). This very old pub has gone by many names in its long life. It was the House of Tudor when it acted as Royalist ammunition store during the Civil War and not so long ago was the Anglers Arms. The current name comes courtesy of Mark Jones (page 220), despite the slightly different spelling.

Whippet Inn North St ✆ 01904 500660 ⌨ thewhippetinn.co.uk. The main focus of this pub is very good quality, adult-only dining with steaks a speciality, but there is a small drinkers-only bar. The wines are good, the beers are local and the cocktail menu is inventive.

Ye Olde Starre Inne Off Stonegate ✆ 01904 623063. Prepare for some ghostly sights while mulling over a pint in the pub that claims to be the oldest in the city. An eye-catching pub sign spans the street – one of the few in Britain to do so. A Greene King pub but a wide range of other guest beers are usually on offer.

AROUND THE MINSTER
YORK MINSTER

The character and ambience of York is owed to a multitude of fascinating and beautiful buildings with a mix of architectural styles from a wealth of historical periods. But if there is one building that truly sums up York, one that most people think of as 'being' York, it is the Minster – or, to give it its full title, the Cathedral and Metropolitical Church of St Peter in York. A colossus in stature and fame – one of the largest cathedrals in the world and arguably the most beautiful example of Gothic architecture – it dwarfs anything that stands around it. The Minster can be seen from several miles away in certain directions, a beacon that rises up through the notorious autumn mists drifting across the Knavesmire, the vast open expanse to the south of the city. This is one of the few positions from which to survey the whole of the Minster. As you move closer to the structure, fragments disappear behind other buildings; even when you are standing right by it, when its sheer size is overwhelming, you cannot possibly see all of it.

What sits before us now is in fact 'Minster Mark ll', the first wooden structure having been built in the year AD627 for the baptism of King Edwin of Northumbria. The current building took 252 years to complete, starting in 1220, and is a masterpiece inside and out, from its delicately carved decorations and mighty flying buttresses to the magnificent **stained-glass windows**. From inside, these windows glint and gleam with every passing sunlit flicker, as if taking on a life of their own. The rose window in the south transept is one of the most famous in the world, not least for the painstaking restoration that was required following the lightning-bolt fire in 1984 that destroyed this work of art. The window joins the red and white roses of Lancaster and York, a symbol marking the

"From inside, these windows glint and gleam with every passing sunlit flicker, as if taking on a life of their own."

end of the Wars of the Roses, a horrific and bloody period of history during which the Plantagenet families of Lancaster and York spent many a year bickering. When Henry VII married Elizabeth of York, daughter of Henry IV, in January 1486 in York Minster, the two 'roses' were conjoined to create the Tudor Rose.

Other windows are equally beautiful, their colours dancing across the gigantic walls and pillars within the Minster, such as the Great West Window, known as 'The Heart of Yorkshire' owing to the shape of the stone carved into it, and the unique Five Sisters Window in the north transept, with five elegant columns of glass. You can take a tour of the Glass Conservation Studio to view the medieval stained glass at close quarters and see the restoration methods used. Tours of the studio, which is housed in the Bedern Chapel close by, take place on Wednesday and Friday afternoons, leaving from the Group Desk in the Minster.

The **Central Tower** is open for visitors who can manage the 275 steps (and an extra charge), giving an astonishingly grand gargoyle's-eye view of the city from 230ft up. Cast your eyes outwards on a clear day and you can also see the distant hills of the Yorkshire Dales to the west and the White Horse of Kilburn on the Hambleton Hills to the

east. In the opposite direction is the part of the Minster that I personally find the most fascinating – the **Undercroft**. In the 1960s the Minster's central tower showed worrying signs of collapse, so its foundations were excavated to create the Undercroft and huge blocks of concrete inserted to prop up the tower. During the works an amazing discovery was made – that the Minster was built directly on top of the Roman fortress headquarters, the Praetorium and Basilica. Since 2013, this Undercroft space has housed an excellent museum detailing all the archaeological finds.

By far the greatest architectural gem of the Minster is the oldest part of the building, the **Chapterhouse roof**. Above the highly ornate ceiling of the octagonal Chapterhouse (which can be seen simply by walking around the Minster), its roof, an upturned conical labyrinth of latticed timberwork, stands as high again as the Chapterhouse does from floor to ceiling. Its weight is phenomenal, the structural strength of all the wood and lead suspended above the Chapterhouse ceiling mind-boggling. Howard Mosley, head of the Visitors' Department at the Minster, describes the Chapterhouse roof as 'a giant IKEA kit', the marks still visible where the carpenters laid out and built the timber frame at ground level before piecing it together in situ. Howard explained that should the Minster ever catch fire again, firefighters are requested to save the Chapterhouse roof before any other part of the Minster. It's a shuddering thought to even contemplate, allowing the rest of the Minster to burn purely to save this one roof, but when you see it for yourself, and the three enormous oak trees that stand suspended in the middle, one on top of the other (having been placed there goodness knows how in 1260 without the aid of modern lifting equipment!), you begin to understand the sentiment and the reasoning.

The Minster grounds

To best appreciate the acoustic qualities of York Minster, listen to one of the concerts held there occasionally or to the attractive peal of the bells on a Sunday morning, slowly dragging persistent slumberous souls into the awoken world. To concentrate on this musical campanology, head for the **Dean's Park**; it's a quiet (but for the bells) and restful green space overshadowed by the north face of the Minster. This is also the

◀ **1** The Treasurer's House and gardens. **2** The grand interior of York Minster.

best vantage point to see the Minster's most recent residents. A pair of peregrine falcons, affectionately known as Mr and Mrs Minster, have bred successfully on the northwest tower every year since 2017 and attract quite a crowd of admirers in the breeding season.

Restoring York Minster

The walls of York Minster might have been built almost a thousand years ago, but this most celebrated of buildings could be likened to Trigger's broom, the prop that made an appearance in the sitcom *Only Fools and Horses*. An unlikely analogy, I know, but in a famous scene Trigger describes how his original road-sweeping broom has lasted for 20 years, adding that it has had 17 new heads and 14 new handles. York Minster is a little bit like that. So soft is the limestone used to build and decorate the Minster that every stone only lasts for approximately 150 years. Hence it's difficult to find much genuinely original stonework.

The stone restoration is a mammoth task so the Minster has its own stoneyard, housed on Deangate. Peer through the gates and you're likely to hear the sounds of giant circular blades slicing through stone like soft butter and when the whirring stops (remembering that the original masons didn't have such a useful tool to summon into action), there's the gentle tapping of the stone-carver's chisel and mallet.

The stoneyard is occasionally open to the public. If you're not in town when a tour is planned, accept that you'll get neck ache and take the time to admire the stonework on the Minster. Generations of stone-carvers have plied their trade and thousands of man-hours have gone into making the Minster look the way it does.

THE TREASURER'S HOUSE

Minster Yard ✆ 01904 624247; National Trust ⊙ Variable – check website

Behind the Minster is the 17th-century Treasurer's House, so called because it stands on the site of the medieval mansion used by the Treasurer of York Minster. Now owned by the National Trust, it was used by a bachelor, Frank Green, to house his collection of antique furniture in period settings. His portrait that hangs in the hall shows quite a friendly looking chap although his frequent notices to staff left around the house suggest a rather pedantic figure – his request for workmen to wear slippers in the house would not pass a health and safety assessment now! There's another chance for a view of the Minster

WHAT'S IN A NAME?

The city of York has lent its name both to the county that it sits in and the Big Apple in the USA but the word 'York' is relatively modern. The oldest documented name we have for this place is Eburacon, meaning 'place where the yew trees grow' in the Celtic language of the local Brigantes tribe. Although this label seems to bear no resemblance at all to modern York, there is a convoluted link between the two involving mistranslation, mispronunciation, laziness and the vagaries of the rules of spelling.

As was their habit, on invading a country the Romans just Latinised the local names, so Eburacon became Eboracum, and remained so for 400 years. They did, however, mistakenly think that 'ebur' was Celtic for wild boar and

consequently adopted the boar as the city's logo. On the Romans' departure the Anglo-Saxons perpetuated this mistake by naming the city Eoforwic – boar-town in old Saxon. When the Vikings took over, they couldn't get their tongue around Saxon pronunciation – the nearest they could manage was Jorvik (with the Scandinavian 'J' pronounced 'Y') and it stuck.

After a brief spell as Everwic under the Normans our lazy tendency to shorten names resulted in Yerk in the 14th century, then Yourke in the 16th century and Yarke in the 17th century, only finally settling on York in the 18th century. In a nice homage to the past, the Archbishop of York uses Ebor as his surname in his signature.

from the drawing room but the Great Hall is really the attraction here, with a hidden minstrel's gallery complete with a small leaded-light window from which to glance at passing visitors below.

For an extra fee (unless you have a York Pass; page 216) you can don a hard hat and be taken down into the house's cold and dirty cellar. 'Why?' I can hear you asking. Well, because this was the site of York's most famous ever ghost sighting.

Harry Martindale was an 18-year-old apprentice heating engineer working alone in the cellar in 1953 when he heard what sounded like a distant trumpet. Soon after, the sight of helmet-wearing soldiers emerging into the cellar through a brick wall caused him to fall off his ladder in shock. As he cowered in a corner, the first soldier walked across the rooms followed by a carthorse and 20 other soldiers. Although it was all over in seconds, fine details were etched onto Harry's memory, including the most bizarre of all – all the figures, including the horse, were only visible from the knees upwards. Fearing ridicule, Harry kept quiet until the 1970s when he was interviewed for a TV programme and the story hit the headlines. Over the intervening years all of Harry's details, initially pooh-poohed by historians, have since been proved to be correct, including the discovery of a Roman road 15 inches below the modern cellar floor level – hence the chopped off feet. Spooky!

A CITY OF GATES, BARS & CHURCHES

The medieval walled City of York had a quartet of fortified entrances which, confusingly, were not called 'gates' but 'bars'. They still exist and are called Monk Bar, Micklegate Bar, Walmgate Bar and Bootham Bar. All four once had a defensive roofed entrance called a Barbican, inside which any would-be invaders could be abused in various unsavoury ways, but these have all been demolished in the past save for the one at Walmgate Bar. The nearby Barbican theatre takes its name from this fine historical feature.

The 'gate' that appears in two of the names actually refers to the road passing through the bar because, just to add to the naming confusion, *gata* is a Scandinavian word meaning street. Many of York's roads retain this old naming system and often describe what went on in a given place. Swinegate was the old pig market, Stonegate was the route by which building stone was moved from the landing quays of the River Ouse to the building site of the Minster, and Coppergate residents were thought to be cup-makers. Incidentally, the shortest street in town bears the bizarre name of Whip-ma-whop-ma-gate which is thought to translate as 'neither one thing nor another' – very apt.

GUY FAWKES IN YORK

When James VI of Scotland travelled south in 1603 on his way to London to become King James I of England, he stayed briefly in York. His lodgings were in the King's Manor in St Leonard's Place, which was, ironically, just yards from High Petergate, the birthplace of his potential murderer, Guy Fawkes. As he had a Catholic wife, it was hoped that James I would provide greater security and tolerance for Catholics than they had known since Henry VIII's abolition of Catholicism in England. It was not to be. Guy Fawkes had become a Catholic some years earlier while at St Peter's School, a quarter of a mile from Bootham Bar, and was aware of the antagonistic feeling occurring among Catholics within the city before taking part in one of British history's most notorious events. Many children still enjoy watching a Guy burn on top of a roaring bonfire each November to commemorate this failed 17th-century coup. However, the students of St Peter's School are notable exceptions as the school considers it unsporting to burn effigies of former pupils.

Many of these gates are, perhaps rather obviously, in the very centre of York where the Viking residents lived. It's these most ancient of streets that provide the character of the city around the Minster, each one similar and yet dissimilar to others, the plethora of independent retailers, restaurants and bars a refreshing change from the cloned high streets found in many towns today.

If there is one street in York that is the city's beating heart it is **Stonegate**. With the River Ouse, the medieval **Guildhall** and the **Mansion House**, home to the Lord Mayor, behind you, Stonegate runs from **St Helen's Square** towards the Minster. It was originally the Via Praetoria that went to the main gates of the Roman fortress long before the Vikings renamed it. There are glimpses of the Minster from time to time, drawing you ever closer towards this giant beast of a building.

But ponder a while along Stonegate; its charm lies within the York paving beneath your feet and the fact that no two buildings are the same. The rooflines, the building materials, the paint colours of the window frames and the decorative iron signs advertising small boutiques, tea shops

"It's these most ancient of streets that provide the character of the city around the Minster."

and ancient inns are all different and all add something to the street's character. It can get busy around Christmas but there's room for all, including the odd busker or two, their independent tunes turning into a cacophony of sound or a melodic harmony depending on their proximity to one another.

For a more serene experience, take a peek into Coffee Yard, a tiny alley off Stonegate, where the medieval **Barley Hall** stands. It was re-discovered in the 1980s, hidden behind the façade of a derelict office block being demolished, and has now been restored to the beautiful timber-framed home it was for the 14th-century Lord Mayor. Community involvement is an element of the building's restoration: there's an oral history project still going on to involve anyone who has ever lived or worked in or around Stonegate.

At the height of religious compliance, well let's face it, forced participation, York possessed a staggering 40 churches within the city walls. An impressive 19 of these medieval buildings have survived with ten still operating as places of worship, and all have their quirky stories to tell, not least three of the closest to the Minster.

St Michael le Belfry, cowering in the shadow of its giant neighbour, saw the baptism in 1570 of an infant named Guy Fawkes who would go on to gain some national notoriety; St Olave's, founded in 1055, is the earliest dedicated to Saint Olaf anywhere in the world; and St Helen's Church on Stonegate is built at an odd angle, out of kilter with neighbouring buildings. It is thought that its Saxon builders aligned it with the original wooden Saxon minster, which was later replaced.

Further afield, St Deny's is built on the site of a Roman temple; All Saints' is the regimental church of the Royal Dragoon Guards; St Cuthbert's is an evangelical house of prayer; and St Martin le Grand sports an elegant clock-on-a-stick suspended over the busy street below. On the other side of the river, St Mary's has Roman building stones incorporated into its very old tower; Holy Trinity was once part of a much larger Benedictine Priory; and All Saints boasts the famous 'Pricke of Conscience' stained-glass window.

The remaining eight decommissioned churches, being listed buildings, thankfully cannot be demolished so have been reinvented in others guises. St Sampson's and St Michael's operate as social centres with cafés; St Saviour's is the headquarters of the archaeological Society, DIG; St Margaret's hosts the National Centre for Early Music; St Mary's is a contemporary art museum; and St Martin cum Gregory's is a stained-glass centre. My favourite of the lot though, is Holy Trinity Church. This little gem of a place, looked after by the Churches Conservation Trust, is tucked away behind busy Goodramgate – a real oasis of peace and tranquillity amid the bustle.

YORK ART GALLERY
St Leonard's Pl ⏣ yorkartgallery.org.uk ⊙ Wed–Sun

This impressive Victorian Classical-style building houses four permanent features; the Centre of Ceramic Art – the largest of its kind in the country – on the first floor, the Artists' Garden (a free contemporary art space behind the building), a café and a shop. The rest of the gallery space is given over to ever-changing exhibitions, ranging from 14th-century church altarpiece art to 21st-century playable indoor golf course installations.

◀ **1** View along the River Ouse. **2** The Museum Gardens and St Mary's Abbey. **3** Micklegate Bar. **4** Stonegate.

THE MUSEUM GARDENS &
THE YORKSHIRE MUSEUM

Shrouded with daffodils in spring and multicoloured blooms in summer, the **Museum Gardens** just north of the River Ouse are many people's favourite place to relax in York, finding a sun-strewn piece of Benedictine wall to prop oneself up against, the empty arches of the delicately carved windows towering above. The distant traffic crossing **Lendal Bridge** disappears as the birdsong whistling from the window ledges takes over, the occasional clanging of the Minster's bells ringing out the passing time.

"Other parts of the abbey remain scattered around the gardens like discarded rubble."

The creamy wall – for there is only one full wall left standing – of St Mary's Abbey, blackened by centuries of decay, belonged once to the largest Benedictine monastery in the north of England. Founded in 1055, it became one of the casualties of Henry VIII's Dissolution. Other parts of the abbey remain scattered around the gardens like discarded rubble, the stumpy foundation stones of once-magnificent pillars appearing to grow from the grass; they are now the back-scratchers for idle bookworms and lunchtime gatherers escaping the bustle of the city streets and offices.

Behind the abbey, just outside a redundant part of the city walls, is **St Olave's Church** in Marygate. Built in 1055, the parish church is the oldest monument dedicated to the patron saint of Norway, King Olaf, who had died in combat 30 years earlier. The church became the foundation for the Benedictine community that built St Mary's Abbey. In a quiet back street, bordered by the Museum Gardens and close to the river, it is a very peaceful and a quite beautiful sanctuary, well away from the hubbub. The six bells are rung every Sunday morning at service in full view of the congregation and visitors are welcome to witness the bell-ringing practice, held every Wednesday evening (◷ 19.00–21.00).

Elsewhere in the Gardens, the **Yorkshire Museum** has an extensive collection of antiquities from the city and around, including the famous Middleham Jewel, unearthed by metal detectorist Ted Seaton in 1985; the exquisite 15th-century diamond-shaped gold pendant inlaid with a single sapphire and engraved with a Latin charm against epilepsy was bought for the tidy sum of £2.5million. The museum has a huge collection of artefacts in its possession and can't display them all

'ALL THE WORLD'S A STAGE'

Back in the 1300s, someone in York had the bright idea of entertaining and educating the peasantry with a series of community plays put on by the Craft Guilds. **The Mystery Plays**, as they were called, were performed during the mid-summer Corpus Christi festival on mobile pageant wagons. The play themes were always religious and, because of their Roman Catholic origins, were banned in 1568 by that royal spoilsport Elizabeth I.

York's Mystery Plays were revived in the 1950s with many modern thespians cutting their dramatic teeth here – Dame Judi Dench once played the Virgin Mary and Ian McShane was a convincing Satan. Nowadays the performances take place every two years and alternate between fixed-stage performances and the traditional pageant wagons. The next cycle in 2024 will be a fixed-stage one.

Of course, you won't have to wait two years to be entertained by other performing artists in York. The main stage play venue is **York Theatre Royal** near Bootham Bar (⊘ yorktheatreroyal.co.uk), with the much smaller Friargate Theatre by the riverside (⊘ ridinglights.org) hosting the acclaimed Riding Lights Theatre Company. I have to say though, that the best dramatic performance I have seen in the city was at **The York Dungeon** (⊘ thedungeons.com/York). For 1½ hours, the audience of eight that I was a part of was baffled, enthralled, amused and terrified in quick succession by a series of very talented actors during a distinctly interactive presentation.

High-profile music and comedy acts tend to appear at the **Grand Opera House** (⊘ atgtickets.com) or the Barbican Centre (⊘ yorkbarbican.co.uk) whereas other more niche music venues include the **National Centre for Early Music** in St Margaret's Church, off Walmgate (⊘ ncem.co.uk) and the excellent **Black Swan Folk Club** on Peasholme Green (⊘ blackswanfolkclub.org. uk) and The **York Vaults** on Nunnery Lane for almost any other sort of music. If you like your entertainment free and unpredictable then go in search of buskers and street artists. The famous Purple Man always seems to be in Stonegate and King's Square usually has something interesting going on. Watch out for the occasional buskers' festival.

at the same time so it operates a rotating exhibition system. Consult ⊘ yorkshiremuseum.org.uk for what's currently on show.

THE RIVER OUSE

Below the Museum Gardens is the River Ouse, whose usually mild-mannered waters entertain visitors on river cruises and dawn-breaking university rowers most days. Sometimes, when the weather has been cruel in the distant Dales forcing the water ever higher, the river forgets its manners, turning into a savage torrent that bullies its way

THE SALMON OF YORK

If asked to name an English salmon river, very few people would suggest the River Ouse, which slides its way through York. But it's not a typically polluted city river, fed as it is by the clear Dales rivers of Swale, Ure and Nidd.

Bob Drake was a lad in the 1940s, struggling to live on wartime rations in York. 'We'd look forward to late autumn nights, just after a high tide, because that's when the salmon would run. A net across the river, hidden under the railway bridge at Poppleton for a few hours, would always land a few fish, five or ten – enough for our family and a few friends. I know it was poaching, but the river was teeming in those days, and they were desperate times.'

What makes this abundance all the more remarkable is that these are the fish that got past the commercial netters way downstream below York, at Naburn and Cawood, the limit of the tide, and they took nine tons of salmon every year – that's a lot of fish. Fast forward to the 1970s. The Dales rivers that feed the Ouse were still as clear and clean as ever, pike, perch, roach and bream still swam under the city's bridges, and trout in its tributaries, but the King of Fish was gone, not one salmon to be seen. What went wrong? The answer lay in the fatal combination of the fish's incredible lifecycle, and what was going on in 1950s West and South Yorkshire.

Atlantic salmon (*Salmo salar*) are famously born in fresh water, migrate to the sea to feast and put on weight, returning a few years later to their home river to mate, spawn and produce the next generation of fish. What complicates the situation in Yorkshire, and which almost resulted in the salmon's

into the front rooms of neighbouring houses and upturning bar stools in the ever-patient **Kings Arms** (page 223). Every time it happens, the landlord marks the flood's height on the wall – the current record is dated 4 November 2000. Ironically, the catastrophic floods of December 2015 were not as high but caused far more damage, and hit the national headlines, because of the failure of the River Foss flood barrier. Water surged from the swollen Ouse up the Foss, which subsequently burst its banks, flooding hundreds of homes and businesses.

When it's not deep under water, the Kings Arms is a great place from which to view aspects of the **Jorvik Viking Festival** (⊘ visityork.org/festivals) an event every February where longboats sail down the river in homage to the time when Viking raiders used to head out to the North Sea to trade around the world. Other events take place around the city including battle re-enactments and saga-telling.

A **river cruise** provides yet another perspective on York. It is one of the best ways from which to view the medieval Guildhall that backs extinction here, is the dominance of the Humber estuary. All of Yorkshire's major rivers join forces as the Ouse, and flow into the sea together in the Humber. The salmon could not survive the level of pollution in the water in the rivers Don and Aire which entered here from industrial Sheffield and Leeds, and either died as young fish on their way out to sea, or as adults on their way back.

If the salmon's story had ended there it would have been a tragedy, but at the turn of this century rumours of a possible comeback were confirmed; some are now making it back up the Humber and returning to their old haunts. 'This is a completely natural recolonisation,' explained John Shannon of the Environment Agency. 'We've not done any stocking of the Dales rivers at all. What we have worked hard at is habitat restoration, and in particular water quality lower down, and the fish have done the rest themselves.'

The future looks good for Yorkshire salmon, and consequently all the other living parts of the river ecosystem, especially the fish-eaters. Not many people see them, because they're very shy and nocturnal, but otters are back in York as well – possibly because gourmet fish are back on the menu.

If you want to stand a good chance of seeing a Dales salmon, you need to be in the right place at the right time. They tend to run upstream in late autumn – November is the peak time – and when the rivers are full and fast. Weirs and small falls, where the salmon have to leap out of the water, are the best places. Try watching from the weir and fish-pass at Naburn or Linton On Ouse.

on to the Ouse close to Lendal Bridge. **City Cruises York** (✆ 01904 628324 ⌖ cityexperiences.com/york/city-cruises) plies the river in a variety of red-and-white cruisers, departing either from Lendal Bridge, close to the Museum Gardens, or Kings Staith, just outside the Kings Arms. The York City Cruise, with on-board commentary, gives a good introduction to York from the river. YorkBoat runs lunch and dinner cruises too if you wish to combine a meal with a river cruise, but one of the most atmospheric of trips is to take the Floodlit Evening Cruise to Bishopthorpe Palace, when the lights of York play games on the water and buildings such as the Guildhall take on another dimension.

You don't need to be afloat to use the river as an exploration tool though. Both riverbanks act as **footpaths** and/or **cyclepaths** up and downstream, right out of the city. If your way is blocked on one bank, just cross one of the many bridges and continue on your way. York's other river, the Foss, allows you to do the same for five miles north to the village of Strensall.

If you are walking along the Ouse and heading upstream towards Clifton Ings and beyond, keep your eyes peeled because you may be lucky enough to see one of Britain's rarest animals. The tansy beetle is found on riverside vegetation here and nowhere else in the country. Look out for these iridescent bronze and green insects feeding on tansy leaves in summer.

TRADERS' & DEBTORS' YORK

Not surprisingly, much of the historical trading area of York grew up between the two rivers, the River Foss flowing into the River Ouse a little southeast of Skeldergate Bridge. Viking traders brought goods in and out of the city via the River Ouse, which flows into the North Sea via the Humber. Many of the Viking artefacts associated with trading have been found in the **Coppergate** area just east of the riverbank while medieval merchants, with a rapidly increasing wealth, chose to position their headquarters, the **Merchant Adventurers' Hall**, in a prominent position next to the River Foss, with water-level storage rooms for goods to be brought in and out.

By contrast to these wealthy merchants' quarters, **York Castle**, originally built by William the Conqueror, has spent most of its years as a prison. In its early years Knights from the outlawed Order of Templars were held here, Edward ll incarcerated and executed his rebellious barons in the castle and Henry Vlll had political enemies hung from the battlements themselves. The Victorians demolished most of the old castle and replaced it with a new debtors' prison in the 1800s followed by the felons' prison in the 1900s. The whole area was, and still is, synonymous with law and justice – the Crown Court is still found opposite **York Castle Museum**, where the various prisons were until their closure in 1934. One of York's most infamous 'traders', if he can be called that for his 'trade' was somewhat one-sided, was Dick Turpin, or John Palmer as he liked to call himself in Yorkshire to escape his crimes further south.

YORK CASTLE MUSEUM

Eye of York ✆ 01904 687687 ⬧ yorkcastlemuseum.org.uk

York Castle Museum was founded by John Kirk, a doctor from Pickering, with a very specific remit – to record the social history of Yorkshire. It

DICK TURPIN

Originating from Essex in the early 1700s where he was known for a string of offences, including petty crime, robbery and murder, Dick Turpin made a swift exit from the southeast of England with the law hot on his heels. The rogue made his way to Yorkshire where he became involved in horse-trading, or rather horse-stealing before selling the beasts back to their rightful owners.

He changed his name to avoid capture but his plan fell apart when he was caught and thrown in to gaol, housed in the old York Castle. Tried in court, he was sentenced to death and taken to the gallows on the Knavesmire to the south of York, rather ironically where the racecourse is today. His grave is in St George's churchyard, behind the castle where he was imprisoned.

The headstone to the grave is unusual in bearing two names – his given one of Richard Turpin together with his illegal alias, John Palmer.

gives a real insight into how we lived in the not-too-distant past, which children in particular seem to find fascinating. I came here first as a child myself, on a junior school trip in the 1960s, and remember being enthralled by Kirkgate, the recreated Victorian street – especially the sugar mice from the old sweet shop. Ironically, there is now a display dedicated to life in the 1960s… hey-ho, time moves ever onwards.

The museum is housed in the Georgian Debtors' and Women's Prisons with part of the exhibition being the unaltered original, giving an atmospheric and uncomfortable sense of what life in the cells must have been like.

CLIFFORD'S TOWER

Tower St ✆ 01904 646940; English Heritage

Four years after his success at Hastings, William the Conqueror arrived in York to 'harry the North', building two defensive castles, one either side of the River Ouse. The ghost of the south bank site is at Baile Hill while all that remains of the once extensive main castle is the keep, given the name Clifford's Tower in the 16th century after the incumbent Constable of the Castle. York Castle has witnessed many gory and heinous acts over the centuries, but its darkest hour was probably during one March night in 1190 when the city's Jewish community took shelter in the keep from a murderous mob. Many chose to take their own lives rather than be lynched, more died in the flames when the tower was set alight and the few survivors were taken and massacred. A memorial

SHANNA HYATT/S

TRAVELLIGHT/S

MERCHANT ADVENTURERS' HALL, YORK

NATIONAL RAILWAY MUSEUM

FAIRFAX HOUSE

PARKERPHOTOGRAPHY/A

tablet at the foot of the tower and daffodils planted by school children on the mound commemorate the shameful death of those 150 victims.

The tower sits in a perfect defensive position, snugly between the rivers Ouse and Foss. The mound is no easier to climb now than it was in 1070, with the exception of a moat to cross and the arrow slits in the circular tower thankfully remaining redundant for anything other than a pigeon's resting place. There are some great views of the city from the top, but that's about all there is now, the tower being open to the elements following an unfortunate incident that blew the roof off in the 17th century when gunpowder was stored there. Clifford's Tower's troubled and controversial history continues today with an ongoing heated dispute over proposals for a modern visitor centre at its base.

FAIRFAX HOUSE
Castlegate ✐ 01904 655543 ⬠ fairfaxhouse.co.uk ☉ Sat–Thu, plus guided tours Fri

To the north of Clifford's Tower, in Castlegate, Fairfax House is considered to be one of the finest examples of an 18th-century townhouse in Britain. Its façade is imposing in a very classical, ordered way, the symmetry just so, the Georgian windows perfectly aligned. You can imagine how this would have been the talk of the town among society, the windows filled with light and chatter during social evenings and carriages arriving to chauffeur away young ladies and gents.

Inside, the rooms have been restored perfectly to the fashion of the day with brightly painted walls and elegant furnishings, including the Noel Terry collection of 17th- and 18th-century clocks, and cabinets full of secret compartments that, in their day, must have held the hidden secrets and affairs of many a society scandal.

JORVIK VIKING CENTRE
Coppergate Shopping Centre ✐ 01904 615505 ⬠ jorvikvikingcentre.co.uk

Between 1979 and 1981, the Coppergate area of town was scoured for clues in one of the largest archaeological digs ever in Britain, revealing a complex of 10th-century Viking buildings and some 40,000 finds. The result was the creation of the Jorvik Viking Centre, one of York's most

◀ 1 The Shambles. 2 Clifford's Tower. 3 The Great Hall in the Merchant Adventurers' Hall. 4 The National Railway Museum. 5 The hallway at Fairfax House. 6 Jorvik Viking Centre.

QUAKERS & CHOCOLATE

On the corner of Castlegate and tiny Friargate is the Friends' Meeting House, the main place of worship in York for the Society of Friends, otherwise known as Quakers. It's a very plain, simple building and deliberately so, owing to the beliefs of the practising Friends. There are no amazing stained-glass windows, no elaborate choir screens or decorative stonework but the result is a very restful building where the sun bounces off the cream-coloured walls and fills the building with light.

The Quakers have a long tradition in York that goes back way before the Rowntree family, but it is the Rowntrees who put Quakerism, or Quaker values, on the map in the city. Although perhaps more renowned for Kit Kat and Smarties, the family played a vital philanthropic role within the city that included creating a garden village for their factory workers in New Earswick and providing land for the two Quaker schools in the city – the Mount School for girls and Bootham School (where Joseph Rowntree, the founder of the chocolate factory, was educated). They also created Rowntree Park on the south bank of the River Ouse in memory of those who lost their lives during World War I. Five walks have been created around the city, highlighting places relating to the Rowntree family, including the building where the cocoa business began before it moved to the current Haxby Road site (now owned by Nestlé) and the Friends' Meeting House. To be honest, they provide a welcome break from the Roman and Viking history that abounds in the city and give you the chance to look at a completely different side to York from the more recent past. In a nice touch, the energy required for completing walks of varying length is measured in Kit-Kat fingers.

Trail leaflets are available from the York Visitor Information Centre in Museum Street. You can also download copies from the Rowntree Society website: ◈ rowntreesociety.org.uk.

visited attractions, beneath the 1980s shopping centre erected on the site. Not always obvious to the thousands of queuing visitors about to descend to this phenomenally successful display (pre-book to avoid the wait) is that they are going to see the genuine Viking archaeology of York in its original position. The site includes timbers preserved in the wet ground, which are only now underground because over them lie the deep deposits created by medieval and later rebuildings of the city. Reconstructions, soundtracks and even authentic aromas from fish markets and cesspits, all highly innovative when the Jorvik first opened in 1984, bring the scenes to life. If you are resistant to the idea of the ride, which you have to take to see it, bear in mind that this is proper archaeology, meticulously researched and far from just a theme park:

the electric 'cars' were the only feasible way to move large numbers of visitors safely around such a compact and fragile site.

Jorvik continues to bring in funds to support the work of the York Archaeological Trust, such as the activities at DIG (✐ 01904 615505 ⏣ digyork.com), housed in St Saviour's Church, Saviourgate, where archaeologists explain what they do and children especially enjoy digging in specially prepared pits of clean 'earth' (actually recycled rubber crumbs) for genuine York artefacts.

THE SHAMBLES

I've always loved the sound of the street named The Shambles, York's finest medieval street. Despite the name referring to the butchers' shops that once lined the street, it so aptly depicts the topsy-turvy nature of the top-heavy houses that lean precariously towards one another on either side of the narrow lane. Each house seems close enough that you could quite easily shake hands with neighbours on the opposite side of the street by merely opening a top floor window.

The Shambles derives its charm from its lack of architectural uniformity, a mixture of brick, timber and rendered buildings. The butchers have long gone, the bow-fronted windows of the tiny shops taken up with a succession of tourist paraphernalia. However, the shrine to Margaret Clitherow halfway along the street is sobering and might curtail any spending. She was the wife of a butcher who harboured Catholic priests at a time when it was not the done thing to do. She was found out and her punishment was to be crushed to death beneath her own front door weighed down by rocks – brutal even by Tudor standards.

THE MERCHANT ADVENTURERS' HALL

Fossgate ✐ 01904 654818 ⏣ merchantshallyork.org ◷ 10.00–16.30 Sun–Fri, 10.00–13.30 Sat

It's the ability to lure passing trade, as shown in The Shambles today, that turned York citizens into wealthy merchants 650 years or so ago. These medieval traders built their communal building, the Merchant Adventurers' Hall, to be able to meet socially and transact their business affairs. It's a fantastic building, with timbers the size of tree trunks and a totally uneven floor that slides into the centre of the room.

From the outside, the hall sits restfully in its own peaceful garden by the River Foss, though this has caused flooding problems in the past as can be seen from the watermarks in the Undercroft, the flood heights steadily rising since they were first recorded in 1831. The coats of arms of 22 of the medieval guilds hang in the Undercroft too, and the accompanying exhibition puts into perspective just how powerful and important they were. The building, including the guild chapel, is still used for regular events both by the current members and by outside organisations, which helps to ensure that it remains a living and breathing part of York.

ACROSS THE OUSE

Wander along The Stonebow, past the hideous concrete monstrosity known as The Stonebow Building, and you come to the market square bordered by Pavement and Parliament Street. It's where all the major banks congregate, but it's also where regular food markets take place and any other festivities that can happen in a temporary marquee; it's the home for many of the events during the annual York Food Festival (⊘ yorkfoodfestival.com).

Continue along High Ousegate and you'll cross over **Ouse Bridge**, the oldest of the bridges in York, to Micklegate.

MICKLEGATE

I find Micklegate one of the nicest – and longest – streets in York. The first few hundred yards, closest to the bridge, are a bit messy, with shops that seem to frequently change hands and the Park Inn Hotel, another of York's buildings that might not be classed as the city planning department's finest hour.

"There are no distinguishing tourist attractions along the street, making it appear blissfully uncrowded."

As you begin to climb the steady slope past this small area in desperate need of a facelift and crossing George Hudson Street, Micklegate becomes a quiet gem. There are no distinguishing tourist attractions along the street, making it appear blissfully uncrowded, but it has some striking Georgian townhouses, built by the wealthy merchants who found the street to be a good trading route when it was the main road into the city centre.

On the opposite side of the street to the shops is **Holy Trinity Church,** a conventionally built stone church, set back from the street line, in its own peaceful grassy graveyard. It's all that remains from a once powerful Benedictine monastery destroyed by Henry VIII. However, the monastery would have been there when previous members of the royal family found their heads being strewn along the top of **Micklegate Bar**, following the Battle of Wakefield during the Wars of the Roses. Micklegate Bar was *the* place for several centuries upon which to find the head of a losing army, traitor or dignitary, royal or not.

THE BAR CONVENT

Blossom St ℰ 01904 643238 ⬙ bar-convent.org.uk

In a Georgian building on the busy corner of Blossom Street and Nunnery Lane, just beyond Micklegate Bar, the Bar Convent is the oldest living convent in England. It was founded in 1686 at a time when persecution of Catholics was rife and has been a major part of the York community ever since. Originally set up as a school for girls, the convent and the founding order has a fascinating history with links to Guy Fawkes and the gunpowder plot.

The convent still has a sense here and there of school-ness inside with long corridors covered in ageing linoleum, but the architectural secret is a covered chapel, designed by a York architect in the mid-18th century to be completely hidden from view. And indeed it is – you would never know it was there from the street. The chapel, which is open to visitors and still in regular use, has a beautiful gilt-decorated dome that is

"Here you can sit with your lunch and not notice a sound coming from the busy roads that surround the building."

completely concealed by a pitched roof from the outside. The **chapel** also has eight exits and a priest hole – necessary security measures at the time it was built.

The convent is a great place to visit to get away from the bustle of the city centre. The plant-filled **Winter Garden**, the entrance hall to the convent, has a striking glass roof and mosaic-tiled floor. It's a quiet place for a cup of tea, as is the peaceful back garden that's tended by the few remaining sisters. For here you can sit with your lunch and not notice a sound coming from the busy roads that surround the building. What's more, you can make the most of the peace and quiet by staying in its highly thought of B&B accommodation (page 248). 'You don't have to be religious to come here and get something out of the place,' one of the staff once said to me. 'It's a place to sit quietly and be able to relax; it has a very soothing environment.'

THE NATIONAL RAILWAY MUSEUM & YORK STATION

Leeman Rd ✆ 03300 580058 ◈ railwaymuseum.org.uk

York has one of the most famous railway stations in the world – with a walkway through to the free-to-view National Railway Museum, complete with one of the world's most iconic trains, the Flying Scotsman. Even if you are not a train enthusiast, something here will make you catch your breath, whether it's the sheer scale of the great steam engines, appearing all the larger if you see them from the ground rather than from platform height, or the charmingly changing period detail of the Royal Carriages from different eras. The Warehouse, an open store for some three-quarters of a million smaller railway objects such as sign boards, benches, buckets and china, is big enough to lose yourself in – it's like being surrounded with props from *Brief Encounter*.

With its Victorian arched, glass and iron canopy, the **main railway station** is also evocative of tearful goodbyes on a black-and-white film set, and is worth a visit even if you are not arriving or departing by train. Short of being underneath the glass roof, the best place to view the station is from the city walls opposite.

On the opposite side of the city walls from the railway station, underneath the arch through which Station Road disappears, is the **former headquarters of the North Eastern Railway Company**. Built in 1906 as a grand status symbol to signify the company's importance, it simply bristles with chimneys and fancy gable ends. The building is now the Cedar Court Grand, York's first five-star hotel and spa.

ACCOMMODATION

This recommended accommodation list is by no means exhaustive, as there are of course a huge range of places to stay in the region. Those featured are my personal choice, with no payment having been made by the businesses concerned. I have tried to suit a range of different pockets, from basic camping to outrageous luxury; and styles – some B&B, some self-catering, some for larger groups. All, however, I feel are 'special' in some way, historically, architecturally or perhaps with a particular 'Slow' take on things.

The hotels and B&Bs featured in this section are indicated by 🏠 under the heading for the town or village in which they are located. Self-catering options are indicated by 🏡 and campsites are indicated by ⛰. Where a recommended pub listed within a chapter offers accommodation, I have mentioned it in the listing. For full listings, go to 🖱 bradtguides.com/nymsleeps.

1 CLEVELAND & HAMBLETON

B&B
Laskill Country House Near Hawnby YO62 5NB
🖱 01439 798265 🖱 laskill.co.uk

Self-catering
Helmsley Garden Cottage & Railway Carriage Bondgate, Helmsley 🖱 01439 771864
🖱 airbnb.co.uk
Merry Hall Boltby YO7 2DY 🖱 07590 649369
🖱 Merry Hall Holiday Home

Campsite
Lordstones Country Park Carlton Bank TS9 7JH
🖱 01642 778482 🖱 lordstones.com

2 ESKDALE

Hotel
La Rosa Hotel East Tce, Whitby YO21 3HB
🖱 01947 606981 🖱 larosa.co.uk

B&B
The Witching Post Inn Egton YO21 1TZ
🖱 01947 895537 🖱 thewitchingpostinn.co.uk

Self-catering
Whitby Lighthouse Hawsker 🖱 01386 897468
🖱 ruralretreats.co.uk

Campsites
Folly Hall Farm Tranmire YO21 2BW 🖱 07774 415395 🖱 follyhallfarm.co.uk
Lythe Caravan & Camping High St, Lythe YO21 3RT 🖱 07496 987688 🖱 thestiddy.co.uk

3 EASTERN MOORS

Hotels

Cottage Lea's Country Hotel Middleton YO18 8PN ✆ 01751 472129 ⌂ hotelpickering.co.uk

Self-catering

Boggle Hole YHA Robin Hood's Bay YO22 4UQ ✆ 0345 3719504 ⌂ yha.org.uk
The Pigsty Fylingthorpe YO22 4TH ✆ 01628 825925 ⌂ landmarktrust.org.uk
Worfolk Cottage Staintondale YO13 0EN ✆ 01482 327574 ⌂ worfolkcottage.co.uk

Campsite

Low Farm Campsite Ellerburn YO18 7LL ✆ 01751 470208 ⌂ lowfarmcampsite.com

4 HOWARDIAN HILLS & RYEDALE

Hotel

The Old Lodge Old Maltongate, Malton ✆ 01653 690570 ⌂ theoldlodgemalton.co.uk

B&B

Newburgh House Coxwold YO61 4AS ✆ 01347 868177 ⌂ newburghhouse.com

Self-catering

Cherry Tree Lodge Welburn YO60 7DX ✆ 07595 542505 ⌂ dogh.co.uk/holiday-cottage
Secret View Cottage Terrington YO60 6PB ⌂ airbnb.co.uk

Campsite

Hobground Campsite Normanby YO17 6XD ✆ 01751 431988 ⌂ pitchup.com

5 WOLDS

Hotel

Burythorpe House Burythorpe YO17 9LB ✆ 01653 658200 ⌂ burythorpehouse.co.uk

B&Bs

Wold Cottage Wold Newton YO25 3HL ✆ 01262 470696 ⌂ woldcottage.co.uk
The Wolds Retreat Kilnwick Percy YO42 1UF ✆ 01759 304832 ⌂ madhyamaka.org

Self-catering

Country Huts on the Wolds Thixendale YO17 9TG ✆ 07824 312514 ⌂ countryhuts.co.uk
Skipwith Station North Duffield YO8 5DE ✆ 01757 282288 ⌂ skipwithstation.com

6 YORK

Hotel

Grays Court Chapterhouse St, YO1 7JH ✆ 01904 612613 ⌂ grayscourtyork.com

B&B

The Bar Convent Blossom St, YO24 1AQ ✆ 01904 643238 ⌂ bar-convent.org.uk

Self-catering

Baille Hill House Bishopthorpe Rd, YO23 1JH ⌂ baillehillhouse.co.uk
The Little House Bishopthorpe Rd, YO23 1JS ⌂ booking.com

INDEX

Page numbers in **bold** refer to main entries.

THE BRADT STORY

In the beginning

It all began in 1974 on an Amazon river barge. During an 18-month trip through South America, two adventurous young backpackers – Hilary Bradt and her then husband, George – decided to write about the hiking trails they had discovered through the Andes. *Backpacking Along Ancient Ways in Peru and Bolivia* included the very first descriptions of the Inca Trail. It was the start of a colourful journey to becoming one of the best-loved travel publishers in the world; you can read the full story on our website (bradtguides.com/ourstory).

Getting there first

Hilary quickly gained a reputation for being a true travel pioneer, and in the 1980s she started to focus on guides to places overlooked by other publishers. The Bradt Guides list became a roll call of guidebook 'firsts'. We published the first guide to Madagascar, followed by Mauritius, Czechoslovakia and Vietnam. The 1990s saw the beginning of our extensive coverage of Africa: Tanzania, Uganda, South Africa, and Eritrea. Later, post-conflict guides became a feature: Rwanda, Mozambique, Angola, and Sierra Leone, as well as the first standalone guides to the Baltic States following the fall of the Iron Curtain, and the first post-war guides to Bosnia, Kosovo and Albania.

Comprehensive – and with a conscience

Today, we are the world's largest independently owned travel publisher, with more than 200 titles. However, our ethos remains unchanged. Hilary is still keenly involved, and **we still get there first**: two-thirds of Bradt guides have no direct competition.

But we don't just get there first. Our guides are also known for being **more comprehensive** than any other series. We avoid templates and tick-lists. Each guide is a one-of-a-kind expression of an expert author's interests, knowledge and enthusiasm for telling it how it really is.

And a commitment to wildlife, conservation and respect for local communities has always been at the heart of our books. Bradt Guides was **championing sustainable travel** before any other guidebook publisher. We even have a series dedicated to Slow Travel in the UK, award-winning books that explore the country with a passion and depth you'll find nowhere else.

Thank you!

We can only do what we do because of the support of readers like you – people who value less-obvious experiences, less-visited places and a more thoughtful approach to travel. Those who, like us, take travel seriously.

Bradt GUIDES

TRAVEL TAKEN SERIOUSLY